Wonderful walks
from
dog-friendly
campsites
throughout the UK

Anna Chelmicka

Hubble&Hattie

The Hubble & Hattie imprint was launched in 2009 and is named in memory of two very special Westies owned by Veloce's proprietors. Since the first book, many more have been added to the list, all with the same underlying objective: to be of real benefit to the species they cover, at the same time promoting compassion, understanding and respect between all animals (including human ones!)

Hubble & Hattie is the home of a range of books that cover all-things animal, produced to the same high quality of content and presentation as our motoring books, and offering the same great value for money.

More great Hubble & Hattie books!
Among the Wolves: Memoirs of a wolf handler (Shelbourne)
Animal Grief: How animals mourn (Alderton)
Babies, kids and dogs – creating a safe and harmonious relationship (Fallon & Davenport)
Because this is our home ... the story of a cat's progress (Bowes)
Bonds – Capturing the special relationship that dogs share with their people (Cukuraite & Pais)
Camper vans, ex-pats & Spanish Hounds: from road trip to rescue – the strays of Spain (Coates & Morris)
Canine aggression – how kindness and compassion saved Calgacus (McLennan)
Cat and Dog Health, The Complete Book of (Hansen)
Cat Speak: recognising & understanding behaviour (Rauth-Widmann)
Charlie – The dog who came in from the wild (Tenzin-Dolma)
Clever dog! Life lessons from the world's most successful animal (O'Meara)
Complete Dog Massage Manual, The – Gentle Dog Care (Robertson)
Confessions of a veterinary nurse: paws, claws and puppy dog tails (Ison)
Detector Dog – A Talking Dogs Scentwork Manual (Mackinnon)
Dieting with my dog: one busy life, two full figures ... and unconditional love (Frezon)
Dinner with Rover: delicious, nutritious meals for you and your dog to share (Paton-Ayre)
Dog Cookies: healthy, allergen-free treat recipes for your dog (Schöps)
Dog-friendly gardening: creating a safe haven for you and your dog (Bush)
Dog Games – stimulating play to entertain your dog and you (Blenski)
Dog Relax – relaxed dogs, relaxed owners (Pilguj)
Dog Speak: recognising & understanding behaviour (Blenski)
Dogs just wanna have Fun! Picture this: dogs at play (Murphy)
Dogs on Wheels: travelling with your canine companion (Mort)
Emergency First Aid for dogs: at home and away Revised Edition (Bucksch)
Exercising your puppy: a gentle & natural approach – Gentle Dog Care (Robertson & Pope)
For the love of Scout: promises to a small dog (Ison)
Fun and Games for Cats (Seidl)
Gods, ghosts, and black dogs – the fascinating folklore and mythology of dogs (Coren)
Helping minds meet – skills for a better life with your dog (Zulch & Mills)
Home alone – and happy! Essential life skills for preventing separation anxiety in dogs and puppies (Mallatratt)
Know Your Dog – The guide to a beautiful relationship (Birmelin)
Letting in the dog: opening hearts and minds to a deeper understanding (Blocker)
Life skills for puppies – laying the foundation for a loving, lasting relationship (Zuch & Mills)
Lily: One in a million! A miracle of survival (Hamilton)
Living with an Older Dog – Gentle Dog Care (Alderton & Hall)
Miaow! Cats really are nicer than people! (Moore)
Mike&Scrabble – A guide to training your new Human (Dicks & Scrabble)
Mike&Scrabble Too – Further tips on training your Human (Dicks & Scrabble)
My cat has arthritis – but lives life to the full! (Carrick)
My dog has arthritis – but lives life to the full! (Carrick)
My dog has cruciate ligament injury – but lives life to the full! (Haüsler & Friedrich)
My dog has epilepsy – but lives life to the full! (Carrick)
My dog has hip dysplasia – but lives life to the full! (Haüsler & Friedrich)
My dog is blind – but lives life to the full! (Horsky)
My dog is deaf – but lives life to the full! (Willms)
My Dog, my Friend: heart-warming tales of canine companionship from celebrities and other extraordinary people (Gordon)
Office dogs: The Manual (Rousseau)
One Minute Cat Manager: sixty seconds to feline Shangri-la (Young)
Ollie and Nina and ... daft doggy doings! (Sullivan)
No walks? No worries! Maintaining wellbeing in dogs on restricted exercise (Ryan & Zulch)
Partners – Everyday working dogs being heroes every day (Walton)
Puppy called Wolfie – a passion for free will teaching (Gregory)
Smellorama – nose games for dogs (Theby)
Supposedly enlightened person's guide to raising a dog (Young & Tenzin-Dolma)
Swim to recovery: canine hydrotherapy healing – Gentle Dog Care (Wong)
Tale of two horses – a passion for free will teaching (Gregory)
Tara – the terrier who sailed around the world (Forrester)
Truth about Wolves and Dogs, The: dispelling the myths of dog training (Shelbourne)
Unleashing the healing power of animals: True stories about therapy animals – and what they do for us (Preece-Kelly)
Waggy Tails & Wheelchairs (Epp)
Walking the dog: motorway walks for drivers & dogs revised edition (Rees)
When man meets dog – what a difference a dog makes (Blazina)
Wildlife photography from the edge (Williams)
Winston ... the dog who changed my life (Klute)
Wonderful walks from dog-friendly campsites throughout the UK (Chelmicka)
Worzel Wooface: For the love of Worzel (Pickles)
Worzel Wooface: The quite very actual adventures of (Pickles)
Worzel Wooface: The quite very actual Terribibble Twos (Pickles)
Worzel Wooface: Three quite very actual cheers for (Pickles)
You and Your Border Terrier – The Essential Guide (Alderton)
You and Your Cockapoo – The Essential Guide (Alderton)
Your dog and you – understanding the canine psyche (Garratt)

Hubble & Hattie Kids!
Fierce Grey Mouse (Bourgonje)
Indigo Warrios: The Adventure Begins! (Moore)
Lucky, Lucky Leaf, The: A Horace & Nim story (Bourgonje & Hoskins)
Little house that didn't have a home, The (Sullivan & Burke)
Lily and the Little Lost Doggie, The Adventures of (Hamilton)
Wandering Wildebeest, The (Coleman & Slater)
Worzel goes for a walk! Will you come too? (Pickles & Bourgonje)
Worzel says hello! Will you be my friend? (Pickles & Bourgonje)

www.hubbleandhattie.com

First published in February 2019 by Veloce Publishing Limited, Veloce House, Parkway Farm Business Park, Middle Farm Way, Poundbury, Dorchester, Dorset, DT1 3AR, England. Tel 01305 260068/fax 01305 250479/e-mail info@hubbleandhattie.com/web www.hubbleandhattie.com. ISBN: 978-1-787110-45-8 UPC: 6-36847-01045-4. © Anna Chelmicka & Veloce Publishing Ltd 2018. All rights reserved.
British Library Cataloguing in Publication Data – A catalogue record for this book is available from the British Library. Typesetting, design and page make-up all by Veloce Publishing Ltd on Apple Mac. Printed and bound in India by Replika Press PTY

Contents

Introduction

I travel about the UK and Europe in my motorhome finding walks and exploring the countryside. When I began doing this my dog, Ruby, accompanied me; later, her daughter, Amber, joined us. These days I am now accompanied by my young Labrador, Pearl. She is lively and energetic but a well-behaved dog, because we go to training classes every week. She makes me laugh a great deal because everything she does is at a bounce; so much so, I often feel I should have called her Bouncy.

Pearl is a very special dog because she is the direct descendant of my wonderful dog Ruby, who helped me recover from a life-changing illness, and adjust to the changed circumstances in which I found myself. As I slowly adapted to my new situation, Ruby was always there, supporting and encouraging me. She was such a special dog and had such a profound effect on my life, my first book, entitled *My Friend Ruby*, is about her.

It was with Ruby that I began my travels in my motorhome: very much a novice. We learnt together. Ruby was so good. I began some research about camping with dogs, taking photographs and recording my findings. I submitted some articles to various magazines, some of which were published. Seeing my work in print gives me an enormous thrill.

I did not anticipate owning two dogs at the same time, but I so enjoyed the whole experience of Ruby having a litter that I considered repeating it, perhaps several times. Therefore, when Ruby had her second litter, which I decided would be her last, I kept the darkest bitch. She was a rich golden colour so it seemed appropriate to call her Amber. Ruby and Amber were very close, and, for several years, the three of us, Ruby, Amber and I, had a wonderful time travelling about all over Europe: Switzerland, Italy, Poland, Germany, as well as France and Luxembourg, made possible by the newly-introduced Pet Passport Scheme. We also travelled extensively throughout the UK looking for places we could all enjoy. All the time I was making notes, taking photos and submitting articles.

When Ruby died it took many months for Amber to adjust, and she was never quite the same dog. The time she and I spent without Ruby was very special. We went out and about in the motorhome, tramping all over the countryside discovering some amazing places.

Just 18 months after Ruby went, at a routine vaccination visit, the vet diagnosed Amber as terminally ill. So very quickly she changed from a fit, active dog effortlessly leaping stiles to an old, slow, sorrowful animal. What was I going to do? It seemed as if in just a short time I would be without a dog. I could not imagine that.

Then I received a marvellous message from the owner of one of Amber's puppies.

Ruby and Amber at Pisa in Italy.

The mating had been successful, and Amber would shortly be a grandmother. So it was, not long after Amber's diagnosis, I collected the darkest bitch from the litter. She was much lighter in colour than either her great-grandmother, Ruby, or her grandmother, Amber, so in keeping with the precious stone theme it seemed appropriate to call her Pearl, though in the intervening months her coat has darkened considerably and now her name is a misnomer.

She and Amber got on well together. Pearl copied her grandmother and just loved curling up with her. They had six months together. I believe having her granddaughter around prolonged Amber's life as teaching the puppy gave her an added interest. We even, all three of us, managed to go out in the motorhome to a couple of campsites and find some different walks, with Amber instructing Pearl in campsite etiquette.

Amber teaching Pearl campsite etiquette.

Pearl is now three, and she and I have carried on the tradition established first with Ruby, then with Amber, of travelling about in my motorhome exploring the UK and Europe, finding walks and enjoying the countryside. Just like her ancestors, Pearl enjoys our jaunts. Whenever I am preparing for a trip, like Ruby and Amber, Pearl quietly slips into the motorhome to be certain she comes along. We have been to many interesting places, and intend to continue our excursions discovering more delightful campsites and wonderful walks!

Walking and motorhoming
(or camping and caravanning)

C3 What is this life, if full of care
We have no time to stand and stare,
No time to stand beneath the boughs
And stare as long as sheep or cows.
No time to see, when woods we pass
Where squirrels hide their nuts in grass.
No time to see, in broad daylight
Streams full of stars like skies at night.
A poor life this if full of care
We have no time to stand and stare. 80

W H Davies

The hurley burley of modern life, especially in this technological age, makes it very difficult to do as W H Davies suggests and find the "time to stand and stare." Tootling along the country lanes in a motorhome and pitching up at a campsite sounds idyllic. Unfortunately, considerable preparation is necessary to achieve this: a campsite has to be found and the journey planned.

The quest to find suitable campsites began the moment I first acquired my motorhome. One of the reasons I decided to get a motorhome was so that I could take my wonderful dog, Ruby, with me when travelling about. Camping with a motorhome seemed the perfect solution as she could come, too. As a consequence, what facilities existed for dogs was a significant factor in ascertaining a good campsite.

At the time, with so many campsite books available and the added perk of exciting new technology in the fast burgeoning internet, I thought this would be easy. Yes, there were many references to dogs. However, these were only with regard to them being welcome. Occasionally in the small print, mention was made of a dog exercise area but no other information was offered. It was only by studying carefully the description of various campsites and reading between the lines did I manage to prise some relevant information. Off I would go with Ruby, not only to visit different parts of the country but also to check out the campsites.

It was very hit and miss. Sometimes, there was nothing specific for dogs: it was

Amber and me – just feet and paws – having lunch at a trig point.
This was a lightbulb moment for me.

just that the campsite allowed dogs on site. On other occasions dog exercise areas were provided, but these were as equally unpredictable. I recall one which was the size of a postage stamp (or seemed to be). After only a few minutes wandering around it, Ruby looked quizzically at me as if to say, "Okay, where do we go now?"

Some sites have small wooded areas or large grassed fields with plenty of space for dogs of all sizes to walk and chase balls, whilst others have nothing specifically designated for dogs, but are near fields or parks where they could be exercised.

There are even campsites that provide washing facilities for dogs, so they can be cleaned up before entering the living space, which is useful, especially if the ground is wet and muddy. If my dog is dirty, however, I put some water in a bucket, wash her with a sponge, then rub her down with a towel. Labradors are easy to clean as they are 'Teflon' dogs. With their short coats the dirt and wet easily rubs off.

Unfortunately, it wasn't until I had arrived and booked into a campsite that I knew whether Ruby was going to be as well catered for as I was, and it was as a direct result of travelling with her that I began to do some research into campsite facilities for dogs. I developed the habit of booking sites at the last minute and for very short periods because of not knowing what facilities might be available, and on some occasions I found it was practical to stay for only a day or two because of the lack of amenities for my dog.

Not long after I started my investigations a new camping and caravanning magazine,

Wonderful walks from dog-friendly campsites

Out and About, was launched. Realizing there was little reliable information regarding facilities for dogs on campsites, I submitted several articles based upon my findings, and was thrilled when several were published in the magazine. Unfortunately, after a couple of years, the magazine folded. Nevertheless, I continued my research.

Having a dog – especially one as active as a Labrador – necessitates lots of walking, and so it was that Ruby re-ignited my interest in country walking, and I even, for a time, subscribed to the magazine *Country Walking*. Besides related articles the magazine published instructions for lots of walks of varying lengths, which hugely appealed to me although, regrettably, I did not do many of them. Firstly, because most of the walks were in popular walking areas, and finding a place to park a big motorhome is frequently problematic. Secondly, breaking camp and preparing the motorhome for a journey, then having to drive back afterwards and re-pitch, rather spoils the outing.

I continued going to campsites and receiving *Country Walking* magazine, but it seemed 'never the twain shall meet.' The solution appeared to be to create my own walks using an Ordnance Survey Map. As it had been many years since I had last used my map reading skills, I needed to update them, and began by practicing reading maps and finding my way about in familiar places. I prepared several walks close to home using OS Maps. While things did not always go according to plan, this was an important learning experience, and I soon gained enough confidence to try out my newly-acquired skills in new and unfamiliar places.

During my research for magazine articles I noticed that some campsites were very close to footpaths and bridleways, so quite long walks seemed possible. Unfortunately, yet again, there was little information and few instructions about any walks in the locality of the campsites, even though in the intervening years the internet had improved enormously and now provided a mountain of information. The problems I encountered trying to find really good sites for Ruby were replicated trying to find sites close to walking trails. Again, while walks were often mentioned, more detailed information was rarely forthcoming until registering at a campsite, by when, of course, this information – though useful – was too late.

This time my newly-acquired map-reading skills and the internet were extremely useful. Once I had found a campsite that suited Ruby I put the location into the OS Maps search box to bring up the appropriate map. From this I could see what footpaths, bridleways and trails were nearby. It was really useful in helping me make an informed decision but very time-consuming and convoluted. Even then, the choice proved unsuitable sometimes. Footpaths might be so overgrown they were unusable, or had simply disappeared. At other times the trail was on a minor road which was very busy and made for unpleasant walking. Occasionally, there were no stiles or gates, and accessing the route required scrambling over walls and fences. Every now and then the campsite was further away from the footpaths than appeared on the map. Even so I did find some excellent sites and lovely walks of varying lengths, and discovered parts of the country that were totally new to me. In the process I learned a lot and my map-reading skills hugely improved, giving me the confidence to be even more adventurous.

As my experience of camping with a dog increased, so my requirements from a campsite changed. Now, I not only wanted a campsite that suited me and my dog, I also wanted one near footpaths so that I could go for long walks through the countryside accompanied by my four-legged companion.

By this time I had two dogs – Ruby and her daughter, Amber – and we travelled about in the motorohome having a wonderful time exploring the UK. However, it still took a considerable amount of time and organization to ensure that the campsites we stayed at fulfilled our requirements satisfactorily. Again, I kept notes and took photographs of my findings.

Even though Ruby was quite old and was not in the best of health she still enjoyed going out in the motorhome with Amber and me. The walks, though shorter, took longer. Eventually, in the May I was forced to make the sad decision to have her put to sleep. Now it was just me and Amber. To help us adjust to the huge loss we both felt I took Amber out in the motorhome to new and different places, and we walked and walked and walked. It was exactly what we both needed. Fortunately, the weather was kind and Amber was fit, leaping nimbly over stiles and enjoying the outings. We discovered some amazing places.

It was whilst stopping for lunch at the top of a hill next to a trig point (a fixed surveying station, used in geodetic surveying and other surveying projects in its vicinity), admiring the view and with Amber sitting beside me, leaning against me totally ignoring my food, which is very unusual in a Labrador, that I had a flash of inspiration. I would note down the route of the walks I did and compile a set of instructions accompanied by some photographs. I would then approach magazines and suggest they publish a series of articles with instructions for walks accessible directly from campsites. I decided in the first instance to submit the proposal to magazines for campervans and motorhomes.

I was thrilled when *Motorhome Monthly Magazine (MMM)* agreed to publish a series of monthly articles during 2016. The editor had a clear plan for how the set of articles would appear in the magazine, and the specifications were very precise, and I soon came to realize that a substantial amount of work was required. Even so I thoroughly enjoyed the whole experience; seeing my work in print was exhilarating and so exciting.

I have used several of the walks previously published in *MMM* in this compilation, and walks from other campsites complete the set. I hope you enjoy the book, find it useful, agree that they are 'Wonderful Walks,' and have as much fun as I have had with all of my dogs, Ruby, Amber and Pearl.

Happy walking!

Visit Hubble and Hattie on the web:
www.hubbleandhattie.com • www.hubbleandhattie.blogspot.co.uk • Details of all books
• Special offers • Newsletter • New book news

9

Respecting the countryside

In the UK we are very lucky to have access to so much of the countryside: a consequence of the 1949 National Parks and Access to the Countryside Act, which many, many people were involved in ensuring was ratified. Its objectives are to protect the countryside and to ensure that it is free for all to enjoy; achieved with the establishment of National Parks and other agencies such as nature reserves.

As times and circumstances have changed, so, over the years, the Act has been modified. Nevertheless, the basic principles have remained the same.

As stipulated by the UK Government's 'Countryside and Rights of Way (CROW) Act 2000,' walkers have the right to –

- access specified areas of the countryside for walking
- use public roads and pavements or public rights of way such as footpaths and bridleways
- use the 'right to roam' on open access land such as mountains and moors, etc
- access private land if the landowner gives permission
- access private land if there is a local tradition or right of access

See https://www.gov.uk/right-of-way-open-access-land for more detail about the exact entitlements and restrictions for walkers, horseriders, and outdoor users (and also Appendix i).

In Scotland the 'Outdoor Access Code' is slightly different. The 'Land Reform (Scotland) Act' came into force in 2003, and established a statutory right of responsible access over most areas of land and inland water. The main points of the 'Scottish Outdoor Access Code (SOAC)' are –

- take responsibility for your own actions
- respect the interests of other people
- care for the environment

Essentially, there are very few restrictions as to where you can walk, ride a bicycle, swim, canoe, kayak or wild camp in Scotland's countryside. The Code leaves it for individuals to use the countryside as they wish whilst respecting their surroundings, the land, people, and, most importantly, to leave it in perfect condition for others to also use (see Appendix i for details).

These extensive and, to my mind, amazing and unique rights over our land carry with them huge responsibilities, which are set out in the Country Code.

Shortly after the 1949 act was passed it was decided that officially formulated guidance was needed for those accessing the land, even though common sense mostly sufficed. So, in 1950, a Country Code was devised, which has been updated over the years, with the most recent modification in 2012.

When walking, please do observe the Country Code, which states –

RESPECT OTHER PEOPLE
- Consider the local community and other people when enjoying the outdoors
- Leave gates and property as you find them, and always try to follow paths and trails

PROTECT THE NATURAL ENVIRONMENT
- Leave no trace of your visit and take home your litter
- Keep dogs under effective control

ENJOY THE OUTDOORS
- Plan ahead and be prepared
- Follow advice and local signs

See Appendix i for detailed and inclusive Countryside Codes.

Enjoy the right we have to explore our wonderful, diverse countryside and appreciate it, but remember your responsibilities and adhere to the Country Code.

You also have the responsibility to keep yourself safe. Though we do not have dangerous animals such as wolves (yet) or bears in the UK, there are dangers. The weather can, in an instant, change a pleasant outing into an emergency, especially if walking in the hills and more remote parts of the country. And accidents can happen. It is advisable to follow the motto of the Scouts and Guides and 'be prepared.'

The walks in this book are not especially challenging so it is easy to be prepared and stay safe. My suggestions are not definitive or applicable to all situations, and they will certainly not prevent accidents, though will help in this regard, and allow you to enjoy the walks more, hopefully.

Maps

Although there are maps of each walk in the book these are for general guidance only, and it is absolutely essential that they are used in conjunction with the relevant Ordnance Survey Map.

Surprisingly, Ordnance Survey Maps have a long history as part of the Board of Ordnance from way back in the 1700s during the reign of George III, providing detailed maps to the military that would be useful in times of war. There was a very real threat of invasion by Napoleon in the late 1700s, and the defending forces needed very detailed information about the south coast area of England.

It was in 1801 that the first one-inch-to-the-mile map was produced – of the

Wonderful walks from dog-friendly campsites

county of Kent – and thus began mapping of the country using the effective Principle of Triangulation, which has resulted in trig points on the top of so many hills. It took many, many years and a veritable army of people to produce the maps. Over time, other people and organizations discovered just how useful the maps were and, eventually, in the 1900s, maps were produced for the leisure market and general public. They became extremely popular, especially with walkers, and Ordnance Survey began producing leisure metric maps as early as the 1970s.

Today, Ordnance Survey Maps, or OS Maps, as the organisation has recently been rebranded, produces two kinds of detailed map for outdoor enthusiasts. The one with the purple cover is the Landranger Series with a scale of 1:50 000, which means that every 1cm on the map represents 500m on the ground. The series with the orange cover is the Explorer Map with a scale of 1: 25 000: every 1cm on the map is 250m on the ground, which is the same as 4cm on the map to 1km on the ground. The imperial equivalent is 2¹/₂inches on the map to one mile on the ground. These Explorer Maps are by far the best for walking as they show more detail, including field boundaries.

In today's digital age there are many other ways of accessing OS Maps. I still buy and use the paper version and, as I have been walking all over the UK, I have a shelf full of Explorer Maps, many of which have become quite tatty with use. However, I do not find it necessary to buy the weatherproof versions as I rarely walk in the rain.

Paper maps should be used for several reasons –
- the walk can be seen in the context of surrounding locality
- if the view is extensive it is possible to identify distant landmarks with a map of a larger area
- it is possible to turn a paper map in the direction of the walk. Digital devices usually automatically revert to a North/South orientation when the device is turned
- with a paper version there are no worries about the battery running down
- also, having a signal is not a necessity. In more remote areas, the lack of a signal is a fairly regular occurrence
- they are vital in case of emergencies, even if digital maps are preferred

Nowadays, OS Maps supplies not only paper maps but also digital maps, and provides a range of products and services to suit various devices: this is THE place to go for mapping needs.

To access OS Landranger and Explorer Maps digitally an annual subscription is necessary, which also allows OS Maps to be downloaded onto other devices via the OS Map App. The Map App is free but some of the features – such as Explorer and Landranger Maps – have to be purchased. Also available to purchase are dedicated GPS units with Landranger or Explorer Maps of the whole of the UK, together with a variety of accessories. More information about Ordnance Survey Maps and the services it provides can be found on the website (https://www.ordnancesurvey.co.uk/).

The service that Ordnance Survey Maps provides is unique, and it continues to embrace new technology to improve the products it is able to offer the general public. It is important that we support OS Maps so that it can continue with this work.

Stay safe with a map and appropriate footwear.

Mobile phone

Nowadays, mobile phones greatly reduce risk if used properly, especially for walkers. As a lone walker it is a vital piece of equipment. When setting out, make sure your phone is fully charged, and be aware that some places have only a weak signal or none at all. If you use apps on the phone, such as mapping or fitness monitoring, be especially mindful of battery usage. Various options exist to ensure battery life. For example, you can carry a power bank (a portable charger designed to recharge your electronic gadgets when on the move), some of which will allow you to recharge your phone two or even more times. If excursions are inclined to be long, the weight and physical size of the power bank is a factor. Alternatively, you could take along a dedicated phone with a pay-as-you-go sim card just for calls and texts.

So, keep safe. Take a mobile phone with you with sufficient battery charge to last for your excursion, irrespective of the length of the outing and size of the group.

Clothing

Although expensive specialist attire is not necessary for general walking, it is essential to wear sensible clothing. Trousers are a better option than shorts, even if it is hot, for protection against prickly plants and stinging nettles. These should be comfortable and, if possible, of a light material so that, should they get wet, they will not become too heavy and will dry quickly (unlike most denim). It is best to wear several layers of thinner garments as this is easier to adjust for a sudden spell of warm weather. I find it useful to take a wool hat, scarf and gloves in case the temperature suddenly drops; it's surprising how much these help. Of course, rain gear is nearly always a requirement as there are often rain clouds just over the horizon.

Wonderful walks from dog-friendly campsites

The one thing that is vital is appropriate footwear. Bespoke walking boots or shoes are essential, as these support the foot and have a good grip: crucial for muddy and uneven surfaces. Most outdoor shops sell a range of specialized walking footwear from the incredibly expensive to the reasonably priced.

Check the weather forecast

Some people are of the opinion that the UK doesn't have climate, only weather, because conditions change so much; not just day-to-day but hour-to-hour. Even though walking in this country is generally a safe, everyday pastime, it can, on occasion, turn into an extremely unpleasant and even dangerous activity if the weather should become inclement. I do not like walking in the rain and mist, and do too much of this type of walking on a regular basis with my dog. I much prefer it to be clear and, if possible, sunny, when I can see more and really appreciate the variety and beauty of the countryside.

Nowadays, with access to a variety of weather forecast apps and programmes for various devices, it is much easier to ascertain the weather hour-by-hour as opposed to daily forecasts. Also, as technology has enabled the gathering of more data and made tracking of weather patterns easier, so the forecasts have become more accurate.

Before setting out, check the weather. Too often people venture out unprepared and mountain rescue teams or the coastguard have to be called out as a result. On two occasions when I have stayed at Glen Nevis Campsite at the foot of Ben Nevis I have witnessed possible emergency incidents, one of which even involved a helicopter hovering dangerously close to the mountainside. I have to confess to it being thrilling to watch, like a film.

If staying at Glen Nevis Campsite, do go down the road to the Ben Nevis visitor centre, which is unlike any other. Extremely interesting and informative, with the emphasis on being safe outdoors, it has a section on maps and navigating, the weather, and also appropriate clothing. There is also a large section about the mountain rescue teams, which are made up of volunteers who go out in all conditions to find those walkers who get into difficulties. I was astounded to discover how many times they are called out, not only to Ben Nevis but also generally. To avoid being a mountain rescue statistic, assess conditions before setting out. Should you need assistance it is extremely helpful to all concerned if your precise location is known, and this can be easily ascertained with the OS Map App, which gives an accurate grid reference for the emergency services to use.

Control of dogs

The UK has another exceptional tradition, which is to allow dogs access to so many places with so few restrictions. It is not like this in many other countries. It is therefore the responsibility of all dog owners to ensure they have control over their animals, do not annoy or upset others, endanger livestock, or in any way jeopardize this freedom.

Owners need to help their dog be confident and relaxed with other dogs not known to them: at the very least they should be able to tolerate passing dogs. This is essential at campsites and on narrow footpaths. Sometimes, space is less than ideal, and dogs have to pass quite close to each other. I find it distressing when dogs react aggressively, barking ferociously and snarling as Pearl and I pass by along the route. On the other hand it is wonderful when Pearl finds a new companion to play with.

It is generally recognized as a necessity to have a dog on a lead at certain times – for example, near livestock; especially sheep. When it comes to larger animals, how a dog is managed depends on the circumstances. My present dog, Pearl, thinks horses are large dogs and wants to play with them, so she becomes rather skittish, which is not ideal behaviour. Ruby, however, was frightened of them as her first close encounter with a horse was beside an electric fence which she accidently touched. As a consequence she was wary of all horses and stayed well clear. I was happy to let her off a lead in a field of horses.

Again, the situation with regard to cattle depends upon circumstances. I have been reassured many times that cattle are harmless except when cows have calves, and one accidently gets between mother and offspring. Generally, the presence of a dog merely arouses their curiosity. Unfortunately, I have had some frightening experiences: having ten or more cows crowding round is rather alarming, and it is not unknown for walkers to be trampled to death by a herd of cows.

Advice is conflicting. On the occasions I have found myself in a field of high-spirited horses or cows I have quickly moved towards the edge of the field by a fence or hedge, because the self-preservation instincts of animals causes most cows and horses to slow down so as not to injure themselves by charging into the hedge or fence. This usually gives some space and time to move rapidly to the exit. I have scrambled over many a gate and stile, shoving my dog ahead of me, and I am extremely cautious when I encounter livestock.

It is obviously important that your know your dog very well when out and about. It is also extremely important to be able to control him, both on- and off-lead. In my opinion the best way to really understand and know your dog, as well as to learn how best to control him is by training.

Training should be a continual, ongoing process, and not just reserved for when he is a puppy. I took Ruby to classes every week for most of her life, and she loved them. She really enjoyed doing all the exercises and learning new tricks, even when she was quite old. Pearl is very young, and she, too, likes attending her classes. Like Ruby she is clever but a very different dog. Because the dogs were so good and well-behaved I felt confident about taking them with me in the motorhome and exploring the countryside. I have travelled extensively over the UK, and even been to several countries in mainland Europe.

Having a well-trained dog who reliably responds to cues makes outings more pleasurable for both of you.

Another responsibility of dog owners which I am happy to say is usually adhered to, is removal and correct disposal in an appropriate waste bin of dog poo. Unfortunately, recently, it has become commonplace for bags of dog faeces to be either tossed into the hedge, hung on the branch of a tree, or left on the side of tracks and footpaths. A disgusting and most objectionable habit. Firstly, it is an environmental act of vandalism; not only does it spoil the countryside but it takes many years for the bag and its contents to decay, even if the bag is biodegradable. Secondly, it is extremely selfish and inconsiderate. There is no provision for these bags to be collected and properly disposed of, and quite rightly there are few volunteers for such an unpleasant task. This has become such an issue in recent months that MPs have joined the debate.

So as not to walk several miles carrying a bag of dog poo, which no one likes to do, the 'stick and flick' method is recommended as an option. The idea is to find a stick and flick the poo out of the way into a verge or hedgerow. This is the method now recommended by the National Trust to visitors on some places it manages. This is not an ideal remedy but is far better than bags of poo decorating the trees and hedges, and littering the countryside.

With so many people taking their dogs with them when walking, a 'Dog Walking Code of Conduct' is becoming customary. The Kennel Club has always offered such advice (see Appendix i), and nowadays other organizations are reminding dog owners of their responsibilities. The most succinct and inclusive code I have come across is that advocated by the Pembrokeshire Coast National Park in the events magazine *Coast to Coast* –

LOOK AFTER YOUR DOG
* keep your dog close and in sight: on the lead if necessary, and always if he won't recall on cue
* ensure your dog wears a collar, identification disc, and is microchipped
* don't allow your dog near cliff edges, rough seas or strong tidal currents
* think of the weather – on warm/sunny days cars and beaches can be too hot for dogs

LOOK AFTER OUR COAST AND COUNTRYSIDE
* always pick up your dog's poo: this is a legal requirement on beaches and places where people walk and play
* take home your bagged dog waste or put it in a litter bin
* ensure your dog is on a lead near livestock, and doesn't approach or chase birds or other wildlife
* when cattle are present keep your dog on a lead
* follow signs and abide by byelaws such as dog restrictions on beaches
* keep your dog on the path when walking in the countryside

BE CONSIDERATE OF OTHERS
* show respect for other people and their dogs
* keep your dog away from horseriders, cyclists and picnics
* don't allow your dog to bark excessively

Remember that not everyone likes dogs, especially small children. For me, having an obedient four-legged companion adds an extra dimension to my walking. It is really enjoyable discovering the many wonderful places in this country. Having been given so many rights in regard to exploring the countryside, we must all make sure we accept and fulfil our responsibilities.

Campsites

Just as each person is unique and yet still part of the human race, so campsites come in all shapes and sizes, are distinctively different, and yet have a commonality. At one end of the spectrum are those sites which are just a flat field with maybe a tap, whilst at the other extreme are the all-singing, all-dancing sites providing a whole range of amenities, sometimes even including fitness centre and spa facilities, which are more like holiday parks. However, most campsites fall somewhere between these extremes.

Two main organizations cater specifically for anyone who likes camping: the Camping and Caravanning Club and the Caravan and Motorhome Club. Over the years, these clubs have grown from very small beginnings to the large organizations they are today, offering their members a whole range of services. Both clubs own and run a considerable number of campsites located throughout the country, which have an easily recognised specific modus operandi. This has resulted in well-designed sites with premium facilities for showering, washing dishes, and doing the laundry, etc, in a neatly-kept and attractive setting. The wardens are always helpful and efficient. These campsites are usually the yardstick by which all others are judged, and even though they rarely have additional facilities such as bars, cafés or swimming pools, they generally represent excellent value for money.

As campsite requirements are particular to each individual, so reviews are not always helpful, whereas facts are, and I have endeavoured to provide factual information about each campsite. Because I have a dog, suitability of a site for her is of paramount importance. Also, as we both like walking (especially my dog), it is also vital that there are footpaths close by to allow us to explore the countryside. These concerns occasionally supersede my own requirements.

What I look for in a campsite, in order of importance –
- dogs are welcome
- a flattish site for the motorhome. I generally prefer this to be grass, though this can become so soft in wet weather the motorhome becomes bogged down and stuck: not a pleasant experience
- footpaths handy to explore the countryside
- electric hook-up so I have the luxury of using my electrical appliances, especially the heater in the winter and, of course, to charge my various devices. As technology develops so there is more and more demand for electricity. A solution for those who like 'wild camping' is a solar panel. I prefer the ease of an existing electric supply

- toilet block so I don't have to empty mine so often
- showers that are more spacious than mine in the van
- wifi or mobile signal so the next stage of the trip can be planned

Then there are those amenities onsite or nearby that increase the comfort quotient –
- a dog exercise area large enough to allow a stretch first thing in the morning and last thing at night, or to chase a ball or frisbee
- a shop where provisions can be replenished
- a pub in which to spend time meeting local people
- a café to indulge in delicious cakes
- a TV connection (on occasion an enjoyable distraction)

Finally, there are those places, usually called 'Holiday Parks,' which provide a variety of entertainment facilities, such as –
- swimming pool
- children's play area
- fitness centre
- spa facilities
- horseriding
- crazy golf
- evening entertainment such as bingo or live shows
- animal petting centre

The range of amenities and facilities found on campsites is vast, thus making each place quite distinctive. One of the pleasures of travelling about is seeing how the campsite description corresponds to reality, and discovering the special characteristics of each site.

Fees for campsites are just as variable as the campsites themselves. Many places

have different rates for different times of the year – high, medium and low season – with even a special, high rate for bank holidays. Some have a concessionary 'mid-week' or OAP rate, and then there are those few sites that charge a straightforward flat rate.

How the fees are constructed also varies. Some, such as the two big clubs, charge separately for each facility – pitch, adult, electric, etc, which is best for sole travellers like me. Other places charge as a package: pitch + 2 adults. Sometimes the package includes other amenities such as electric hook-up and TV. Of course, campsite fees change year-to-year, particularly if they have upgraded their amenities. This is all very confusing. The only way to be certain of the charges is to check at the time of booking.

Then there is, for me, the issue of charges for dogs. Many campsites – including all of the 300+ sites that are run by the two main clubs – do not charge. I cannot understand why fees are as high as £3.00 per dog per night in some instances.

I have noticed a recent trend for what is usually referred to as 'super' or 'service' pitches, which is generally a hardstanding with all services supplied to it. So, on the area's perimeter will be a water tap, electric hook-up, TV connection, wifi signal and waste drain. Obviously, there is an extra charge for such pitches. As with campsites that provide swimming pools or bars, etc, these additional provisions are an enjoyable luxury, but not all of which I require.

I am happy with well-managed and maintained resources such as those provided by the 'club' campsites. Not all of the campsites I visited were of this standard, but they did all have electric hook-up, toilets and showers, whilst a few had additional facilities such as a shop, etc. Similarly, the facilities for dogs varied, and Pearl has appraised these in her section, Pearls of wisdom.

With all the hustle and bustle of modern life it is a pleasure to experience a simpler, slower pace for a time, and be able to watch the flowers grow, hear the birds sing, and gaze at the sunsets as they splash the sky with colour.

The book

The campsites are located throughout the country. The UK is divided into 7 regions –
Wales, North East (Cleveland, County Durham, Lincolnshire, Norfolk,
Northumberland, Tyne & Wear, York, Yorkshire East, Yorkshire North, Yorkshire South,
Yorkshire West), North West (Cheshire, Cumbria, Isle of Man, Lancashire, Merseyside),
Central (Cambridgeshire, Derbyshire, Herefordshire, Leicestershire, Nottinghamshire,
Northamptonshire, Rutland, Shropshire, Staffordshire, Warwickshire, Worcestershire),
South East (Bedfordshire, Berkshire, Buckinghamshire, Essex, Hertfordshire, Kent,
Isle of Wight, London, Oxfordshire, Surrey, Sussex East, Sussex West, Suffolk), South
West (Cornwall, Devon, Dorset, Gloucestershire, Hampshire, Somerset, Wiltshire), and
Scotland.

The three campsites from each region are selected from different counties, and I
have included a couple of extra campsites because they are particularly special.

The book comprises 24 campsites with detailed instructions for 45 walks. Each of the
chapters is a region of the UK. The walks are in alphabetical order of the county in which
the campsites are located. First, there is a brief summary of the unique characteristics of
the county, followed by a description of the campsite. Then there is the most important
section – Pearls of wisdom – detailing what my dog thinks of the campsites and walks.

Following this are directions for the walks. First is the short walk of 4-6 miles
(6-10km): this is divided into four sections. Next are directions for the longer walk of
8-11 miles (13-18km): this is divided into 8 sections.

The final section is a brief account of the activities and attractions in the immediate
locality, within an approximate 10 mile (16km) radius of the campsite. It may be possible
to walk to some of these, although there is not always a convenient route.

The campsites and walks have been purposely selected to illustrate the huge variety
and diversity to be found in the UK, and include campsites with basic facilities, as well
as some with a range of amenities. Similarly, the walks traverse a range of landscapes,
including –

- hills and mountains (Scotland, Wales, North West)
- valleys and flat fields (Central, South West)
- towns and cities (Scotland, North West, North East)
- with an historical interest (North East, Scotland)
- forests (North West, South East)

- coastal (Wales, South East)
- close to wildlife (North East)

All of the walks are possible with dogs, and if they are well-behaved the jaunts are easier and more enjoyable. Dogs need to be agile to manage the stiles, fences and walls, and there is the very occasional 'sheepproof' stile which may require a helping haul and shove for them to get over if they are too big to lift.

These walks are not particularly challenging as most of the routes are along tracks and across fields. However, a reasonable degree of fitness is necessary, as is a moderate level of stamina, as there are stiles and gates to climb over and some quite steep hills. Consequently, these walks are not suitable for pushchairs. As for children, parents should decide which walks are appropriate for their child.

This book can be used in various ways –

- for a weekend break to just one campsite, and doing the walks from that campsite
- for longer trips of about a week, exploring a region and visiting all three campsites and doing the six walks
- for an extended expedition, visiting several regions and either doing all of the walks in each region or selecting just one campsite, and so experiencing a taste of the region

However the book is used, please remember that this is not a comprehensive list of walks from campsites, but rather a selection.

Appendix ii contains essential information for all of the campsites (such as contact details, directions, etc), and charges are correct at the time of publication. Appendix i states in full the various Countryside Codes.

Visit Hubble and Hattie on the web:
www.hubbleandhattie.com • www.hubbleandhattie.blogspot.co.uk • Details of all books
• Special offers • Newsletter • New book news

21

The walks: Wales
(Monmouthshire, Pembrokeshire, Powys)

Monmouthshire — mountains and canals

OS MAPS EXPLORER OL13 BRECON BEACONS NATIONAL PARK

The mention of Wales conjures up a picture of deep valleys sliced out of the surrounding hills by gushing rivers. Clinging to the sides of the valleys are small towns and villages that have sprung up as a result of the many coal mines established throughout the area. Today, most of the coal mines have closed, but the landscape is as arresting as it has always been, especially the Brecon Beacons, the mountainous region at the head of the valleys, whose name derives from the ancient practice of lighting fires (beacons) to warn of danger or attack by invaders. More recently, this custom has been resurrected to commemorate special events.

Situated between south and mid-Wales, the Brecon Beacons stretch from Llandeilo in the west to Hay-on-Wye in the east, and covers some 520 square miles (1350 sq km). The area has many similarities with the better known symbolic landscape of south Wales – hills, rivers and valleys – though its characteristics are distinctly different. The terrain rises more steeply, for example, with many hills attaining heights of over 2000ft (610m), and thereby qualifying as mountains.

Spectacular views from mountain tops.

There are several mountains in the Brecon Beacons. The Sugar Loaf, just to the north of Pyscodlyn Farm Caravan and Camping Park, is referred to as a mountain, but is, in fact, 46ft (14m) short of the required height. According to the dictionary definition it is, however, 'a natural elevation rising more or less abruptly from the surrounding level and attaining an altitude which ... is impressive or notable,' so the term 'mountain' seems appropriate. This very much reminds me of a delightful film – *The Englishman Who Went Up a Hill But Came Down a Mountain* – starring Hugh Grant and Colm Meaney, the latter best known for his role in the Star Trek series, in which the issue of what is a hill or a mountain is the central theme.

Throughout the mountains of the Brecon Beacons are many rivers, waterfalls, valleys and caves, and dotted about are small towns, picturesque villages and tiny hamlets. The scenery is spectacular, particularly from the mountain tops. But it must be remembered that, although the countryside is magnificent, soaring skyward, it is, in fact, a working landscape. The grassy, heather-clad mountains are the result of many centuries of human activity.

Agriculture and farming have been hugely important for the region, despite the presence at various times of the Roman army and Norman conquerors. Initially, farms were established on the drier uplands, but nowadays are to be found in the more fertile lowlands. Pyscodlyn Farm Caravan and Camping Park is a working farm situated in the River Usk valley. A dairy herd can, on occasion, be found in the adjacent fields, as well as sheep, which usually graze in the higher fields. This rural way of life was not hugely affected by the industrial revolution. The coal seam ran out at Merthyr Tydfil, but there was some quarrying and mining to the south and east of the hills. The environment of the Brecon Beacons is constantly changing, and these days road-building, erection of power lines and wind farms, changes of agricultural practices and urban expansion are contributing factors.

As far back as 1957 it was realized that the Brecon Beacons is a special place with stunning scenery and rich history, so the area was designated a National Park under the auspices of the National Trust. It continues to acquire impressive honours, one of which is the British Horse Society (BHS) Access Award, as special effort has been made to establish riding routes in the Park: what a fantastic place in which to do so! In 2005, membership of the European Geopark Network was granted, and the area also received UNESCO Global Geopark recognition, and is officially recognized as one of Europe's most important geological landscapes. In 2013 it qualified as an International Dark Sky Reserve: considering the level of light pollution this is a significant achievement.

Today, not only is the Brecon Beacons National Park a wonderful place for walking as there are many tracks, some of which have been used for centuries by drovers taking livestock to market, but is also an incredible place for an activity holiday. The choice is so varied: horseriding, cycling, sailing, orienteering, fishing – the list goes on. In addition are the wonderful towns and villages to explore. There are so many things to do. Yet the Brecon Beacons National Park remains primarily a marvellous unspoilt landscape of moorland and mountains.

Wonderful walks from dog-friendly campsites

CAMPSITE: PYSCODLYN FARM CARAVAN AND CAMPING SITE

The wide entrance to this site very quickly narrows to a single lane as it passes between the farm buildings and approaches the farmhouse, so bigger units will need to proceed with caution. Once registration at the farmhouse has been completed (they take only cash and cheques), the site soon opens out onto a large, flat field with a smaller one off on the right for tents. Even though there are several static vans and permanent caravans there is plenty of space, with 30 electric hook-up points available. There are two amenities blocks – one each for ladies and gents – and both have washing-up facilities. The ladies are clean, modern and well designed with delightfully large shower cubicles. The toilet blocks are some distance away from some of the pitches.

PEARLS OF WISDOM 🐾

For me, this is one of the best campsites. Just a leap across a narrow road is a humongous field for exploring, or chasing balls and frisbees, with all kinds of smells under the thick hedging. Later, I discovered that if we went through the gap in a hedge there was another ginormous field which was just as exciting. Having to sit by the campsite gate and wait for the cue to

The campsite from a nearby hill.

cross the road was sooo difficult. On top of all this the fabulous path beside the river went on and on. Sometimes, the pesky sheep meant my owner restricted my movements ... these animals are just too silly to bother with.

The campsite gate where Pearl had to sit before crossing the road to the dog exercise area.

SHORT WALK – UP A HILL OR A MOUNTAIN?

Distance: 5.5ml (8.8km)
Duration: 3.5hr (challenging in places)
Terrain: Several steep hills; rocks to scramble over at the summit. Wide, grassy tracks, footpaths, stony tracks, fields, road and stiles. Also, there are sheep roaming freely on the slopes of the mountain

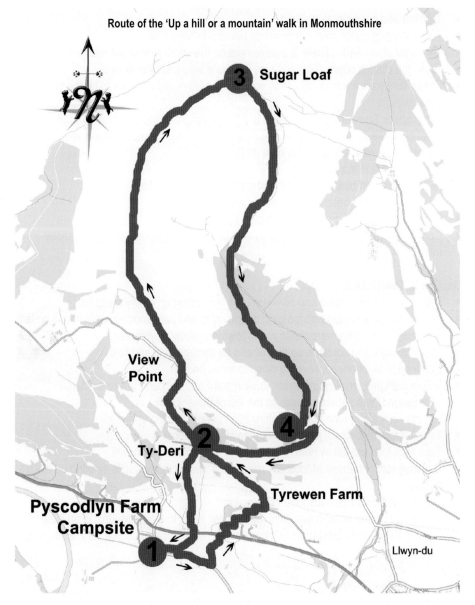

Route of the 'Up a hill or a mountain' walk in Monmouthshire

as well as in some fields. Be vigilant if accompanied by a dog

Section 1: 1ml (1.6km)

- Exit site via route to dog exercise area in SW corner and go through gate onto road
- Bear left and go through gate into field (the dog exercise field)
- Continue on, keeping close to the hedge on the right and cross the stile in the hedge next to gate

- Turn left and continue along road
- Turn left along minor road, which winds upward to busy A40
- Turn right along A40. (There is a pavement on the south side of the road)
- Cross the road in 50yd (45m) and turn left along lane just after house
- Follow lane as it winds up hill. (It is very wet in places and appears to be the bed of a small stream)
- Turn right at Tyrewen Farm (there is building in progress so route may change slightly)
- Pass old white farmhouse on left and bear left along track towards newer steel barn (there is a painted footpath sign on a wall)
- Turn sharp left in front of barn
- Follow track past buildings on left and go through gate into field
- Continue straight ahead towards yellow waymarker
- Bear left along track and go through gate by white houses
- Continue straight ahead to crossroads with bench and signpost (in km) on grassy mound

Section 2: 2ml (3.2km)
- Bear right around mound and continue onto lane going up a very steep hill
- Follow lane past signposted footpath on the right, and past another white house on left
- Continue ahead onto narrow stony path towards yellow waymarker
- Take right fork and continue up the hill and go through gate into field
- Continue straight ahead, keeping close to fence on left
- Follow path and fence round to left to view point and car park (there is a large information board showing routes to the top of Sugar Loaf)
- Exit car park along path to left of information board climbing up the hill
- Take left fork at footpath junction, keeping close to fence
- Take right fork and follow path as it gradually moves away from wall
- Continue straight ahead at footpath crossroads (path clearly visible snaking up the hill ahead)
- Turn left at next crossroads footpath junction
- Follow path to top of mountain climbing last few yards to trig point (this is an ideal place to have lunch. Best to sit in the lee of the mountain as it can be very windy and chilly)

Section 3: 1.5ml (2.4km)
- At trig point do not retrace steps, but follow path along the ridge in an easterly direction
- Bear right along a stony path down off the ridge.
- Turn right just below ridge onto grass path
- Take right fork partway down hill
- Continue straight ahead at next footpath crossroads
- Follow path and turn left at next junction along earth track
- Continue along track which becomes grassy, ignoring all paths leading off
- Follow as it goes downhill and twists to right and left

- Continue along path around sweeping bend to the right with several small grass mounds on left
- Turn immediately left
- Continue ahead and take right fork, still going downhill
- Follow path round to right towards road

Section 4: 1ml (1.6km)

- Turn left along road
- Turn right at T-junction along cul-de-sac road (this road leads to the crossroads with km signpost and bench)
- Bear left at junction and, just past the mound go, through gate with yellow waymaker on left beside house (Ty-Deri)
- Descend steps and over stile into field
- Turn right and go downhill and over stile in fence just past gate on left (dogs can squeeze through the gate)
- Continue on downhill bearing left, and over stile opposite
- Follow path downhill and cross another stile into field (this stile is in the fence by the pylon. There is a gate just before this that may be easier for dogs to use)
- From gate, continue straight ahead across field, bearing left towards buildings in corner
- Cross stream and small wooden fence beside large iron gate onto footpath by house on left
- Continue along narrow footpath past houses on left to busy A40
- Turn left along grass verge to driveway
- Cross road and turn left and over stile into dog exercise field
- Turn right and go through gap in hedge
- Bear left across field to gate in corner, and go
- Cross road and go through gate opposite into campsite

Long walk – Water 1 and Water 2

Distance: 9ml (14.4km)
Duration: 5hr
Terrain: Riverside footpaths, fields, roads, lanes, tracks, gates and lots of stiles, some difficult for large dogs to cross and sheep in many of the fields. Only a couple of short hills

The footpath snaking up and away.

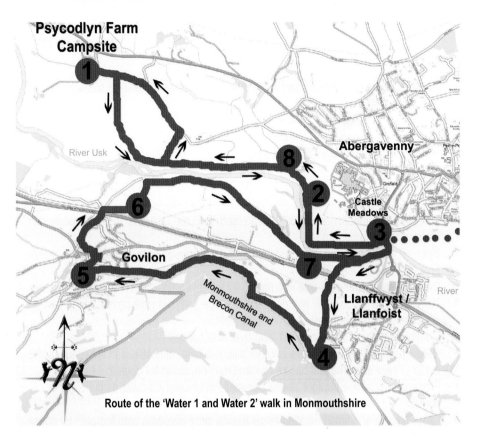

Route of the 'Water 1 and Water 2' walk in Monmouthshire

Section 1: 1.25ml (2km)
- Exit site via route to dog exercise area in SW corner and go through gate onto road
- Continue straight ahead
- Turn right in 150yd (140m) and over stile in hedge into field, just before house
- Straight ahead along edge of field and over stile opposite, by tree
- Continue straight ahead along edge of field close to fence on right, and over stile in right-hand corner
- Bear left across field and over stile in left corner
- Bear right onto path beside River Usk
- Follow path beside river, crossing several fields and stiles that have special 'dog gates'
- Stay on riverside path and cross stream via narrow wooden bridge
- Follow path and river round to right and cross another wooden bridge on left onto narrow footpath; turn right
- Continue along footpath beside river through trees and over stile into field (take care: in places path is very narrow)

Section 2: 1.5ml (2.4km)
- Continue straight ahead still following riverside path as it sweeps round to left to stone road bridge
- Bear left and go through gate and up steps onto road
- Turn left, cross road and, in 50yd (45m), go through entrance to Castle Meadows

- Continue along tarmac path beside the river
- Turn left and follow path round to right and through gate into car park
- Bear left along pavement to the park entrance
- Cross road and bear right; up steps into another smaller car park
- Bear right across car park out to street
- Keep right along Castle Street towards public toilets (along Castle Street is the Castle and Museum, which are well worth a visit though dogs are not allowed. The street beside the Angel Hotel leads to the centre of Abergavenny with shops, the market hall and theatre. Here there are many places to stop for refreshments)
- Retrace steps to Castle Meadows and the stone road bridge

Section 3: 0.75ml (1.2km)
- Turn left; cross stone bridge towards Bridge Inn
- Turn right just before pub and cross road to cul-de-sac opposite
- Continue along road beside river, past church and cemetery
- Turn left along a lane towards busy road
- Continue straight ahead through tunnel and gate towards garden centre
- Turn right along road with garden centre on left and cross B424
- Continue straight ahead along lane, keeping church on left and steadily climbing
- Take right fork and climb steps on right immediately before tunnel onto canal tow path

Section 4: 1.5ml (2.4km)
- Turn right and continue along towpath with canal on the left
- Cross bridge and turn right to continue along tow path with canal now on right
- Exit towpath on left just past boat club sited on opposite bank

Section 5: 0.5ml (0.8km)
- Turn right and cross a small wooden lattice footbridge
- Bear left to lane between houses
- Follow lane and cross road
- Bearing slightly left, continue along lane opposite
- Turn right and continue along road to junction
- Turn left and cross bridge to pub on left (a good place to stop for lunch)
- Exit/pass pub and

A stile ahead into the next field.

continue straight ahead, with bridge now on right, and cross road to Mill Lane opposite, heading towards A465
- Cross road, pass through railings and descend steps to tunnel
- Turn left and go through tunnel
- Turn right along path between two fences, and go through gate ahead
- Continue along track and go through another gate just past house on left

Section 6: 1.5ml (2.4km)
- Turn immediately left and over stile into field
- Straight on and cross another stile into next field
- Continue straight ahead, skirting garden to waymarker
- Turn right along path close to river and over stile into field
- Straight ahead across field, moving away from river, and over stile in corner on right
- Continue straight ahead, keeping close to fence on left, and cross another stile into another field
- Straight on across field and cross another stile onto track
- Cross track and stile opposite into another field
- Straight across this field and over stile ahead into next field
- Keep close to fence on left and over stile in left corner onto footpath above brook
- Pass stile on right and continue along track into field
- Continue straight on and over stile
- Follow river to gate and over stile by house

Section 7: 1ml (1.6km)
- Straight up track which then becomes the road and passes cemetery and church, and leads to main road
- Turn left and cross bridge (there is a pavement only on one side of the bridge)
- Turn left and descend steps to riverside path
- Follow path with river on left and over stile into copse
- Continue along path to bridge

Section 8: 1ml (1.6km)
- Turn left to cross bridge and continue along path over field
- Cross narrow footbridge and three fields
- Turn right immediately after crossing stile, keeping close to hedge on right and heading towards white house
- Continue on, crossing two stiles to enter lane that leads to road
- Turn left and follow road to campsite, ignoring all turnings off
- Enter the campsite via gate from dog exercise area

IN THE LOCALITY
FISHING
With so many rivers, canals and reservoirs in the vicinity there is plenty of opportunity to

fish. The nearest water is the River Usk, and day tickets to fish for trout or salmon along a mile-and-a-half on one bank of the river can be purchased from the campsite.

CYCLING
There are numerous routes for cycling fans to explore. The campsite can provide some suggestions, and can also arrange bike hire.

GOLF
On the outskirts of Abergavenny are two golf courses: the Monmouthshire Golf Club and the Wernddu Golf Club. Information regarding golfing matters is available from the campsite owner, Ken, who is a keen golfer.

RIDING
Being a BHS Access Area there are many routes on the Brecon Beacons especially suitable for horses. With several licensed trekking centres close by, riding the trails offers the opportunity to view the National Park from a different aspect.

SUGARLOAF VINEYARD
Just 1.5 miles (2.4km) away is the Sugarloaf Vineyard. The five acres of vines are cultivated on the lower south-facing slopes of the Sugar Loaf Mountain on Dummar Farm. Over the years, a number of distinctive, smooth quality Welsh wines have been produced, many of which have been awarded 'Quality Status' by The European Wine Standards Board. It is an enjoyable place to visit. The Vineyard Trail is extremely interesting and informative. Refreshments are available at the licensed coffee shop, including a sample of local cheeses which perfectly complement a glass of wine. Of course, vines as well as the wines are available to purchase.

ABERGAVENNY
Being on the edge of the Brecon Beacons on the confluence of the rivers Usk and Gavenny, Abergavenny is known as the gateway to the National Park. Its unique position was recognized by the Romans, who established a fort here, and the Normans, who built a large castle. Throughout the centuries the town has been an important venue for various fairs and markets.

Abergavenny prospered during the Industrial Revolution when weaving and tanning were important, and, although there are now no major industries, it remains a vibrant town. Markets are still held several days a week, and are very popular with both locals and visitors. In addition, various festivals are held during the year, and attract many people.

ABERGAVENNY CASTLE AND MUSEUM
The ruins of Abergavenny Castle lie close to the centre of the town overlooking the river Usk. Built in 1087, it is a fine example of a motte and bailey-type castle, and has a long and fascinating history. The most notable incident was the massacre of Welsh noblemen in 1175. Then, in the 19th century, the castle 'keep' on the mound was converted into a

hunting lodge, which now houses the Abergavenny Museum. Five permanent displays chronicle the history of the town and castle, in addition to various artefacts of local interest. Admission to the castle and museum is free; however, dogs are not allowed.

TITHE BARN OF ST MARY'S PRIORY CHURCH

This building – initially part of a monastery – has been important to the community for centuries. The monks needed somewhere to store the tithes or taxes paid to them so built the tithe barn next to the church. From 1542 and the dissolution of the monasteries, the barn was used for a variety of purposes. Today, people visit it to see the Tapestry Exhibition and learn about the church, as well as to participate in various workshops.

BRECON AND MONMOUTHSHIRE CANAL

This isolated canal runs 35 miles (56km) from Brecon to the Pontymoile Basin, mostly through the Brecon Beacons National Park. However, originally it was two canals: the Brecknock and Avergavenny Canal and the Monmouthshire Canal. These were used to transport goods, mostly iron ore to and from Newport. Nowadays, only a few boats use the canal because it is not connected to any other waterways, so it is peaceful and tranquil and a haven for wildlife. Flowing through the lovely wooded Usk Valley, it is considered the prettiest canal in Britain: a true hidden gem that is popular with walkers and cyclists.

RAGLAN CASTLE

Ruin though it may be, this is one gargantuan castle – and everything about it is big! Built for show rather than defence, even so, it withstood a fierce attack during the English Civil War, and was systematically destroyed. Afterwards, it was not considered worth restoring, and became a source of local building materials firstly, and then a romantic ruin: finally, it is now a tourist attraction. It is a short drive from the campsite, or a bus runs every two hours from the campsite directly to the castle.

BIG PIT

Also only a short drive away, but more difficult to get to because it is in the next valley, is the Big Pit National Coal Museum: an actual working coal mine from 1860 until 1980. All of the buildings have been conserved and restored so that visitors can learn and experience what it was like to work in a mine. Many of the machines are in working order and are used by visitors on the underground tour. The museum is free and is open most days. It is best to wear sensible footwear and warm clothing.

Pembrokeshire — sea, sand and space
OS MAPS EXPLORER OL35 PEMBROKESHIRE/GOGLEDD SIR BENFRO

Extending out into the Irish Sea, Pembrokeshire is enclosed on three sides by water; on its fourth, side to the east, is the county of Carmarthenshire, and to the north east Ceredigion.

Pembrokeshire is one of the best known Welsh counties, primarily due to its long coastline and amazing sandy beaches. These, and the surging waters, are particularly popular with surfers. Despite it being one of the largest counties in Wales, it is, in fact, one

The long coastline and amazing sandy beaches.

of the least populated, which bestows upon it a particularly companionable atmosphere. It's also very quiet and peaceful; due, in part, perhaps, to it being one of the few motorway-free counties. Near the shore there are only narrow roads with little traffic, except during the height of summer, so the sounds of rolling seas and sighing winds have little competition.

Several of the beaches have been awarded various accolades, including the International Blue Flag and Green Coast and Seaside Awards. To qualify for these, some beaches have a policy of no dogs, so dog owners should familiarize themselves with the exact restrictions of each beach.

With so many award-winning beaches, it's no wonder that this area is popular with holidaymakers. Tourism is an important part of the county's economy nowadays, whilst, in the past, it was mining and fishing. Though there is no mining now, there is still some fishing, but only from Milford Haven. It's a similar story with agriculture. Farming – especially dairy, arable and the renowned seed potato – is vital to the economy, although its importance has decreased markedly over the years.

Pembrokeshire may be sparsely populated but it does have its share of notable people. The writer Beatrix Potter was one of many who spent her childhood holidays in the county. Hollywood actor Christian Bale was born here; so, too, in 1457 at Pembroke Castle, was Henry Tudor, who became Henry VII, despite his tenuous claim to the throne through his mother. His Welsh connection and heritage proved extremely useful. He landed his army in Pembrokeshire and, with much local support, marched on to Leicester where he defeated Richard III at the Battle of Bosworth Field. So it was that a Welshman, Henry Tudor, became King of England.

As with many coastal areas a trail mirrors much of the stunning coastline. The 186-mile (300km) Pembrokeshire Coast Path, allows access to harbours, numerous beaches, small and large, and many spectacular views. This amazing landscape, including cliffs, dunes and wooded estuaries, is part of Pembrokeshire Coast National Park, the only one in the UK. It is quite possible to walk around three sides of the county.

Wonderful walks from dog-friendly campsites

With such an extended coastline, Pembrokeshire has six lifeboat stations: essential with so many visitors participating in a variety of watersports, including diving on the many wrecks found offshore.

In addition, there is the wildlife. Several colonies of birds nest on the cliffs; in the surrounding waters there is a resident seal population, and quite often dolphins and porpoises, and very occasionally whales, too.

It's no wonder that, in 2015, the Pembrokeshire Coast National Park was listed among the top five parks in the world by the *Huffington Post's* travel writer.

CAMPSITES: LLEITHYR FARM HOLIDAY PARK; ST DAVIDS LLEITHYR MEADOW CARAVAN AND MOTORHOME CLUB SITE

The surprising thing about these two sites is that they are right next door to each other. On one side of a hedge are the tents and various units of the farm site, and on the other the caravans and motorhomes of the club site, with usual high standard facilities.

Lleithyr Farm Site is more suited to families. It allows tents and has a range of amenities. At the edge of the camping field is a small modern amenities block. Across the road in the static caravan park is another toilet block. In an adjoining field is a trail around several animal enclosures, allowing a closer look at sheep, donkeys, etc. There is also a play area, a comprehensive shop, a bakery (summertime only), and laundry. Then there is a footpath which passes reception and continues on up to the fields. As this is a working farm, sheep are often nearby, so dog owners should be vigilant.

The surrounding roads are narrow, and although entrance to the club site is straightforward, getting to Lleithyr Farm is a little less so. On approaching the campsite, units are directed into the static park, from where it is necessary to walk across the road and down a driveway to reception in order to register. There is a bus stop right outside the farm campsite, with frequent buses to Whitesands beach, or St David's if the short walk is too much.

PEARLS OF WISDOM 🐾

My time at this campsite was so-so. Most of the places to walk close to the campsite were tarmac and unexciting, except when we met other dogs, which we often did as neither site has a dog exercise area. Although there was not much traffic it was rather boring. What a shame that the route to all of the wonderful places was via so much tarmac. I really enjoyed the walks over the fields, moor, and along the path beside the sea. Mind you, I had to be careful, not only because there were sheep, but also because the edge of the path sometimes dropped steeply to the sea.

I also loved it when the cliff path crossed the beach where I could take a dip. Sometimes my ball was tossed about by the water, and I found myself leaping over and diving under the white froth, and then being swept back onto the beach. Though it was a bit scary, it was great fun!

SHORT WALK – MOOR COASTAL PATH
Distance: 4.5ml (7.2km)

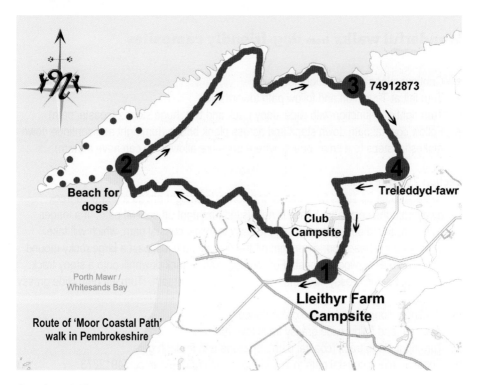

Route of 'Moor Coastal Path' walk in Pembrokeshire

Duration: 3.5hr
Terrain: Coastal footpaths, moor, tracks, fields, roads, lanes, gates, stiles, beach. Sheep in some fields and some long, steep hills

Section 1: 1.5ml (2.4km)

- Exit campsite out onto road via gap in hedge beside a telegraph pole in left corner
- Continue along road to beach
- Turn right at road junction signposted 'Youth Hostel'
- Follow driveway round to left to Youth Hostel
- Bearing slightly right, go straight ahead between buildings to narrow footpath leading to trees and hedges, and through kissing gate
- Turn immediately left and follow path around hill and down to wide track
- Turn right, continuing along path around hill
- Take left fork (right goes to top of hill 'St Davids Head') towards headland
- Follow path and take left fork again: headland now on right

Dogs are allowed on this small beach.

- Continue along path through heather
- Turn left at T-junction and follow path towards sea
- Turn right at T-junction with wide stony track and two huge stones (coastal path)
- Follow coastal path down steps and across plank bridge (turn right and continue down makeshift steps to a small beach, where dogs are allowed so can have a swim)

Section 2: 1.5ml (2.4km)
- Retrace route up steps from beach and continue straight ahead along wide track away from the sea (if the beach is not visited turn right off coastal path. If a longer walk is required continue on along the easy to follow coastal path, which will take you round the headland. Turn right off the coastal path just past a large rocky mound at waymarker on wooden post. Follow wide grassy track downhill onto a stony track. Bear right along grassy track that narrows to stony footpath. Turn left onto wide grassy track)
- Continue along track to open grass space
- Keep left and follow wide grassy track towards sea
- Turn right along track (coastal path), up slope and through gate
- Continue along coastal path to 2nd signpost with grid reference 74912873

Section 3: 0.75ml (1.2km)
- Turn right up hill along narrow footpath
- Climb hill (very steep) past freestanding gate to top (fabulous views)
- Follow path past five-bar gate on left to fence on left
- Continue downhill and go through gate on to farm

Section 4: 0.75ml (1.2km)
- Turn right and go through gate into field (signposted)
- Cross field, keeping close to hedge on right, and over stile in corner
- Step down to left and cross another stile into field
- Cross field, keeping close to hedge on right, and over stile opposite
- Continue straight on with fence now on left
- Bear left at corner through gap in hedge and down to wide stony track
- Turn left and follow track over two stiles, past campsite reception on left
- Turn right along path into campsite by toilet block

LONG WALK – LITTLE CITY (ST DAVIDS) VIA SEA VIEWS
Distance: 7ml (11.2km)
Duration: 4hrs
Terrain: Coastal footpaths (narrow in places with some steep drops), tracks, fields, roads, lanes, gates, stiles. Some long, steady climbs

Section 1: 0.5ml (0.8km)
- Exit campsite out onto the road via gap in hedge beside telegraph pole in left corner

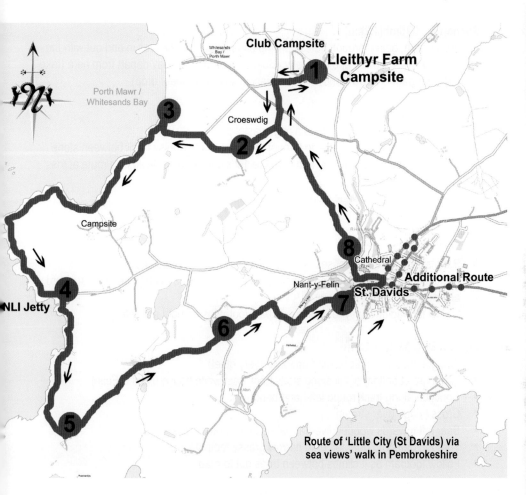

Route of 'Little City (St Davids) via sea views' walk in Pembrokeshire

- Continue along road to beach
- Turn left at junction onto footpath, opposite signpost 'Youth Hostel'
- Follow path to B4583 and cross to road opposite
- Continue along road
- Turn right along a stony track by 'Croeswdig' at left-hand bend (signposted)

Section 2: 0.75ml (1.2km)
- Follow track to left-hand bend
- Turn right and over stile beside gate into field
- Cross field towards low stone building (actually, it's a roof), passing standing stone on right and over stile onto road
- Continue straight ahead onto stony track towards sea
- Turn left along narrow footpath (coastal path) immediately before first house, and follow down to sea (signposted)

Wonderful walks from dog-friendly campsites

Section 3: 1.75ml (1.2km)
- Follow path, going through gates passing campsites, as it weaves in and out with the coast to RNLI slipway and boat jetty. Boat trips around the bay depart from here (take care: the path is narrow and, in some places, there is a sheer drop)

Section 4: 1ml (1.6km)
- Cross jetty driveway to continue along coastal path
- Turn left at 2nd signpost and go through gate onto wide grassy track between stone wall on left and wire fence on right (ignore 1st signpost to St Davids via route across National Trust)
- Go straight ahead to wide stony track with buildings on left

Section 5: 1ml (1.6km)
- Turn left and go through farmyard
- Bear left, passing two houses on left and barns on right (signposted)
- Continue on between buildings along wide stony driveway, through another farmyard and out onto tarmac driveway
- Follow tarmac driveway to crossroads past footpaths on right and left

Section 6: 0.75ml (1.2km)
- Straight ahead and along road opposite (very quiet)
- Turn right at bottom of hill along stony track past white house (Nant Y Felin)
- Continue along track round left-hand bend
- Cross bridge over stream
- Bear left towards wooden five-bar gate across mown grass
- Through gate and bear left onto narrow grassy footpath
- Follow footpath as it climbs between trees out to road

Section 7: 0.75ml (1.2km) (omitting Visitor Centre)
- Continue along road and take right fork along Catherine Street
- Follow road round left-hand bend onto Goat Street
- Turn right at junction
- Continue ahead still on Goat Street to gardens in Cross Square (continue straigh ahead along High Street (A487) for Oriel y Parc Gallery and Visitor Centre. There are lots of cafés and pubs in the city so a good place to stop for refreshments)
- Retrace steps to gardens in Cross Square and cross A487 to narrow street opposite, The Peebles, with café on left corner
- Continue along The Peebles under arch and above Cathedral grounds
- Follow lane round to right, down to Cathedral, and over wooden bridge between church and ruins towards Cathedral shop

Section 8: 1.5ml (2.4km)
- Continue straight ahead onto stony track with ruins on left

- Take right fork and continue to road
- Continue along road, climbing steadily
- Follow minor road round right-hand bend and cross B4583 to footpath opposite
- Continue along footpath to road
- Turn right along road passing the Caravan and Motorhome Club site on left, and go through gap in hedge by telegraph pole into campsite

IN THE LOCALITY
BEACHES AND SURFING
The numerous beautiful sandy beaches, together with remarkable breakers, are ideal for surfing, and attract many surfers. Whitesands, just a short walk from the campsites, is especially popular. Dogs are not allowed here, but, just a short distance north along the coastal path is a small beach where dogs are allowed. Despite there being no road to this beach, it is frequently teeming with dogs and their admirers.

WILDLIFE
There is an abundance of wildlife for the eagle-eyed to spot, from flora and fauna to birds and sea creatures. A resident seal colony can sometimes be seen basking on isolated inlets at the foot of the cliffs and on the islands in the bay. A boat trip not only visits the colony but also increases the possibility of seeing dolphins and, for the very fortunate, possibly a whale. Book at the offices in St Davids but note that the boat leaves from St Justinian's, three miles away on the coastal path. A wide range of boat trips are offered, some of which allow dogs.

DR BEYNON'S BUG FARM
Just over two miles (3.2km) from the campsite to the NE of St Davids is a most unusual 100-acre working farm where visitors are welcome, especially at its research centre for invertebrates (insects). Here is an ideal place to learn about and explore bugs!

ST DAVIDS CITY
(YES: THERE SHOULD BE AN APOSTROPHE BUT IT IS OMITTED, OFFICIALLY)
The city very much epitomises the county of Pembrokeshire, being small but perfectly formed. With a population of only approximately 2000, it is one of the smallest cities in the UK, having the requisite cathedral which is very imposing.

City status was first granted in the 16th century, retracted in 1888, and reinstated by Queen Elizabeth II in 1994. Even though St Davids is situated on the far western tip of Wales, it has always been an important place. It is here that St David, the patron saint of Wales, was born and is buried, so the city is considered the 'spiritual' capital of the country. For 1500 years – and especially during medieval times – it was a place of pilgrimage, but, after the reformation, its significance markedly declined: the resultant neglect meant that it became rather shabby.

In recent times better transport links and tourism have revitalized the city, and it is now a bustling, thriving place with many shops, galleries, cafés, pubs and restaurants.

Wonderful walks from dog-friendly campsites

Charming cottages on Goat Street in St Davids.

Most interestingly, it has no boarded-up shops, no fast-food outlets, large chain stores ... or even traffic lights! Cross Square is the heart of the city and hosts a market every Thursday. Goat Street is where all the crafts are located. Shops are along Nun Street and New Street, and on the outskirts of the city is the National Park office and Visitor Centre.

St Davids Cathedral

Although the building is in the valley beside the river Alun, the Cathedral dominates the city. It occupies the same site as the monastery that St David founded in the 6th century, and so for centuries was an important place of pilgrimage, attracting many thousands of pilgrims. Its history has been tumultuous, having been destroyed and rebuilt many times. The impressive Bishop's Palace beside the Cathedral is now just a ruin, but the Cathedral itself has undergone extensive renovation, especially during the last sixty years.

Nowadays, as it always was, it is a church that serves the community, and there are daily services, with hymns from the cathedral choir (which includes girls). Every Whitsun the city is treated to a variety of events as part of the St Davids Cathedral Festival. Of the many tombs in the cathedral, the two most renowned, are that of St David and Edmund Tudor, father of Henry VII.

Powys — Beside the dams
OS Maps Explorer 200 Llandrindod Wells & Elan Valley

When just a child – more years ago than I care to remember – I visited the Elan Valley on a cycling holiday. I remember little apart from the effort it took to cycle up the hills and the splendour of the dams. The image that has stayed with me all these years is of a large, round building rising out of the dam, probably housing some machinery, crowned with a sumptuous green dome. A truly awe-inspiring sight. As for the dams, I knew nothing about them except that they were built to supply clean water to the city of Birmingham. As an adult I promised myself I would one day return and learn more, but life got in the way. Quite by chance, whilst searching for suitable campsites with footpaths close by, I found Elan Oaks Camping and Caravan Site situated just over two miles (3.2km) outside of Rhayader, and close to one of the Elan Valley dams. This seemed serendipitous so I

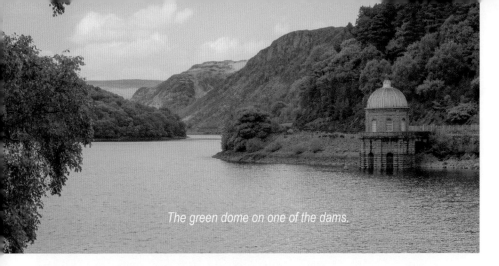

The green dome on one of the dams.

decided to explore the region. As with so much of Wales, the south eastern side of the Cambrian Mountains in Mid Wales is sliced by rivers such as the Elan, Claerwen, and Wye, cascading towards the sea.

During the Industrial Revolution the population of Birmingham, like many other cities, grew rapidly. With poor sanitary conditions, diseases such as cholera and typhoid were rife. It was realized that a clean water supply was required, and the area around the Elan and Claerwen rivers, with deep narrow valleys carved out of the hills, higher than average annual rainfall of 72 inches (180cm), impermeable rock, and all at an altitude higher than the city, was deemed suitable. So Birmingham Corporation bought the surrounding land, and in 1893 building work began on an elaborate reservoir proposal.

Not surprisingly, there was some opposition to the scheme. Firstly, the area had to be cleared: inhabitants were relocated and some buildings demolished, whilst others were flooded, including Nantgwyllt house and gardens, which was linked to the poet Shelley. Bizarrely, the ruins can be seen today when there is a drought and water levels drop. Francis Brett-Young was inspired by this unusual scene to write *The House under the Water* in 1932. Nantgwyllt church was rebuilt beside Garreg Ddu dam.

On the site of Elan village, wooden huts were built to house the workers, and additional buildings, such as a hospital, bath house, library, shop and canteen, were also built due to the number of people. Even a school was built and, using 19th century cutting-edge technology, the streets were lit at night.

To resolve the problem of transporting such huge quantities of equipment, materials and workers, a railway line was constructed along the valley from the town of Rhayader; this took an astonishing three years. It has been a long time since trains used this line. Fortunately, it was converted into a cyclepath and so allows easy access to the stunning views of the reservoirs and surrounding valleys, and a straightforward route to more remote areas of this part of Wales.

The Victorians' plans for the reservoir complex were ambitious. Originally, it was proposed to build seven dams – four in Elan Valley; the remaining three in Claerwen Valley – and an aqueduct to transport the water to the city using gravity, but it took 11 years to complete the dams in Elan Valley and the aqueduct alone, and these were officially opened in 1904 by King Edward VII and Queen Alexandra. As with all huge projects, things did not go according to plan, and it was not until 1952 that the Claerwen Valley

Wonderful walks from dog-friendly campsites

The base of one of the dams.

dam was opened by our own Queen Elizabeth an incredible 48 years later, by which time the original scheme had been modified, and just the one dam in Claerwen Valley was completed. Nevertheless, more than sixty years after completion, the complex is still as dramatic and awe-inspiring.

Seeing the dams and reservoir close up allows one to marvel at the epic feat of civil engineering they involved, and truly appreciate the enormous scale of the project and incredible achievements of all concerned. The Victorians radically changed the landscape and, in so doing, created an environment that is a haven for wildlife and a marvellous amenity for visitors to enjoy. It is a picturesque, unspoilt area and the views are extraordinary, in part because of the dams and reservoirs. It is simply an amazing place to visit.

CAMPSITE: ELAN OAKS CAMPING AND CARAVAN SITE
There is no reception on site so late bookings should register at the electric shop on North Street in Rhayader. There is a pay and display car park opposite but parking is tricky. The campsite is divided into three areas: the first is the Caravan and Motorhome Club CL section, which accommodates five units; the second is the main site which has 12 hardstanding pitches, and the third is a very large camping field.

The amenities block, including laundry and dish-washing room, is in the first section. It is a modern, sumptuous building, but with only three unisex shower/toilet cubicles, it is over-stretched when the site is full, despite portable toilets in the camping field. A code is required to access all amenities and the barrier in and out of the site. It is a neat, extremely well cared for site in a wonderful location.

A conveniently located campsite.

Pearls of Wisdom 🐕

There was so much choice close by it did not matter that there was no specific place for me to run. If I really wanted to chase my frisbee I could do so in the large camping field if it was not too crowded. Though the path beside the campsite was tarmac it went on and on, and the smells along the edges were intriguing. By the buildings was a lovely grassy route beside some water where – hurray! – I could have a dip. Lots of interesting places to explore, but sometimes my outings were restricted by these pesky sheep who popped up everywhere.

Short walk – A Crossroads
Distance: 5.75ml (9.2km)
Duration: Approx 3hr
Terrain: Some clearly defined wide tracks, footpaths, fields, a cycle path and some quiet minor roads. There are several gates and some stiles. Most of the hills are steady climbs and descents but with the occasional steep incline

Section 1: 0.5ml (0.8km)
- Exit campsite via gate to right of entrance barrier
- Continue straight ahead across road to gateway opposite
- Go up driveway
- Turn right in 50yd (45m) immediately before long stone barn and cross wooden stile by hut (sheep-proof)
- Continue ahead and through gate opposite
- Bear left up hill toward tree (steep climb) ignoring gate on left
- Continue along edge of field and over stile in gap in fence (difficult for big dogs)
- Straight ahead, keeping close to fence on left
- Turn right at corner, going downhill towards buildings
- Turn left near bottom and go through gate into farmyard
- Continue straight ahead through another gate

Wonderful walks from dog-friendly campsites

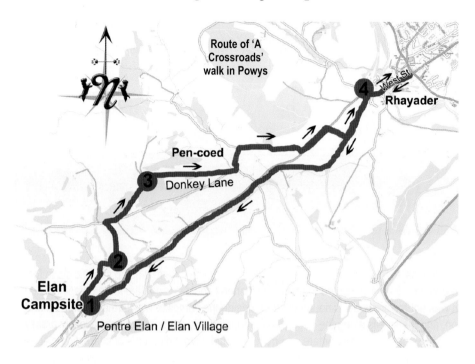

- Bear right out onto stony track

Section 2: 1ml (1.6km)
- Continue along stony track
- Take left fork up hill
- Follow track round bend and through five-bar gate out onto grassy track between fields (the climb here is gentle and steady)
- Straight ahead onto footpath at left-hand bend, and through gate onto road
- Turn right and continue along road
- Take left fork onto stony track into woods just before cattle grid

Section 3: 1.75ml (2.8km)
- Turn right at crest of hill and through gate onto grassy track, known locally as Donkey Lane but labelled Pen-coed on maps
- Continue straight ahead onto road
- Take left fork along narrow road past white house on left
- Turn right at T-junction and continue to main road
- Turn left (take care as this is a busy road during holiday times. There is a wide grass verge on the north side of the road)
- Turn right at lay-by on right and go through gate into field
- Cross field, keeping close to edge, and through gate opposite into next field
- Cross this field and climb over gate opposite

- Continue straight ahead on very grassy track to cyclepath
- Turn left heading towards Rhayader, going through two gates to the road
- Turn left and continue straight ahead over the bridge along Bridge Street, on to West Street and to the Clock Tower in the centre of the town (good place to stop for refreshments)

Section 4: 2.5ml (4km)
- Retrace steps along West Street and Bridge Street
- Turn left and through gate onto cyclepath
- Follow cyclepath to campsite, going through several gates, crossing one road and following path out beside the road for a short distance

LONG WALK – DAMS GALORE!
Distance: 9.5ml (15.2km)
Duration: 5hr
Terrain: Several long, very steep climbs as well as steady climbs and descents. Some clearly defined wide tracks, footpaths, several streams to cross, cycle path, and a minor road. Some fields, moorlands, lakeside paths, gates, stiles, and steps

Section 1: 1.25ml (2km)
- Exit campsite via gate to right of entrance barrier.
- Turn left, cross driveway, and go through gate onto cyclepath
- Follow cyclepath past church on left and across another driveway
- Bear right towards road and continue along cyclepath beside road with fence on left
- Turn left immediately past fence
- Follow footpath and cross footbridge over river
- Turn right and go straight ahead through Elan village to double bridge
- Continue on past bridges and through gate onto riverside footpath
- Continue along footpath and cross 'dog-friendly' stile into wood
- Follow twists and turns of footpath until it emerges onto a tarmac lane
- Turn right and go through gate (keep dogs under control as steep drops in places)

Section 2: 0.75ml (1.2km)
- Continue ahead with the dam building on the right (to see the base of the dam turn right and follow the building around to the other side. It is possible to walk across the dam to the opposite side, and even reach the Visitor Centre)
- Turn left up steps at corner of building and go through gate at top (the steps are long and steep).
- Turn right and walk around outcrop of rock on left to footpath beside lake (to the right is a view of the top of the dam)
- Continue along rocky footpath at base of cliffs
- Turn left up steps (very steep)

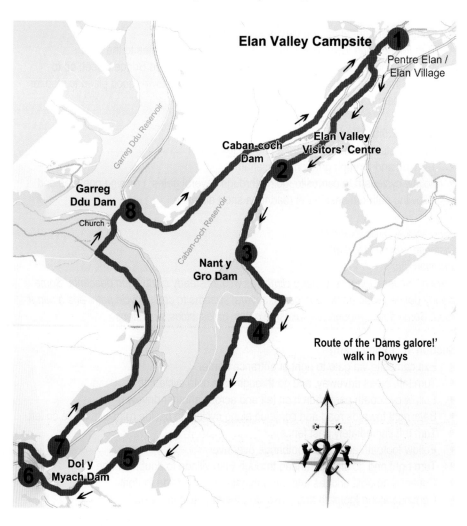

Elan Valley Campsite

Pentre Elan /
Elan Village

Caban-coch
Dam

Elan Valley
Visitors' Centre

Garreg
Ddu Dam

Church

Nant y
Gro Dam

Route of the 'Dams galore!'
walk in Powys

Dol y
Myach Dam

- Continue along footpath and through gate in fence on left
- Turn right and continue along path with lake still on right
- Bear left up hill at waymarker, through oak trees and another gate onto lakeside path
- Follow path around left-hand bend away from lake

Section 3: 1ml (1.6km)
- Bear left up hill at waymarker (a long, steep climb) past the ruins of Nant y Gro Dam
- Continue on wide track going uphill and around to left
- Turn right just before cluster of fir trees at waymarker
- Follow path as it zig-zags downhill to cross stream ahead
- Continue along path uphill opposite, and down to small waterfall

Through the gate onto the cyclepath.

- Cross waterfall via wooden plank bridge 10yd (9m) on left upstream
- Follow path round to right and uphill, keeping close to fence on left

Section 4: 1.5ml (2.4km)
- Through gate ahead: now fence is on right
- Continue along path heading towards trees, climbing steadily
- Follow path with trees on right and through gate ahead
- Continue on downhill with trees still on right

Section 5: 0.75ml (1.2km)
- Follow path as it gradually moves away from trees. Cross two fields and two streams and go through gate to cross another stream via a wooden plank bridge
- Follow wide stony track, keeping close to fence and water on right, and through gate ahead
- Stay on stony track going downhill with fence still on right
- Cross another stream and go through another gate still on stony track (on the right, glimpses of the dam can be had, and there are some lovely places on the riverbank to stop and have lunch)

Section 6: 1ml (1.6km)
- Continue along stony track and keep right past Longhouse
- Along road and cross bridge
- Continue straight ahead to T-junction by car park
- Turn right and continue along road (though this road only goes to the dams it does get busy during weekends and holidays so take care)
- Bear left up slope at layby with information board (another steep climb)

Section 7: 1.5ml (2.4km)
- Bear right downhill at waymarker

- Continue following narrow path as it goes up and down, and through gate high above the dam
- Continue on uphill
- Bear right at waymarker along wide track, going slightly downhill, and through gate
- Take track on right going down to road
- Turn left and follow road to long bridge, passing church on left
- Turn right and cross bridge

Section 8: 1.75ml (2.8km)
- Turn right and go through gate onto cyclepath
- Continue along cyclepath past Visitor Centre below (this is a good place to stop for refreshments and discover more about the area. Take one of the footpaths off to the right that drop down to the car park. Going through the car park away from the Visitor Centre and along the access road will bring you back to the cyclepath)
- Cross over access road to Visitor Centre
- Turn left and continue along cyclepath to campsite

IN THE LOCALITY
CYCLING
Though the area is hilly there are several cycle routes. The old railway line has been converted into a cyclepath, and climbs steadily northward to the Craig Goch Dam; it's suitable for all ability levels. The views of the reservoirs and surrounding area are spectacular. Using lanes and quiet roads in the area it is possible to devise circular routes, but, because of the hills, these are best suited to more competent cyclists. Bikes can be hired from a shop in Rhayader or from the Elan Valley Visitor Centre.

FISHING
The surrounding area is eminently suitable for fishing. The waters are considered so exceptional they were selected to host the Commonwealth Fly Fishing Championships. Fishing permits are obtainable from the Post Office in Rhayader.

BIRDWATCHING
The lakes created by the dams and the remoteness of the hills are ideal conditions for a huge variety of birds. A bird hide is accessible from the road via a small wooden gate in a copse on the north side of the disused dam of Dol y Mynach Reservoir. However, it is the survival of the Red Kites in the Elan Valley that is most remarkable. At one time, this bird of prey could be found in large numbers all over the UK, but because he feeds on carrion, was considered vermin and systematically eradicated. In recent times it was only in remote areas such as the Elan Valley that a few pairs survived. Realization that the Red Kite was close to extinction resulted in a change of attitude which allowed the species to thrive. The birds now resident in the valley are all descendants of the small group who managed to survive in the region.

GIGRIN FARM RED KITE FEEDING STATION

The farm is situated on South Street, half-a-mile South East of Rhayader. Every day in the afternoon the local birds of prey are fed. Mostly this is the Red Kite, but other species such as crows and buzzards join in this freebie. It is an amazing sight to see so many magnificent birds.

NANT Y GRO DAM

Built to provide water for the people living in Elan village who were involved in building the dams. In 1942, it was used by Barnes Wallis to test his famous 'dambuster' theories. He managed to successfully blow up the dam, leaving it in ruins which have remained untouched since then.

ELAN VALLEY VISITORS CENTRE

Located at the first and lowest dam in the Elan Valley, Caban Coch dam, the centre is an excellent place at which to learn about the dams and surrounding countryside. It has a gift shop, comprehensive tourist information section, an exhibition area, and a café that serves a range of food. The outside is spacious with lovely places beside the water for picnics, as well as a large car parking area. It is free to use but there is a charge for parking.

MEDIAEVAL LONGHOUSE

In the Claerwen Valley close to Dol v Mynach Reservoir is the Llannerch y Cawr Longhouse, that dates back to the 16th century. A simple, single-storey building, the farmer and his family lived at one end and the livestock at the other, separated by a passage. It was restored in 1999, retaining many of the traditional features. Now the two halves are rented out as holiday lets.

RHAYADER

The name Rhayader means 'Waterfall on the Wye,' being a corruption of the Welsh 'Rhaeadr Gwy.' This small, bustling town is situated only a few miles from the source of the river Wye, and has the distinction of being the first on the river. It is also an important centre for the local farming community, and is the venue for a regular livestock market. On the major routes linking North and South Wales, Rhayader has always been a natural stopping point for travellers; perhaps this explains the proliferation of eateries!

The Clock Tower at the crossroads of the town is supposedly the midway point between North and South Wales. With its long and eventful history, Rhayader has many large, imposing buildings, and there is an informative town trail obtainable from Tourist Information.

The walks: North East England
(East Yorkshire, North Yorkshire, Northumberland)

East Yorkshire — Bird watching made easy

OS MAPS EXPLORER 301 SCARBOROUGH, BRIDLINGTON AND FLAMBOROUGH HEAD

Being an island, Britain has an extremely long coastline, often with rocky headlands and promontories jutting out into the sea. One such place is Flamborough Head in East Yorkshire on the east coast, just south of Scarborough, which extends approximately 6 miles (9.6km) into the North Sea, and chalk cliffs of over 430ft (130m) plummet to the sea far below.

Cliffs plummet to the sea.

The cliffs stretch from Sewerby round Flamborough Head to Buckton, and attract many different birds; especially seabirds. In fact, one of the most important colonies of seabirds in Europe can be found at Flamborough Head, which is a significant factor to this area being designated a Site of Special Scientific Interest.

In spring and early summer the cliffs are inhabited by various gulls, as well as the quite distinctive Puffin. In high summer the cliffs are crammed with tens of thousands of other seabirds, including Auk and Gannets. This is an amazing experience that involves all of the senses. Large numbers of birds swoop and dive; then, as you approach their nesting site, the pungent smell is almost overwhelming. Just as you become accustomed to it, the screeching and squawking increases in volume until almost deafening. The sight of all these birds squeezed wing-to-wing, beak-to-tail on rocky outcrops is simply incredible.

One of the most important seabird colonies in Europe.

At one time the eggs were harvested and primarily sold for food, although some were sold to the leather industry because the albumen was used in patent leather manufacturing. To get to the eggs men were lowered on ropes down the cliff face, with only a cloth cap stuffed with straw for protection. This was known as 'climming.' As many as 400 eggs were collected every day, and yet, astonishingly, serious injury was rare. This practice ceased many years ago. In 1971, an RSBP reserve and visitor centre was established at Bempton Cliffs, where, besides helping visitors understand the complexity and significance of this area, it monitors bird activity, including the migratory species that arrive in the autumn.

These chalk cliffs are the edge of Yorkshire Wolds, which stretch in a southerly arc towards Hull. The land between the sea and the Wolds is mostly flat, the fields stretching right up to the cliffs, and is used for arable or to keep sheep. Though there are villages and small market towns dotted about, it is the coastline that dominates the region.

On each side of the cliffs are long stretches of beautiful golden sands and popular seaside resorts, one of which can be found just south of Flamborough Head, at Bridlington. These days the resort is more sedate, though still has the usual seaside attractions such as amusement arcades, funfair rides, and donkey rides. There is a large shopping complex and, close by, a long, wide, fabulous promenade, particularly appreciated by those using mobility scooters, judging by the battalions of them out in force.

Wonderful walks from **dog-friendly campsites**

The promenade is also a boon to me and other dog owners, as we can enjoy a beach walk, despite dogs not being allowed on the sands during the summer months. There is also a picturesque, bustling harbour from which it is possible to take a boat trip to see some of the many caves; go fishing, or simply watch the boats bring in their catch.

The coastal path around Flamborough Head is easy to follow (the views are stunning), and leads out to the lighthouse that warns shipping of the treacherous coastline. Despite this, over the years, the rocks have claimed many ships. The lighthouse was built in 1806 to replace a chalk version, and the in 1996 it became automated so the lighthouse keepers were no longer needed and left. However, it is open to the public during the summer.

Although chalk is quite resistant to the battering it gets from the North Sea, over many hundreds of years caves, coves, chasms, arches and stacks have been hacked out by the relentless sea, and this process is continuous. Even today, sections of the cliff crash into the sea periodically, and often the footpath has to be re-routed. So do take care walking the clifftop path, especially as, in places, the path is very close to the cliff edge: ensure your dog is under close control.

CAMPSITE WOLD FARM CARAVAN AND CAMPING

Being on the outskirts of Flamborough, the campsite is ideally situated to explore this area. Because it is part of a working farm, the owners are busy with various farm chores. It is a no-frills site but does have the convenience of electric hook-up, modern toilets, and showers.

The camping field comprises two small meadows stretching down towards the cliffs. In places these slope quite steeply, though there are several fairly level areas, especially on the side with hook-up. Those pitches with hook-up are rather close together, but there is a lot of space for tents. The new, small toilet and shower block is at the top of the field near the farmhouse, so some distance from several pitches. It's clean, neat and tidy, but queues could soon form when busy, I imagine. A pound coin is needed to operate the showers. The water taps are mostly scattered around the top meadow, so are also quite a distance from some pitches.

My welcome was warm and friendly. The site was quiet and peaceful, and the views were captivating. Access to the network of footpaths was easy. In addition, the charge was reasonable, especially for those touring on their own.

PEARLS OF WISDOM 🐾

As we arrived I noticed that there were fields everywhere. How exciting: lots of places to explore, I thought!

But what a disappointment ... not only was there no designated area for me, but very few places overall for short, stretch-the-legs outings. Luckily, when there were only a few visitors it was possible to chase after my frisbee in the camping field. The footpath close by did lead to some amazing places, but it was a good job I am fit and agile enough to leap over some of the stiles: the only way we could go because of all the fencing. Those silly sheep (again!) ... they made such a noise, like they were taunting me.

Then there were the birds, who made an enormous din. The smell of these was so overpowering I had difficulty smelling anything else. There was a lot to investigate during the walks but I had to be really careful of the steep drops, and pay close attention to my owner.

SHORT WALK – BIRDS, BIRDS AND MORE BIRDS!
Distance: 5ml (8km)
Duration: 2hr
Terrain: Mostly flat; cliff top path, fields, stony track and roads. Care should be taken along the Headland Way as parts of it are quite seriousy eroded

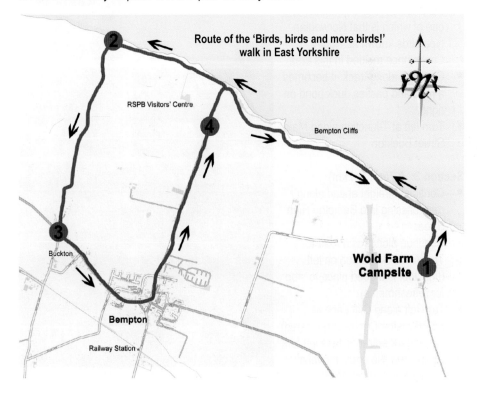

Route of the 'Birds, birds and more birds!' walk in East Yorkshire

Section 1: 1.75ml (2.8km)

- Exit campsite via gate in 'Puffin Meadow'
- Turn right and follow grass track up slope
- Through right-hand gate with 'RSPB' notice beside it
- Bear right across this field to corner of fence that juts out
- At this corner turn left and follow fence to stile (this is sheep-proof)
- Over stile onto clifftop path – 'The Headland Way' – and turn left
- Follow Headland Way through RSPB reserve past Bempton to where path branches into three separate paths (beware: the single path on the right which passes through

gateposts is VERY dangerous as it has slipped down to the sea)

Section 2: 1ml (1.6km)

- Take the double track on left and follow across fields away from cliffs

Puffin sculpture on the cliff top path – 'Headland Way' – close to the RSPB reserve.

- Turn right at junction along track (signposted). This is Hoddy Cows Lane; it is not known for sure why it is called this, and there are several explanations, one of which is that Norwegian-type birds known as Hoddy Crows once resided in this area
- Continue along track: it becomes a road and passes duck pond on right
- Turn left at T-junction along Main Street Buckton

Section 3: 0.75ml (1.2km)

- Continue straight ahead along road passing into Bempton High Street
- Continue along main road to The White Horse pub on left (this, too, is a good place to stop for refreshments)
- Turn left along Cliff Lane to RSPB Visitor Centre (signposted)
- At car park entrance take left fork signposted 'No entry' for vehicles into picnic area and Visitor Centre. This, too, is a good place to stop for refreshments
- Go left towards Visitor Centre toilets
- Straight ahead through gate on right of building onto path behind building

Section 4: 1.5ml (2.4km)

- Turn right and follow path to cliffs
- Turn right along Headland Way to stile in fence, which is now on right
- Over stile and straight ahead across fields to campsite

Long walk – The Coastal Sweep
Distance: 9.5ml (15.2km)
Duration: 4hr
Terrain: Mostly flat; cliff top path, fields, stony track and roads. Care needed along The Headland Way as parts of it are seriously eroded

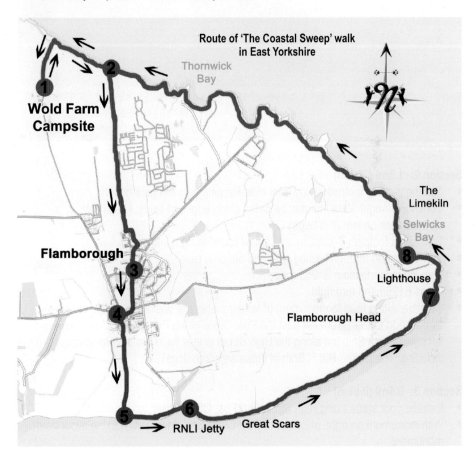

Route of 'The Coastal Sweep' walk in East Yorkshire

Section 1: 1ml (1.6km)

- Exit campsite via gate in 'Puffin Meadow'
- Turn right and follow grass track up slope
- Through right-hand gate with 'RSPB' notice beside it
- Bear right across this field to corner of fence that juts out
- At this corner turn left and follow fence to stile (which is sheep-proof)
- Over stile onto clifftop path – 'The Headland Way' – and turn right
- Follow Headland Way to signposted footpath on right just before large caravan park clearly visible ahead

Wonderful walks from dog-friendly campsites

Access is easy from the campsite to the Headland Way.

Section 2: 1.5ml (2.4km)
- Turn right along footpath away from cliffs keeping caravan park on left
- Continue straight ahead on narrow paths along edges of fields, keeping close to caravan park on left (it is huge)
- Turn left at footpath T-junction, and follow round to right into sports field
- Straight ahead through kissing gate and out onto road
- Turn left towards main B1255 road
- Cross B1255 and turn right
- Continue along road to monument (if refreshments are desired, perhaps elevenses, take a short detour. Turn left past the Post Office along Post Office Street, then turn left again at the Ship Inn along the High Street where there are several shops, including 'The Coffee Hut.' Both of these welcome dogs)

Section 3: 0.5ml (0.8km)
- Retrace your steps along High Street and Post Office Street to monument on B1255
- With monument on right, at corner of Post Office Street turn left, walking away from monument
- Follow road past castle ruin and round right-hand bend
- Just after row of white cottages on the left, go through gate into churchyard of St Oswald's Parish Church
- Take path to left, walking around church, and exit via white gate onto Lily Lane; then turn right

Section 4: 0.75ml (1.2km)
- Straight ahead past Butlers Close on left to T-junction
- Turn left into West Street
- Continue on following road as it twists first left; then right
- Keep straight on as road becomes a track and enter Beacon Farm

- Go straight ahead across farmyard to gate and onto a wide track
- Follow track along fields towards sea and cliffs, where there is a seat to rest and enjoy the view

A conveniently-placed seat from which to admire the view.

Section 5: 0.5ml (0.8km)
- Turn left at T-junction onto 'The Headland Way' (signposted)
- In about 0.5ml (0 8km), a long flight of steps leads to stony beach: this is South Landing where Flamborough Lifeboat Station is based. There is a shop attached to the station, and money raised from this is used to support the lifeboat
- Cross Sea Road and climb long, steep flight of steps back up to cliff top

Section 6: 2.25ml (3.6km)
- Turn right towards headland
- Beside seat and sculpture take right fork onto Headland Way (there is a sculpture trail around this part of the headland)
- Continue along Headland Way, almost two miles (3 2km), as it twists and turns, and goes up and down along top of cliffs towards lighthouse that can be glimpsed across the fields

Section 7: 1.5ml (2.4km)
- Take path that bears left up slope with lighthouse just visible over the hedge
- Follow path into field but keep close to hedge on left and continue straight ahead to Lighthouse, car park and café (here is a good place to stop for refreshments; also tours of the lighthouse when open)

Wonderful walks from dog-friendly campsites

- From café turn left along road towards car park exit
- The Headland Way path is signposted on right. Descend short flight of steps: turn right and then left, climbing to top of cliffs
- Follow Headland Way past golf course along cliff top to North Landing

Section 8: 1.5ml (2.4km)
- Take path to right of car park and follow to Thornwick Bay
- At road turn right and follow drive to café but keep close to fence on left, following it to the left
- At corner of fence turn left
- A short distance along on right is a signposted path
- Through kissing gate and continue straight ahead
- At fork take right path to cliff top (there is some serious erosion along this stretch of The Headland Way, so take great care The route is often diverted for safety reasons, so follow any signposted diversion)
- Continue along Headland Way to stile in the fence on left that leads into the field back to campsite

IN THE LOCALITY
BIRDWATCHING
The Headland Way, which is easily accessed by a private footpath from the campsite, runs for miles along the top of steep chalk cliffs. Rising to 430ft (130m), these cliffs are sheer and home to one of the largest sites of nesting seabirds in England.

There are many excellent viewing points along the Way: at Bempton Cliffs there is an RSPB Visitor Centre, and views from the clifftop walk are spectacular, with many coves, sea caves and stacks – large pillars comprising layers of rocks – along the coast line.

DANES DYKE
This ancient earthwork runs across the headland from the cliffs to the beaches near Bridlington, where there is a Nature Reserve. Here can be found many woodland trails and an impressive beach. The Dyke passes close to the campsite, but the footpath along it going towards the Nature Reserve is overgrown, unfortunately, which makes for very difficult walking.

THE YORKSHIRE BELLE
Cruises on this boat run from Bridlington Harbour round Flamborough Head, occasionally even going as far as Bempton Cliffs. They take between one and two hours, and dogs are welcome onboard.

FLAMBOROUGH LIGHTHOUSE
Standing proudly on the headland, this imposing structure is visible from far and wide on land and sea. The present example was built in 1806 by John Matson of Bridlington, and is open to visitors between March and September: do check tour times.

BRIDLINGON

This is a typical seaside town with a wonderfully long sandy beach (dogs not allowed in summer) and harbour. With lots of boats coming and going, this is an exciting place to visit.

JOHN BULL ROCK FACTORY AND CANDY KINGDOM

Just three miles (4.8km) south of Bridlington in Carnaby is this rock-producing factory, where you can touch, hear smell, see, and taste the rock on your way around the factory.

SEWERBY HALL, ZOO AND GARDENS

As the zoo and gardens are just south of Flamborough, it is possible to walk here from the campsite (obviously, dogs will not be allowed in the zoo and hall). The gardens are open all year round from dawn until dusk; the hall is open Easter to the end of September. A land train runs from Sewerby to Bridlington every half-hour.

North Yorkshire — Sport of Kings
OS MAPS EXPLORER 302 NORTHALLERTON & THIRSK
YELLOW MAP WALKS AROUND AND ABOUT THIRSK

As well as being the largest of the Yorkshire counties, North Yorkshire is also one of the biggest in the UK; certainly the largest in England. It stretches from the east coast to just a few miles short of the west coast across the North of England, and encompasses two national parks: the North Yorkshire Moors in the east and most of the Yorkshire Dales in the west. These are separated by the wide, fertile Vale of York and Vale of Mowbary.

Because Yorkshire covers such an extensive area, its impact upon the history of England has been significant. During the 15th century the leading families of Yorkshire wanted to influence the Kings of England, which frequently led to confrontation, especially with the powerful families of Lancashire. As the symbol of Yorkshire is a white rose and that of Lancashire is a red rose, this protracted period of historical brawling is known as 'The War of the Roses.'

This conflict finally ended in 1485 when Richard III of York was defeated at Bosworth by Henry VII (Tudor) of Lancaster. To seal his victory and unite the two sides, Henry married Richard III's niece, Elizabeth of York. It is because Henry won at Bosworth that, today, England's symbol is the red rose. Coincidentally, just recently, Richard's remains were found under a car park in Leicester. They are now interred in Leicester Cathedral, close to where he died.

Perhaps this definitive defeat, in addition to the type of landscape and location of the county, explains the unusually fierce loyalty of Yorkshire folk. Locally, the region is often referred to as 'God's own County.' The people may appear reserved – or even brusque – but they do welcome visitors, though acceptance takes a tad longer. Maybe this is why it took so long (until 1990) for the Yorkshire cricket team to admit players born outside of the county.

North Yorkshire is a very rural county, and over half of it is a national park or an AONB (Area of Outstanding Natural Beauty). In contrast to the rugged hills and peaks of the national parks, the vales are fairly flat with gentle rolling hills, and the fast-flowing streams have become slower, wider, and more imposing as they wend their way to the North Sea.

Though it is sheep country and the ancillary wool-related commerce has been important to the area since the Middle Ages, the industrial revolution had minimal impact. The grand houses of the wool merchants, the wealthy abbeys, various monuments and striking ruins, and many charming market towns such as Thirsk are evidence of a once-prosperous time.

Nestled in the Vale of Mowbary close to both the Yorkshire Dales and the North Yorkshire Moors is the delightful market town of Thirsk, which, like many of the towns in this area, has a long and intriguing history. There is mention of it in the *Doomsday Book*, and the cobbled square dates from medieval times. The enormous Clock Tower overlooking the square is a recent addition erected in 1896 in remembrance of the marriage of Queen Elizabeth II's grandparents, King George V to Princess Mary of Teck. It replaced a dilapidated market cross. Pubs, cafés and shops surround the square, many of them small, local, and independent. Every Monday since 1293 a market has been held in the town, which nowadays sells everything from local produce to clothing and hardware.

Birthplace of Thomas Lord, who founded Lord's Cricket Ground in London, these days Thirsk is better known as the home of James Herriot, the nom de plume of Alfred Wright, whose books recounting the exploits of a country vet are based upon his experiences. The town boasts a charming compact cinema, library, leisure centre, art gallery, and also, on the outskirts, a racecourse.

Since 2015 the 'Yarnbombers' have invaded the town. Crocheted and knitted decorations first appeared to brighten the place for the Tour de Yorkshire, mysteriously appearing overnight to the delight of townsfolk and visitors, and disappeared as equally suddenly. These delightful decorations now appear regularly to mark special occasions, and are enjoyed by everyone. Further details, and an informative town trail, are obtainable from the Visitor Centre. All-in-all, Thirsk is a lively and bustling town with an interesting history.

CAMPSITE – THIRSK RACECOURSE CARAVAN AND MOTORHOME CLUB
Situated on the outskirts of Thirsk, the campsite is, as the name suggests, within the confines of the racecourse, and within walking distance of two conveniently-sited supermarkets. The amenities are of the usual Club standard, albeit somewhat cramped. The main racing stand overshadows the 59 pitches, which are accessed via the premier entrance, and located in the car park for owners, trainers and premier ticket holders. Thus, on days when there is racing, all units have to move to the rally field. This is on the north side of the racecourse adjacent to the start of the 8 furlong races. Though this is an inconvenience as the only facility is the chemical toilet, it does offer the opportunity to experience horseracing from a unique perspective.

PEARLS OF WISDOM 🐎
The onsite exercise area was a bit something-and-nothing: just a narrow patch of grass

The town of Thirsk is brightened with knitted decorations by the Yarnbombers.

beside the wall. There were some interesting doggy smells, and it was big enough to chase my frisbee, but the traffic noise was very distracting. I was very pleased when we went to a much bigger, more exciting place.

I did not like the long walk we had to take along the pavement before I could run about, investigate, and sometimes play with other visiting chums. The tracks and fields I was taken to were fantastic but, again, the walk along the road was very restrictive and boring. All the walks I did were a mixture of strict lead walking and free roaming. I much preferred the roaming!

SHORT WALK – BESIDE THE BECK
Distance: 4ml (6.4km)
Duration: 2hr (longer if climbing Pudding Hill)
Terrain: Flat, except for Pudding Hill; roads, footpaths tracks, footbridges, kissing gates, stiles

Section 1: 1.25ml (2km)
- Exit campsite via entrance
- Turn left along Station Road past Lidl
- Cross road bearing right towards petrol station
- Turn left along alley in 20yd (18m (signposted)
- Continue along alley into Castle Green
- Take left fork across

Watch the races from the campsite.

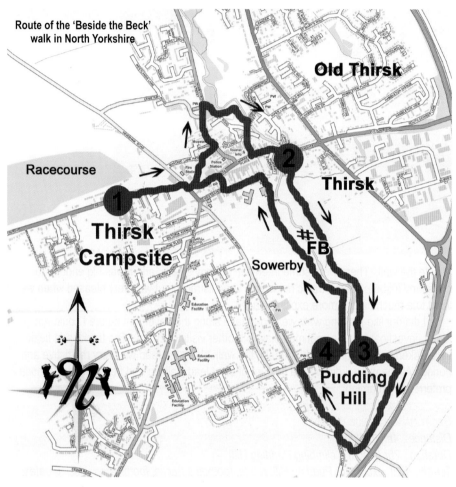

Route of the 'Beside the Beck' walk in North Yorkshire

Old Thirsk

Racecourse

Thirsk

Thirsk Campsite

Sowerby

FB

Pudding Hill

N

green and go through kissing gate onto road
- Turn right along road and out onto main road
- Turn left past Herriot Museum and continue on towards church
- Turn right opposite church into Marage Road
- Keep left onto tarmac path, staying close to fence on left
- Follow path beside the Beck
- Turn right before footbridge and go through kissing gate
- Follow path still beside Beck through another kissing gate and out onto road by bridge
- Continue straight ahead through Market Square on right
- Turn left along Finkle Street, past library on right and over bridge
- Turn right along driveway between garage and flats
- Keep to left of car park; continue straight ahead towards trees, passing fence on right, and through kissing gate into field by information board
- Cross field and go through kissing gate opposite

- Take right fork
- Follow path across field and over stile

Section 2: 0.75ml (1.2km)
- Continue along footpath with Beck on right, passing footbridge on right
- Bear left to cross another footbridge
- Bear right and follow path across two small fields and through kissing gate into big field
- Turn right along edge of field with hedge on right, and go through kissing gate in corner into next field
- Bear right along edge of field (beware barbed wire fence on left). Go through another kissing gate into field
- Continue straight ahead and go through kissing gate onto road

Section 3: 0.75ml (1.2km)
- Turn left away from bridge
- Continue along road to left-hand bend
- Turn right through kissing gate. 'Pudding Hill' is on the left with views over Thirsk.

Pearl enjoying a swim in the Beck.

- Continue along path beside Beck; through kissing gate into next field
- Follow path beside Beck and through kissing gate onto road beside busy road bridge overhead.
- Cross road to information board
- Continue ahead across green, bearing right to old 'Pack Horse Bridge'
- Cross bridge, turn right, and follow path back to road
- Cross road, bearing right onto wide main road
- Turn left at junction onto main road with big houses each side
- Continue along main road

- Turn right and follow narrow road on left side which becomes a hedged footpath
- Continue along footpath back onto road
- Turn left along road and immediately left again before bridge, and go through kissing gate into field

Section 4: 1.25ml (2km)
- Cross field and go through kissing gate onto path beside Beck
- Follow riverside path through another kissing gate and past footbridge on right, keeping close to the Beck

Former mill beside the Beck.

- Take path bearing slightly left away from Beck, heading towards clump of trees and hedges to go through kissing gate onto playing fields
- Continue straight ahead towards low building (leisure centre)
- Go through gap, keeping building on left
- Continue straight ahead across car park to entrance
- Turn left and continue along road to cinema on left
- Turn right and cross road to continue along Castlegate
- Turn left along alley with butcher shop on corner into Castle Green
- Follow path across green towards Lidl
- Cross road to Lidl entrance
- Continue along Station Road to campsite entrance

LONG WALK – ROUND AND ABOUT
Distance: 7.75ml (12.4km)
Duration: 4hr
Terrain: Mostly flat; fields, stony tracks, footpaths kissing gates, stiles, roads and bridge across a railway line and a level crossing (there are gates and big notices warning of dangers at the crossing, but the area between the rail lines is filled in so it is easy to walk across)

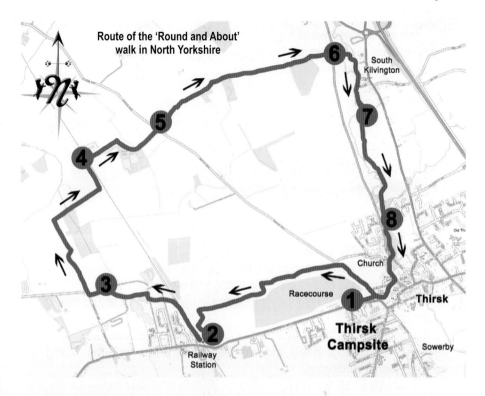

Route of the 'Round and About'
walk in North Yorkshire

South
Kilvington

Racecourse

Church

Thirsk

Thirsk
Campsite

Sowerby

Railway
Station

Section 1: 1.25ml (2km)
- Exit campsite via entrance
- Turn left along Station Road
- Turn left along road immediately past Lidl
- Continue along road, which becomes narrow, past campsite and athletic club on left
- Turn left, through barrier onto wide track
- Follow track as it turns right and left past gate which overlooks racecourse onto narrow footpath along edge of field
- Continue along footpath as it turns left into 2nd field
- Follow footpath along two edges of field
- Turn left at next corner and continue along path into copse and to railway station car park

Section 2: 1ml (1.6km)
- Bear right across small car park; up steps to bridge over rail tracks and out onto road
- Turn right along road
- Turn right at first driveway
- Keeping right, go through gate into tarmac path with rail tracks on right
- Continue as path becomes wide, stony track; then grassy
- Turn left into field

- Bear right across field towards house
- Cross road and continue across field, bearing right towards house
- Follow path into trees
- Turn left at fence and follow path around edge of campsite on left
- Cross footbridge; turn right. Cross 2nd footbridge; turn left
- Continue along footpath with campsite still on left, turning right, left, right again into field
- Follow path along edge of field round to left at corner, and now parallel to road
- Turn right through 2nd gap in hedge: about halfway along, turn out onto road
- Turn left along road

Section 3: 1.25ml (2km)
- Turn right at junction and continue along road to left-hand bend
- Continue straight onto footpath
- With hedge on left follow path right and left along edge of field
- Turn left at corner and go through gap in hedge onto wide track
- Turn immediately right along grassy track between telegraph poles and go through kissing gate
- Turn immediately right and continue ahead along edge of three fields to railway line
- Turn left, still along edge of field, and follow path beside railway for 200yd (183m,) heading towards buildings

Section 4: 0.75ml (1.2km)
- Turn right to cross railway lines (cross with great care; as if on a very, very busy road)
- Continue straight through farmyard and follow driveway to road

Section 5: 1.25ml (2km)
- Cross over and continue straight through Woodhill Farm to bridleway
- Follow driveway past Moat Farm, and through barrier onto wide track that runs along edge of two fields
- Continue straight past footpath junction along edge of another field to road

Section 6: 1ml (1.6km)
- Bear slightly right and cross road to path opposite with signpost 'No Camping' on right
- Continue along short path between trees, and through kissing gate into field
- Cross field and go through gate opposite and cross footbridge
- Turn right and follow path heading towards buildings, and cross another footbridge
- Turn right immediately, keeping wall on left
- Follow footpath beside Beck, keeping close to it on right (entrance to pub is possible through small field on left)
- Over stile into field
- Continue straight and over stile opposite
- Bearing slightly right, continue ahead and over stile opposite

Section 7: 0.75ml (1.2km)
- Go straight towards corner of hedges away from river, passing under two trees
- Bear right towards metal-type bridge, and through stile with bridge on right
- Follow path along edge of field and through another gate
- Go straight towards trees and through kissing gate
- Follow path with Beck now on right again
- Cross footbridge and continue ahead

Section 8: 0.5ml (0.8km)
- Cross another footbridge into park
- Follow path through park parallel to road past church and out onto Marage Road
- Cross road and take right fork with church on right, and continue ahead to Kirkgate
- Turn right along Masonic Lane (Picks Lane)
- Turn left and go through kissing gate into Castle Park
- Follow path to metal fence and along alley to main road
- Cross road to Lidl entrance
- Continue along Station Road to campsite entrance

IN THE LOCALITY
THE WORLD OF JAMES HERRIOT MUSEUM
This is situated in the centre of Thirsk in the very house that housed the veterinary practice, as well as being the family home of Alf Wright, better known as James Herriot, author of the *All Creatures Great and Small* series of books. The museum celebrates the life and work of an ordinary country vet in 1940s and 1950s Yorkshire, with a collection of distinctive items. Also on display are the props and sets used in the TV series. Interestingly, most of the outdoor filming for the series took place in the Yorkshire Dales because it was more picturesque than Thirsk and surrounding environs. The Herriot Trail, which tracks the various locations used, is available from Tourist Information.

THIRSK MUSEUM
The history of the town and many interesting local artefacts are displayed in the house where Thomas Lord, founder of Lord's Cricket Ground, was born. The museum contains information regarding local life, customs and legends.

BUS TO YORK
From Thirsk Market Square runs a regular hourly bus service to the city of York. The journey takes about an hour and dogs are allowed on the buses.

FALCONRY UK BIRDS OF PREY CENTRE
Th centre is based in the grounds of Sion Hill Hall, five miles from Thirsk, and displays are held thrice-daily. A whole host of magnificent birds of prey, including hawks, owls and eagles, reveal their superlative skills. Special bookings are also possible.

Wonderful walks from dog-friendly campsites

Sion Hill Hall
When Percy Stancliffe and his wife, Ethel, bought Sion Hill Hall in 1911, they discovered the Manor House, which had stood for 600 years, was unsafe, and so had to be demolished. They commissioned Walter Brierley to design a new one, which was completed in 1913. Herbert William Mawer bought the house in 1962 and, over the years, furnished it with antiques of all kinds. Since his death in 1982, a charitable trust has looked after the house and its five acres of beautiful gardens.

Sutton Park National Park Centre
Only five miles (8km) to the west of Thirsk is the edge of the North Yorkshire Moors, Hambleton Hills, the highest part of which is at Sutton Bank, where the hills rise so steeply from the vale that vehicles – particularly caravans – have only restricted use of the A170. This does not prevent the road (1-in-4 gradient) from being closed every three days, on average, to recover stuck vehicles.

Once the top is reached the views of the Vale of York and Mowbary are spectacular. They can be enjoyed from the Sutton Park National Park Centre, where there is also information about the area, bike hire, a bird feeding station, walking trails, and tearoom for refreshments.

Northumberland — in the steps of Roman Soldiers
OS Maps Explorer OL 43 Hadrian's Wall

Hadrian's Wall is so-called because it was built by the Romans on the orders of the Emperor Hadrian, and straddles the country from the east coast at Newcastle to Carlisle on the west coast as it passes through three counties: Northumberland, Cumbria, and Tyne and Wear.

In many places, little remains of the actual wall, unfortunately. The significance of the structure was not realized until the 1830s, for which John Clayton is the man to thank, as he appreciated the need to preserve what remained of the wall. In addition to studying and excavating the edifice, he began buying land surrounding it, and, with astute management, was able to begin restoration that, unfortunately, ceased on his death. Eventually, the National Trust became responsible for the site, and the work of protection, investigation, and restoration resumed. Now, in Northumberland, at Housesteads, it is possible to see the remains of one of the best preserved forts situated along the wall.

As you leave the Visitor Centre at Housesteads and round the shrubs, the first glimpse of the path sweeping across the Northumberland landscape up to the fort is breathtaking. The fort fills the horizon – and that's just the archaeological remains. The original complete complex must have been stunning. As your eye meanders along the path, realization that the moving specks you can see are actually people emphasizes the immense scale of the scene. Slowly approaching the fort reinforces initial impressions: it is huge.

Looking back at the vast panorama of the Northumberland landscape is equally awe-inspiring. The enormous hills rolling into the far distance like immense waves are majestic and spectacular. The Romans may have built an enormous garrison but this is dwarfed by the vast Northumberland landscape. To build anything in this remote, difficult terrain is an amazing achievement; to construct a place teeming with people I find difficult to imagine as the land and sky seem too big and intimidating.

With so many Roman soldiers deployed along the wall, maintaining an efficient supply route was essential, especially in times of conflict. The Romans were nothing if not efficient, and, about half-a-mile south of the wall they built a road parallel to it that was flatter and straighter, and it was along this thoroughfare that traffic could travel more easily between the forts and milecastles (small forts). It was also along this road that reinforcements could be quickly deployed to potential trouble spots. Hence, the name 'Military Road.'

Walking along this is easier than along Hadrian's Wall Trail. It's still possible to experience the beauty and vastness of the landscape, and marvel at the complexity and magnificence of the wall. However, walking Hadrian's Wall Trail adds an extra dimension: the views, the wall, the effort, the time, the landscape, the weather, the people – *all* contribute to an extraordinary experience.

Just south of the Wall is Military Road, which soldiers used to get to trouble spots quickly.

The Hadrian's Wall Trail, which runs for 84 miles (135km) beside the wall, is actually very new; opened by the National Trust in 2003. It is now so popular that the mostly grass path is prone to extensive damage from the numerous boots pounding the trail. As a consequence, the National Trust asks that walkers plan their visits for between May and October when the weather is drier.

Because of the fragile nature of the wall it is not permitted to walk along the top. Obviously, it is not possible to complete the trail in one day unless you are descended from

Wonderful walks from dog-friendly campsites

Superman, but there are many circular and linear walks that are entirely feasible to do in a day.

Because of its close proximity, the wall is important to the town of Haltwhistle, which also lays claim to being the centre of the UK. Around the town a trail of blue plaques mark some of the more significant events of the town's tempestuous past, when both Scots and English claimed sovereignty. It's a pleasant place to visit with many interesting buildings.

Campsite – Herding Hill Farm

Nestling among the hills of Northumberland just above Haltwhistle Burn, the campsite is ideally suited for visiting both Haltwhistle and Hadrian's Wall, as well as places further afield. At the campsite entrance there's a bus stop for the AD122 Hadrian's Wall country bus, which goes to many interesting Roman sites along the wall. A few minutes' walk away down the hill is a pub; not dog-friendly, sadly. Only a mile from the campsite is an impressive section of Hadrian's Wall which includes the extensive remains of Milecastle 42.

Hadrian's Wall snaking across the Northumberland countryside.

The campsite offers a range of camping experiences. Beside 20 touring pitches there's a large field for tents and some Wigwams and Tipis. The amenities block is well organized with a dishwashing area, a laundry, and a large drying room. Quite unusually, in the ladies there is also a bath (I don't know about the gents!) The shop stocks the usual camping accessories, toiletries, a few children's toys and gifts. A home-cooked pizza can be delivered to your pitch at weekends in the summer. If you are really stiff after a long walk there's a sauna available to hire. For the children there is a play area based on a Roman theme, and animals to pet. It is a well-equipped campsite in a picturesque and convenient location, although rather expensive for the solo traveller.

Pearls of wisdom 🐾

It didn't take me long to become really familiar with the exercise area, and its long, thin

Herding Hill Campsite.

shape meant it was not really suitable for Frisbee chasing. The field next door was huge, full of nooks, crannies and crevices, and a lovely place, but I found it really difficult having to walk demurely along a short section of road to reach it.

Lots of our walks were very up and down, and necessitated quite a bit of roadwork, despite us having a ride on a bus. At every turn there seemed to be strange animals. My owner said the ones with a large white stripe round the middle were cows. We didn't go too near them. On the campsite were smaller but very fat round things that grunted and snorted (think she called them pigs). There were also tall black things with long necks and a funny name: alpacas, I think? I didn't mind getting close to them as there was a fence between us.

SHORT WALK – MIDDLE ENGLAND
Distance: 4ml (6.4km)
Duration: 2hr (longer if stopping at Haltwhiste)
Terrain: Fields, footpaths, track, roads, wooden step stiles, kissing gates, and some steep hills

Section 1: 0.75ml (1.2km)
- Exit campsite via reception onto Shield Hill
- Turn left and continue along road
- Turn left just after brow of hill at footpath signposted Haltwhistle
- Over wooden step stile or through gate
- Take footpath straight ahead, skirting hill on left
- Bear left along footpath over mound, and through what appears to be a gap in an old wall
- Turn right along path parallel to stone barrier on right and mound on left
- Turn left at junction along grassy track
- Continue along path, bearing right as it winds downhill
- Bear right along path to stone wall, keeping fence on right
- Over stone step stile over wall at marker
- Straight ahead to another marker, keeping stone wall on right

Wonderful walks from dog-friendly campsites

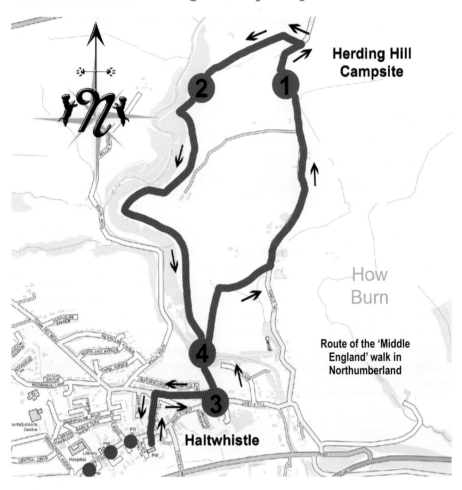

Herding Hill Campsite

How Burn

Route of the 'Middle England' walk in Northumberland

Haltwhistle

- Bear left towards wooden step stile beside gate

Section 2: 1.25ml (2km)
- Over stile and turn left, keeping close to fence on right
- Go through gate in corner of field
- Turn right and continue along path down steps to wide stony track beside Haltwhistle Burn
- Turn left along riverside path, keeping Haltwhistle Burn on right
- At footpath crossroads turn right down steps into copse to the water
- Cross bridge and ascend steps
- At top turn left along path to kissing gate and out onto road
- Go along road to main thoroughfare

Section 3: 0.5ml (0.8km)
- Turn right and continue along road to entrance of Sainsbury's car park

Pearl and the centre of Britain in Haltwhistle.

- Turn left into car park.
- Straight ahead past store on left to lane opposite signposted 'Market Place'
- Go along lane between houses and out onto Main Street (opposite is The Market Place: a charming square with seats and various displays marking the supposed centre of Britain. To the left of the square is a beautiful church, and to the right down a lane is the Black Bull pub that is dog-friendly. To explore Haltwhistle further turn right along Main Street to the town centre. There is a blue plaque trail to follow. Information about this can be found on a board in Sainsbury's car park or at Tourist Information further down the street)
- Retrace steps through Sainsbury's car park to road
- Turn right along road
- Turn left down private road, through kissing gate onto footpath
- Descend steps to Haltwhistle Burn

Section 4: 1.5ml (2.4km)
- Cross bridge and climb steps opposite

73

- Continue straight on through kissing gate into field
- Go straight ahead uphill, keeping close to wall on left
- Through another kissing gate
- Walk about 20 paces to cross marshy ground
- Turn right and walk around field to kissing gate in far corner by house
- Through kissing gate onto Shield Hill
- Turn left and continue along road to the campsite (take care walking along the road: although not very busy, traffic can be fast)

LONG WALK – PATROLLING THE WALL
Distance: 8ml (12.8km)
Duration: 4hr
Terrain: Clear, easy-to-follow route. Several very steep climbs and descents. Extremely stony and uneven in many places

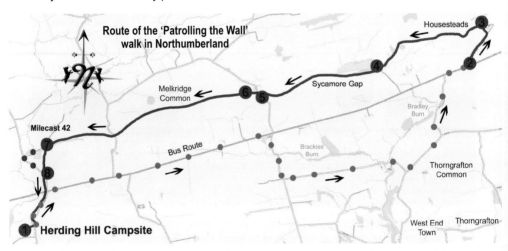

Considering Hadrian's Wall was built nearly 2000 years ago it's amazing so much of it is still standing. After the Romans abandoned it many centuries ago, the stone was plundered, especially for road building, and it is only recently that the importance and significance of the wall has been recognized (in 1987 it was designated a UNESCO World Heritage site).

As further findings are unearthed, so it becomes even more apparent what an extraordinary structure it is. Walking the Hadrian Wall Trail allows one to really appreciate its magnificence.

Section 1: Bus AD122

- Take the shuttle bus from the campsite to English Heritage/National Trust site 'Housesteads.' For the Romans, travel was made on foot or horseback, whilst we are fortunate enough to be able to hop on and off a bus, and the AD122 provides a great way to see the wall, as it runs between Hexham and Haltwhistle, stopping at various Roman sites, including Once Brewed, Vindolanda, and Housesteads. The service runs approximately every hour, but only from around Easter to October to coincide with the National Trust's request to walk the Wall Trail during drier weather. The precise bus timetable varies each year, depending on funding, so check times beforehand. Please use the service: without it many of the interesting areas of Hadrian's Wall are difficult to access by regular public transport. The bus stop is right outside the campsite entrance

Section 2: 1ml (1.6km)
During the building of the wall, which began in about AD 122 (the number of the bus!), it was decided to also build forts at intervals along it. These varied in size from the large ones that housed garrisons of soldiers and sometimes their families, to the small 'milecastles' that were constructed every Roman mile to protect a gate and control passage across the wall.

Altogether, 16 large forts were constructed, and Housesteads is the best preserved of all the Roman forts along Hadrian's Wall, as well as one of the largest, being able to accommodate 800 soldiers.

Just outside the walls was a civilian settlement, which, over the years of Roman occupation, grew into a very large town. The original name of the fort was 'Vercovicium,' which translates as 'the place of the effective fighters.' Further details and information about both the fort and Hadrian's Wall can be found at Housesteads Visitor Centre situated adjacent to the fort remains. This is an extremely interesting place to visit (National Trust and English Heritage work together to manage this impressive historical artefact).

- From the bus stop go through car park to the Visitor Centre. Walk through gift shop (you do not have to pay the entrance fee if you are not going to look at the archaeological remains. Unfortunately, dogs are not allowed into the fort)
- Take the path out of the Visitor Centre and follow as it winds around the shrubs and up to the fort on top of the hill
- Keeping fort on the right, leave tarmac path and walk up grassy slope (on your left in a stone, barn-like building is a café; the only opportunity for a refreshment stop)
- Keeping close to wall of the fort on right, continue straight ahead to Hadrian's Wall and through kissing gate

Section 3: 1.5ml (2.4km)
- Turn left and take path beside the wall, and go through kissing gate onto stony track
- Continue along stony track beside the wall, and through kissing gate onto tarmac road
- Turn left along road after 30yd (27m)

Section 4: 1.5ml (2.4km)
- Turn right at signpost onto footpath going up a hill (this is now Military Way; Hadrian's Trail moves to the other side of the wall and is quite difficult. Also, this route gives a

clear view of the Sycamore Gap)
- Continue along Military Way until it drops steeply and continues round an outcrop of rock, with Hadrian's Wall on the far side of fence
- Through gate beside building, and cross field to kissing gate by signpost onto road (for refreshments turn left along road going downhill for about 0.5 ml (0.8km) to a pub with large car park)

Section 5: 0.5ml (0.8km)
- Turn right, keeping close to wall for a few yards
- Turn right again and go through another kissing gate back onto Hadrian's Wall trail
- Turn left uphill along path as it bends left, keeping close to the Wall on left. On the right is a small car park; there are no facilities here apart from the occasional ice cream van
- Through the kissing gate and cross road
- Through another kissing gate with the Wall now on your right

Section 6: 2.5ml (4km)
- Continue along trail to small fort at Milecastle 42

Section 7: 0.5ml (0.8km)
- Turn left and take path across field towards pub
- Bear right across this large field, heading towards road*
- Go through kissing gate onto road

*(if there are cows in the field go through kissing gate on right at bottom of steps just past fort on right. DO NOT GO UP THE STEPS. Continue straight ahead to next kissing gate. Follow path around quarry lake to car park. Turn left at car park entrance. Follow road as is bends to the left. Continue along road passing kissing gate on the left)

Section 8: 0.5ml (0.8km)
- Turn left along road to crossroads
- Cross the road
- Continue straight ahead, keeping pub on left up Shield Hill to campsite on right

IN THE LOCALITY
HADRIAN'S WALL
There is plenty to see along the entire stretch of the Wall from Carlisle Castle in the west to Arbeia Roman Fort and Museum in the east, including Birdoswald Roman Fort and Vindolanda. Various events are held from April to September. Information can be found at Tourist Information or online.

ONCE BREWED TOURIST CENTRE
This has a dual purpose: as a Tourist Information Centre, and a Centre for Northumberland National Park. If you wish to familiarize yourself with the area it is worth visiting, as

it provides a wealth of information as well as the opportunity to purchase local crafts, souvenirs and refreshments. The AD122 bus stops here.

HALTWHISTLE

This town has a long turbulent history as both Scots and English have claimed sovereignty at various times. There are several information boards as well as an interesting blue plaque town trail. Nowadays, the close proximity of the Wall has resulted in a thriving tourist industry.

The town's other claim to fame is that it is at the centre of Britain. Located in the town is Mr George's Museum of Time, which houses a collection of clocks, watches and tools supposedly used by 'Mr George the Clock Man,' who can be found in a series of children's books written by Diana Bell, who based the character on her father, who was a clock repairer.

HEXHAM

This is a delightful market town to visit – especially its abbey and gaol – and is easy to reach as it is on the AD122 bus route. Tuesdays and Saturdays are market days.

BIRDWATCHING

This can be done anywhere, and the only equipment required is a pair of binoculars.

CYCLING

It is just as easy to explore the area by bicycle using 'Hadrian's Cycleway.' The 160ml (256km) route stretches the length of the Wall, and mostly follows signposted cyclepaths and quiet minor roads, with only a few steep hills. Again, information is available at Tourist Information.

STAR-GAZING

For much of Northumberland, light pollution is minimal, so it is possible to see a great many of the billions of stars overhead. As a consequence, in December 2013, the National Park was awarded International Dark Sky Status, making it officially the best place in England to enjoy the heavens. The only Dark Sky Discovery Site is within walking distance of the campsite at the now-disused Cawfields quarry (hopefully, in time, there will be more of these sites). The autumn and winter months are the best time for star-gazing as mid-summer nights do not become properly dark. Though the moon is wonderful to see, it makes it more difficult to see some of the stars, as does cloudy weather.

GEOCACHING

This is outdoor treasure hunting! You need geocaching membership and a GPS device. When you have found the 'cache' (which can be absolutely anything), you log your find, and if you take anything you must leave something of equal or greater value. I am told this is what makes it exciting as you have no idea what you will find. The campsite is part of a 26 geocache circuit, so is a good starting point.

The walks: North West England
(Cheshire, Cumbria, Lancashire)

Cheshire — stop and look

OS MAPS EXPLORER 267 NORTHWICH & DELAMERE FOREST

Cheshire is probably best-known to most people, like me, as the name of a cheese, and from Lewis Carroll's *Alice in Wonderland* and her encounter with the grinning but disappearing Cheshire Cat. This is hardly surprising as Cheshire is squeezed between the wide mouth of the River Mersey and Liverpool to the north west; the huge conurbation of Manchester to the north east; Newcastle and Stoke-on-Trent to the south east, and Wales to the west. It is primarily a place people pass through on their way elsewhere.

As a consequence, for many decades the transport system across the county has been excellent, enabling travellers to quickly and efficiently cross it. The M6 slices up through the middle of the county on its way north, and the M56 and M53 cut through the north of the county serving the River Mersey.

It is exactly the same with the railways. Because of its location, Crewe, in the south of Cheshire, was at one time the centre of the railway industry, and, even today, it is an important junction, but only as somewhere to change trains.

Likewise, when the canal system was being developed in the 17th and 18th centuries, crossing Cheshire was of such importance that several canal systems were built: the Shropshire Union Canal; Trent and Mersey Canal; Macclesfield Canal, and Bridgewater Canal, as well as the smaller Rochdale, Ashton and Peak Forest Canals. In addition, spanning the very north of the county is the enormous Manchester Ship Canal which allowed larger seagoing vessels to sail several miles inland to Manchester.

Nowadays, very few of these canals are used for commercial purposes, although they do enhance Cheshire enormously as a wonderful leisure facility connecting many of the towns, and as examples of the many amazing engineering feats that have occurred.

Cheshire is a mostly rural county, sparsely populated in comparison to others. The many small towns and villages are chiefly bedroom communities for the larger cities nearby. The county separates the mountains of Wales in the west from the hills of the Peak District that spill over into the eastern fringes of the county. Several rivers meander across the county, and pockets of greenery, such as Delamere Forest between Chester and Wirral, are dotted about, making for a richly diverse county.

The most industrialized part of the county lies in the north along the banks of the River Mersey, where several engineering companies manufacture a range of goods connected with cars and aeroplanes. Further east, near Northwich and Middlewich, salt is still worked as it has been since Roman times. Consequently, it has been convenient for chemical companies to locate there. And even further east, silk and cotton is produced, for which Cheshire is famous. However, it is the fertile soil of central Cheshire that has had the greatest impact as it is ideal for cattle, and there are numerous excellent dairy farms. The cheese produced is world-renowned.

Apart from the hills of the Peak District in the east, much of Cheshire is flat, the largely unspoilt rural landscape interspersed with charming villages and small market towns where local produce can be purchased, particularly on market day. The slight inclines, such as Pale Heights on the short walk, allow a surprisingly extensive view. Many of the counties encompassing Cheshire can be seen, which reinforces the impression of the county being squeezed in-between them.

Then there is Chester itself – the capital of the county – still an important settlement since established as a vital Roman stronghold in the first Century AD. It has a rich and varied history. With the River Dee and Shropshire and Union Canal passing through the city, Chester is a marvellous place to explore. There is so much to see, do and learn as there is with the county itself. Most people travel across Cheshire unaware of the delights to be found once off of its main busy thoroughfares.

CAMPSITE – DELAMERE FOREST CAMPING AND CARAVANNING CLUB SITE

This is not a big site; just 80 pitches. There is little open space, and no play area for children, but with a dog exercise area, and three gates giving direct access to the forest there is plenty to occupy both children and dogs.

It is a typical club site with the usual well designed facilities block kept spotlessly clean, located at one end of the campsite next to the reception-cum-shop, so some pitches are quite a distance from the toilets and shower. On Friday evenings fish and chips are available from a mobile van. Though Delamere Station is next to the campsite, passing trains do not create a significant disturbance but do allow easy and efficient access to places several miles away. This is a characteristic club campsite in an excellent location, and convenient for a range of activities.

PEARLS OF WISDOM 🐾

Wow, just a short bound, a squeeze under a gate, and there I was facing row upon row of

trees. What a huge forest – and lakes, too! – some of which actually sprouting trees and some of which smelling rather strongly. I was happy to have a dip in any

The forest is easily accessed from the campsite.

of the lakes but my owner was adamant I stay out of most of them. Last thing at night we even had a short excursion into the wood and then back through the campsite dog area. We spent all day in the forest with me exploring, chasing squirrels, and even having a dip, and not once was there a boring road, though the trains were rather close. It was absolutely thrilling. However, I could have done without a hose wash down afterward ...

SHORT WALK – FOREST AMBLE AND SCENIC PANORAMA
Distance: 4.5ml (7.2km)
Duration: 2.5hr
Terrain: Forest tracks and footpaths, some fields, gates and stiles with some gentle slopes and a steady climb

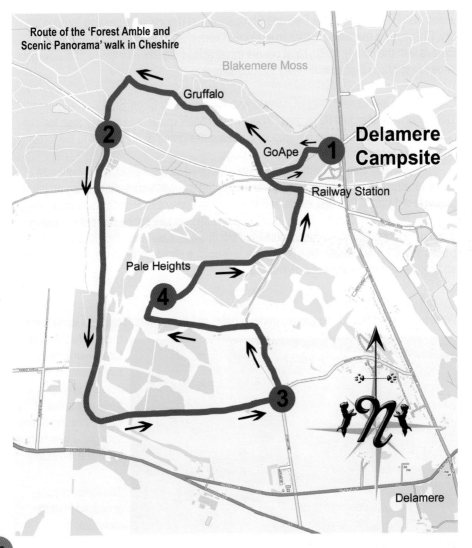

Route of the 'Forest Amble and Scenic Panorama' walk in Cheshire

Section 1: 1ml (1.6km)
- Exit campsite via dog walk gate nearest reception
- Through gate into forest
- Bear left along path, keeping close to water on right, and follow round to left back to main track
- Turn right and follow the path with rail tracks on the left
- Continue straight ahead past 'GoApe' picnic hut towards car park
- Turn right along path to GoApe, then immediately left and pass between two wooden pillars to a stony track
- Turn right and follow path round barrier
- Continue along path to left at footpath junction (signposted)
- Continue along wide track past footpath off to right
- Go straight ahead at footpath crossroad, passing wooden 'Gruffalo' on right
- Turn left at next wide junction along track signposted 'Moor Trail 7 miles'
- Keep left at right hand bend off stony track onto footpath
- Cross bridge over railway

Section 2: 1.25ml (2km)
- Keep to left track at next big junction, climbing slightly and following round to left
- Turn right at brow of hill past two half-stiles – one with yellow waymarker – onto narrow footpath beside stream
- Turn left at T-junction signposted 'Sandstone Trail'
- In approximately 50yd (45m) turn right at next junction signposted 'Nettleford Wood'
- Continue along track as it climbs, passing farm on left, and through a kissing gate
- Go straight ahead past track on left and big junction, down a slope and round left-hand bend
- Turn left onto footpath signposted 'Stoney Lane'

The Gruffalo found in the forest.

Section 3: 1.25ml (2km)
- Continue ahead up a slope and follow narrow footpath, keeping close to fence on right, and through kissing gate
- Continue along edge of field and through a metal kissing gate
- Turn sharp left and go through abutting wooden kissing gate into a grassy valley
- Straight on, keeping close to fence on right
- Follow path over stream and up valley, and through a gate by a trough
- Bear right and follow wide grassy track up slope and through gap in hedge

- Turn sharp right and go through a large gap in hedge
- Continue straight ahead towards mast with hedge on left
- Turn left along tarmac lane
- Continue straight ahead, going right around the 2nd mast (Pale Heights)
- Follow the tarmac path along brow of hill to the Cheshire Monolith (very interesting: each standing stone is carved with the name of the county that can be seen from this viewpoint)

Cheshire standing stones situated on Pale Heights.

Section 4: 1ml (1.6km)

- Exit path between Staffordshire and Derbyshire standing stone
- In a few yards take left fork towards trees and hedge
- Go through gap in hedge and continue straight on along stony path
- Follow path as it winds downhill through the trees
- Turn left at junction, cross stream, and turn sharp right
- Turn right at T-junction, then fork left

- At junction, continue following path as it bears left to the road
- Through kissing gate onto road
- Turn left; climb slope
- Turn right and cross bridge over rail tracks
- Turn right into forest towards GoApe
- Turn sharp right and follow path through the forest to the campsite, keeping close to the rail tracks on right

LONG WALK – CITYSCAPE

A city map from Tourist Information is more helpful for this walk than the OS map listed at the start.
Distance: 8ml (12.8km)
Duration: 4hr
Terrain: Pavements, lanes and parks. Care should be taken crossing several roads
Catch the train from the station next door to the campsite. Chester is two stops down the line. You can pay the conductor on the train, as there is no ticket office, or online facility. The price is the same

Section 1: 1ml (1.6km)

- Exit the station via City Road
- Continue along City Road to the bridge over the canal

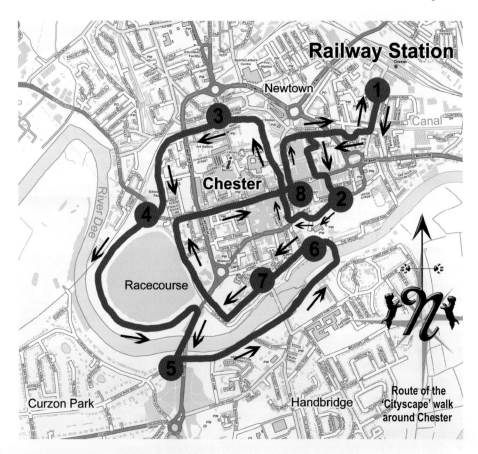

Route of the 'Cityscape' walk around Chester

- Cross the bridge and turn left down the steps by Old Haggerty Pub onto the canal tow path
- Turn left and walk under the bridge with the canal on right
- Continue along tow path to Canal Side
- Turn left down Back Queen Street
- Turn right at T-junction onto York Street
- Follow the road round to the left onto Queen Street
- Turn left at T-junction along Foregate Street
- Turn right down Love Street
- At T-junction cross road and turn right
- Entrance to Grosvenor Park on left (a good place to let your dog have a run off-lead before continuing)

Section 2: 1.25ml (2km)
- Retrace steps to park entrance on Vicar's Lane, and continue along the road towards the arch
- Bear left and cross road to walk ramp entrance around the Roman amphitheatre

- Through gate at the end and turn left: cross road; go under road arch; turn left
- Turn left again immediately to go through an arch in the wall, then up steps onto the wall
- Turn right to walk across the top of Newgate Arch over road
- Continue along the wall over the amazing Eastgate Arch, and past the cathedral to King Charles Tower
- Follow the wall to the left as it passes beside Shropshire Canal to Northgate (here, you can descend from the wall onto Northgate Street and walk to the cathedral and Town Hall where Tourist Information is located. Also, this is a good place to stop for refreshments)

Section 3: 0.75ml (1.2km)

- Retrace steps onto the wall at Northgate
- Turn left into Water Tower Street
- Continue along the road to steps on right leading up to the wall walk
- Follow ramparts over dual carriageway to tower
- Follow ramparts round to left and along the road to Watergate
- Turn right down Watergate Street; go through racecourse entrance.

The Roman Wall around Chester.

Section 4: 1.25ml (2km)

- Take 1st turning right along path beside racetrack
- On the far side of the course duck through two rails onto footpath beside River Dee
- Continue along path to arch ahead
- Turn left and go up narrow steps immediately BEFORE the arch
- Continue on as path climbs above the racecourse to steps ahead that lead up to some black railings on right, and the road
- Turn right and cross bridge over River Dee on Grosvenor Road
- Turn right off bridge, down steps to footpath

Section 5: 1ml (1.6km)

- Turn right towards river and right again under an arch (before the arch it is possible to descend the bank to the water's edge so your dog can have a swim)
- Continue along path as it becomes a tarmac cyclepath, keeping close to the river on left
- Turn right; cross road then sharp left onto path through a park signposted 'City Centre'

(another place you can access the water's edge for your dog to swim – note it can be a bit muddy)
- Take left fork close to river
- At road, turn left, cross, and then take steps back onto riverside path
- Follow path to footbridge
- Turn right up steps; then left to cross bridge

Section 6: 0.5ml (0.8km)
- Turn right towards boats
- Turn left up steps beside public toilets
- Continue ahead to ramp entrance around amphitheatre
- Go through gate at the end and turn left: cross road; go under arch; turn left
- Turn left again immediately and go through an arch; then up steps onto the wall

Section 7: 1.25ml (2km)
- Turn left and follow wall walk to the river
- Follow wall walk path as it descends to road. Cross it; pass close to river; cross another road and return to ramparts around the castle
- Turn right at 'Watergate' along Watergate Street and on to Eastgate Street

Section 8: 1ml (1.6km)
- Turn left onto Frodsham Street
- Continue on to canal towpath
- Turn right along towpath to Old Haggerty pub
- Up steps to City Road
- Turn right along City Road to train station ahead

Eastgate Street in Chester, notable for its unique, two-tiered shops.

IN THE LOCALITY
DELAMERE FOREST (CYCLING/OUTDOOR ACTIVITY/WILDLIFE/BIRDWATCHING)
The forest is so-called after the French for 'of the lake' – 'de la mere,' and is the largest wooded area in Cheshire, and includes Old Pale and Eddisbury Hill. Several of the many footpaths and tracks are also suitable for cyclists, and bikes can be hired from a shop next to the Visitors Centre close to the campsite. Deep in the forest only a few minutes' walk from the campsite is a 'GoApe' centre where all the walks and climbs are in the tree tops:

viewed from the ground there seems to be an entire city amongst the bushy tree canopy. 'GoApe' also arranges tours of the forest on segways; this is great fun. In addition, the forest is a treasure trove for wildlife and birdwatching enthusiasts, especially close to Blakemere Lake where the huge numbers of birds produce a cacophony of sound audible for many miles.

Throughout the year, the forest plays host to various events, and information about these is available at the Visitors Centre, where there is also a café. All very interesting and exciting.

Delamere village

A small, peaceful place stretching along the road near the railway station, Delamere is notable for the forest, campsite and station, which also boasts a café.

Blakemere village

On the outskirts of Cuddington, and accessible by train from Delamere station, is Blakemere village. First established as a craft centre in 1994, over the years it has expanded, and is now a shopping outlet with many small independent shops, and a range of family activities.

Delamere railway station

Travelling by train is so much more convenient than taking a motorhome or car as parking concerns are eliminated, and it also enables visits to places some distance away. Trains run from Delamere station to Chester or Manchester with several stops en route, including Northwich and Knutsford. The trains run approximately hourly throughout the day. A day out in Liverpool is possible with a change of train at Chester.

Beestone Castle and Woodlands Park

Ten miles (16km) south of the campsite is this spectacular medieval ruin on the top of a high crag rising out of Chester plain. It is managed by English Heritage, and is open from April to September.

Chester

Founded by the Romans on the banks of the River Dee is this most remarkable town. Amazingly, the defensive wall they built around the city still remains intact today, despite Chester's fluctuating fortunes. Then there is the Shropshire Union Canal that passes through the city, and the oldest racecourse in the country. In addition, there are several other fascinating features of the city to explore, especially the unique shopping rows. The walk along the Wall, that allows dogs, is a wonderful way to see Chester.

Cumbria — The tourist hotspot
OS Maps Explorer OL4 The English Lakes (North Western) Keswick, Cockermouth & Wigton

Hearing the words 'Lake District,' the image that probably comes to mind is one of lakes, hills and hikers, and the individual most responsible for this trend is Alfred Wainwright (1907-1991), who spent many years walking over the highlands of Cumbria, generally referred to as 'fells.' Wainwright made extensive notes and drew detailed pictures whilst walking, and, in the late 1950s, after collating this information, he began publishing a series of guide books entitled *Pictorial Guide to the Lakeland Fells.* He self-published the books, which, considering the date, was a very 21st century practice.

Over the years, millions of his books have been sold, and these splendidly erudite guides of the Lake District transformed how Britain's countryside was perceived. Wainwright relentlessly explored the Lake District and surrounding area writing various guides, and also appeared on TV. In the 1970s he devised the long-distance coast-to-coast path from the Lake District to North Yorkshire, that, although it does not have National Trail status, is a very popular route. Without doubt, Wainwright's influence has been, and still is, enormous. As stated in the *Independent* newspaper, "... his name is unquestionably in the Cumbrian air ..." undeniably due to the fact that he surveyed practically all 214 fell tops.

Whereas Alfred Wainwright wrote walking guides, around 150 years previously, in the early 1800s, William Wordsworth and his friends, who were known as the 'Lake Poets,' wrote poems. The splendour and beauty of the Lake District stimulated their imaginations, and inspired them to produce several, still-popular, anthologies.

Then, in the 1900s, Beatrix Potter wrote stories and drew pictures. As a conservationist, she also appreciated the countryside and recognized its importance. The 14 farms and 4000 acres (1620 hectacres) she purchased were left to the National Trust on her death in 1943 on condition that Hill Top at Sawrey, her favourite place, remained unchanged and open to the public.

Because of Alfred Wainwright, Wordsworth, and Beatrix Potter, the Lake District, with its easy lakeside strolls and challenging hill climbs, is probably the most well-known region in the UK for walkers, be they experienced hikers or casual amblers. The region has a multitude of footpaths, the majority of which are well signposted, which makes it a very popular destination, especially in the summer. Consequently, many walking routes are like motorways, with a constant stream of walkers: hardly surprising, really, considering that some 15 million people come to explore the region's fells and countryside every year.

The Lake District is so-called because there are 19 major bodies of water, only one of which – Bassenthwaite Lake – is actually a lake. The rest are either 'meres,' 'tarns,' or 'water,' such as Grasmere, Stickle Tarn, and Derwentwater. The largest 'lake' at almost 160sq ft (15sq m) is Windermere, but Wastwater is the deepest, and the smallest is Brotherswater at only 2.2sq ft (0.2sq m).

Between the lakes are the mountains. Officially regarded as the 'Cumbrian Hills,' these are more commonly known as 'The Lakeland Fells.' The most familiar is Scafell Pike which, at 3000ft (914m), is the highest mountain in England. These higher fells are rocky crags whilst the lower ones are mostly characteristic moorlands, farmland, and some woods. Even though the Lake District is the most mountainous region in England, with many lakes dotted around, it is the most populated National Park. Nevertheless, there are just a handful of major settlements.

Wonderful walks from dog-friendly campsites

Nowadays, tourism is crucial to the economy of the region, but during the last century, forestry assumed a greater importance, and farming is still essential – and has been since Roman times. The main livestock is sheep, and several breeds, such as Herdwick and Swaledale, are native to the area. Sheep are especially useful in preserving the landscape that appeals to so many of the visitors: besides controlling vegetation, the ubiquitous dry stone walls were erected to contain them. Nowadays, many of the footpaths and bridleways are between fields and fenced off, thereby making outings more enjoyable for both dog and owner.

Large lakes, high hills, majestic mountains and spectacular skies: these are the unique characteristics of the Lake District, and amount to a winning combination for a multiplicity of outdoor activities, quite apart from walking. Selecting a campsite was difficult because so many were suitable. A selection of different walks were possible from the two campsites I have included because they are close to Derwentwater, a large lake, and one of the larger towns, Keswick, as well as Castlerigg, a typical 'fell.'

CAMPSITE 1 – CASTLERIGG HALL CARAVAN AND CAMPING PARK

Located on a hillside, this campsite overlooks Derwentwater, and its creative terracing areas take full advantage of the amazing views. The amenities block is modern and generous, although is reached via quite a steep walk from some pitches; access concerns should be mentioned on booking.

There are three types of pitch: basic – hook-up only; standard – fully serviced, and superior – standard with a view. In addition, there is a shop, laundrette, dog wash, campers' kitchen, free wifi, and restaurant, which is especially obliging to those requiring gluten-free food. It is also possible to hire electric bikes – a boon for the hills. The facilities are extensive and the price reflects this.

PEARLS OF WISDOM 🐾

Not one but two dog exercise areas here – that is something – but what a total let-down: so tiny they are only suitable for the shortest of strolls. My owner was especially peeved as she was charged quite a hefty fee for me. It's just as well that, a stone's throw up the quiet road, are the footpaths by Brockle Beck; a marvellous place to explore, though very rocky, with lots of going up and down. In fact, all the walks are like this. We discovered a lovely short circular walk around the campsite that crosses a bridge over the water, and I greatly appreciated the many fenced-off paths as I was not restricted by sheep all over the place. A bonus was to be allowed to accompany my owner when she went in to eat.

CAMPSITE 2 – CASTLERIGG FARM CAMPING AND CARAVAN SITE

Just across the road from Castlerigg Hall is this campsite, which has the same address and postcode, although contact details are different (very confusing: take note). Here, too, facilities are comprehensive, with a shop and restaurant, though not as efficiently organized or as lavish. Also, the views are less spectacular. Consequently, it is less expensive, especially during high season, and there's no charge for dogs. As a solo traveller with a dog, although not as luxurious, this was better value.

Lakes, hills and hikers in Cumbria.

Spectacular views from Castlerigg Hall campsite.

PEARLS OF WISDOM 🐕

I really liked this campsite, which is much better than the one just across the road. Though there was only one exercise area for me, it was always fun to explore because it was surprisingly big, and I could amble along this way and that. Also, there is plenty of space for me to chase my frisbee, and meeting other dogs was awesome. I have to say I could

Wonderful walks from dog-friendly campsites

have done without the washing facilities next to the amenities block (I would rather have a swim than a wash).

SHORT WALK – TO THE LAKE
Distance: 4ml (6.4km)
Duration: 2hr
Terrain: Fields, footpaths, tracks and roads with many gates and some stiles and a few short quite steep hills. Can be very wet in places

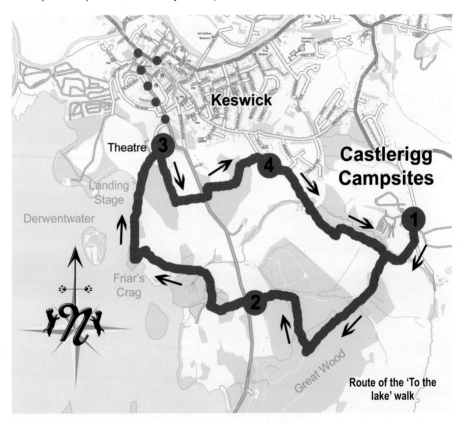

Route of the 'To the lake' walk

Section 1: 1.5ml (2.4km)
- From campsite entrance turn south and proceed uphill
- Ignoring footpath on left, bear right along footpath signposted 'Keswick'
- Through gate and cross wooden bridge
- Turn right and follow yellow waymarker path beside stream
- Through gate and continue along path at edge of field, still following stream below
- Turn left along fenced path between fields signposted 'Great Wood'
- Go straight ahead downhill into Great Wood, and cross brook using stepping stones
- Turn right at footpath crossroads just past brook
- Continue along very rocky track down long hill

- Turn right at footpath junction by large beech tree
- Continue on down rocky, wet grass track, first round to left, then right
- Turn left on a bend with 'footpath' on an unusual small white plaque
- Follow path, keeping close to wall on left, and go through gate ahead into field
- Cross field and go through gate opposite onto road (take care of narrow verge)

Section 2: 1ml (1.6km)
- Cross road and bear slightly left to footpath opposite
- Continue straight ahead and follow path round left-hand bend to 'Keswick' signpost
- Turn right, go through gate and follow path as it winds to the lake (due to flooding, the course of the path has changed. As it is repaired, the route may change. Follow route indicated towards lake)
- Through gate and follow path around edge of Derwentwater on left to gate (a good place for your dog to have a swim)
- Through gate and turn left up stone steps to Ruskin monument
- Continue along path to viewpoint over the lake (an ideal place to sit and admire the view, and watch all the boats criss-crossing the water)
- Take path to the right along edge of the headland, past coves and moored boats on left, ignoring all footpaths to the right
- Continue straight ahead skirting lake, past 'Keswick Launch Company' mooring berth on left and 'Theatre by the Lake' complex on right (the theatre café is a good place to stop for refreshments. To visit the town of Keswick, continue along the path past the theatre and car park to Lake Road, and along here into Keswick)

Section 3: 0.75ml (1.2km)
- Bear right just past theatre complex, and cross car park towards public toilets
- Continue straight ahead along edge of car park, keeping close to toilet block on right
- Turn right along footpath in far right-hand corner of car park
- Bear left at fork in footpath
- Turn left at footpath crossroads, and follow narrow track to road
- Cross road to path opposite (busy road: take care)
- Turn left and walk along path parallel to road
- Follow path as it turns first right and climbs, and then left and descends

Outdoor activities on Derwentwater.

- Bear left at junction on right-hand bend to kissing gate
- Through gate and straight ahead to road

Section 4: 0.75ml (1.2km)
- Turn right along road and continue round first left-, and then right-hand bend
- Cross bridge with Spring Farm on right
- Continue straight ahead, keeping Tea Room and Farm Shop on left
- Through gate ahead and follow path as it winds through the wood
- Take left fork and cross bridge (if the bridge is still down, turn right at fork. Follow the path left up the hill to the signpost 'Great Wood.' Continue straight ahead to bridge. Cross bridge and go through gate and up onto road. Turn left to campsite entrance)
- Follow path through gate onto road, and turn right into campsite entrance

LONG WALK – UP AND OVER TO THE MYSTIC STONES
Distance: 8.5ml (13.6km)
Duration: 5hr
Terrain: Fields, moor footpaths, tracks and quiet roads with several gates and some stiles, and some very steep hills. Tracks are easy to see but often the ground is very uneven with stones jutting out at all angles. Views are amazing

Section 1: 0.75ml (1.2km)
- From campsite entrance turn south uphill
- Ignoring footpath on left, bear right along footpath signposted 'Keswick'
- Through gate and cross wooden bridge
- Turn right and follow yellow waymarker path beside stream
- Through gate and continue along path at edge of field, still following stream below
- Turn left along fenced path between fields signposted 'Great Wood'
- Straight ahead downhill into Great Wood, and cross brook using stepping stones

Section 2: 1ml (1.6km)
- Continue straight ahead at footpath crossroads just past brook
- Through woods along track parallel to hill, but gradually descending
- Turn left at T-junction at bottom of a steep slope signposted 'Ashness Bridge'

Section 3: 0.5ml (0.8km)
- As a path of large stones on left climbs, bear right across a wooden bridge
- Follow path to right
- Continue down steps, keeping close to wall on right
- Follow path to left, which becomes single track

Section 4: 1ml (1.6km)
- Continue along track through ferns to gate, ignoring all paths on right going down, and on left going up

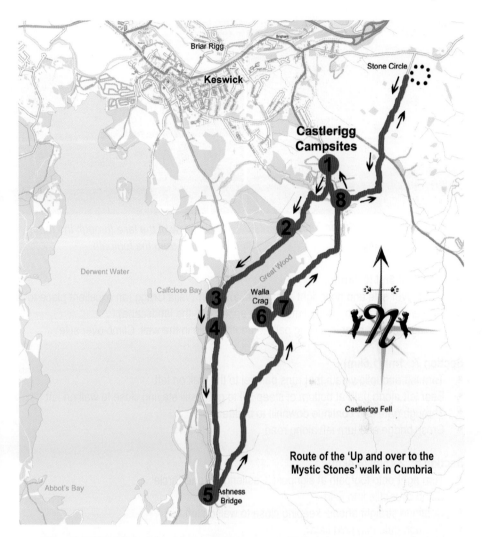

Route of the 'Up and over to the Mystic Stones' walk in Cumbria

- Through gate to road
- Turn left to Ashness Bridge (this is a popular spot, so care should be taken because, with a car park the other side of it, there are always vehicles using this small, single lane bridge)

Section 5: 1ml (1.6km)
- Take path to left of bridge going up a hill
- Through gate or over stile, and continue straight with fence on right
- Turn left as the path goes up the hill away from the fence
- Through another gate and straight ahead to hill top up a steep, rocky path
- Continue along path as it winds round Castlerigg Fell to stile in wall (the views are breathtaking)

Wonderful walks from dog-friendly campsites

Hills surrounding Castlerigg Farm campsite ...

... and a view of the lake through the ferns from the footpath.

Section 6: 0.5ml (0.8km)
- Climb over stile and bear right along path to top of Walla Cragg (an excellent place to stop and have lunch, giving time to truly appreciate the landscape)
- Facing the wall, bear left along path to another stile in the wall. Climb over stile

Section 7: 1ml (1.6km)
- Turn left and follow path that runs parallel to the wall on left
- Bear left along path at bottom of steep hill to gate, still staying close to wall on left
- Through gate and continue downhill to bridge.
- Cross bridge and turn left along road

Section 8: 2.75ml (4.4km)
- Turn right onto footpath at signpost 'Castlerigg Stone Circle'
- Climb over stile into field
- Continue straight ahead, keeping close to wall on left
- Through gate into next field
- Continue straight ahead, still close to wall, and go through another gate
- Turn left onto track that leads into a field
- Follow path close to fence on left, and go through another gate into field
- Continue straight ahead and through kissing gate onto road
- Cross road to minor road opposite (Castle Road)
- Continue along Castle Road to the stones (access is via a stone step stile in a wall on the right)
- Retrace steps along Castle Road and fields to the stile leading onto access road
- Turn right along road to campsite entrance

IN THE LOCALITY

The area was badly hit by floods during the winter of 2015. Every effort has been made to repair the damage caused, but it is an ongoing process. I noticed that many of the footpath signposts have been renewed, and now include not only distance but also time to destination: a most useful improvement. The two walks from the campsite are still possible with only one modification, surprisingly. You can show your support by visiting the area.

CYCLING

Although there are many hills in the area – some quite steep – cycling is a popular activity. There are many designated cycle routes through the striking landscape using numerous country lanes and off-road tracks. Some of these routes can be found in a useful publication *Biking around Keswick*, available from the Tourist Information office or the bicycle hire shop, Keswick Bikes.

BIRDWATCHING

In the skies of the Lake District fells it is possible to see several rare species of bird. The possible return of the golden eagle around Haweswater is the most exciting event, although recently only one has returned, and efforts are being made to find him or her a mate. Numbers of buzzards have increased here, as have those of peregrines, ravens, and ospreys. At the RSPB viewpoint at Dodd Wood, high above Bassenthwaite Lake, the recently returned ospreys can be seen most days fishing, sitting, feeding and flying. Pictures and videos of fledgling ospreys in the nest can be seen at the Forestry Commission Whinlatter Visitors Centre.

OUTDOOR ACTIVITIES

Three outdoor adventure companies are based in and around Keswick: Chase Adventure, Keswick Adventure Centre, and Keswick Extreme. Consequently, there is plenty of opportunity to experience a range of outdoor activities, including the well-known ones of canoeing and rock climbing, and more contemporary ones such as ghyll scrambling (http://www.ghyllscrambling.co.uk/ghyll-scrambling-in-the-lake-district).

KESWICK

Situated between Derwentwater and the Skiddaw Mountains is the attractive market town of Keswick, just a short walk from both campsites. One of the largest settlements in the Lake District, it's popular because it is a good base from which to explore the area, so there are many restaurants and cafés.

However, this charming town has several interesting attractions of its own. There's the Keswick Museum and Art Gallery that houses a range of artefacts reflecting life in the area. The local Keswick Brewery runs tours that include tasting sessions. Hidden away in Museum Square in the centre of Keswick is The Puzzling Place, full of illusions and riddles that will give your brain a workout, and on the banks of Derwentwater in a stunningly scenic setting is the newly-refurbished Theatre by the Lake, complete with café and bar.

Until recently, Keswick was an important centre for the manufacture of pencils, as a result of the discovery in the 16th century of graphite near Seathwaite. The Pencil Museum in the northern end of the town illustrates the importance of this industry. More unusually, this museum allows dogs to accompany their owners inside. Right in the centre of the town is Moot Hall, once an assembly gathering place, but now housing the Tourist Information office. Since being granted a market charter by Edward I in 1276, a market has been held here twice-weekly on Saturdays and Thursdays.

On Derwentwater shore at Friars Cragg is a memorial to John Ruskin, who considered Keswick "... almost too beautiful a place to live in." Also situated on the lakeside is Keswick Launch Company, which operates a boat service around the lake that berths at seven jetties dotted around the shore. This service allows passengers to disembark and explore the area on the far side of this huge lake, and return to the town later. I did contemplate doing this but eventually took just the lake tour with my dog.

CASTLERIGG STONE CIRCLE

Just north of the campsite is the earliest of many such stone circles dotted around the UK, strikingly situated on a hill with views across to Skiddaw. There are 38 stones approximately 30 metres in diameter, with ten stones forming an inner rectangle. The origins of the structure are unknown, although it is thought to have been constructed for ceremonial use. Now owned by the National Trust, it is managed by English Heritage.

Lancashire — Pendle and the witches
OS MAPS EXPLORER OL21 SOUTH PENNINES

Sandwiched between the large conurbations of Manchester and Liverpool to the south, the dramatic landscape of the Lake District of Cumbria to the north, and the sea to the west, Lancashire is rather overshadowed by its long-time adversary, Yorkshire, to the east. Rivalry is fierce, and has been for many centuries, although, nowadays, this is chiefly confined to the sports field.

It all seems to have stemmed from the 1400s when control for the throne of England was hotly contested by various royal relatives and their supporters. One group was known as the House of York; the other the House of Lancaster, and their disagreement endured for almost 40 years. Fortunately, it was not one long continuous conflict but a series of sporadic and frequently very violent confrontations. This dispute was later referred to as the War of the Roses because the symbol of both Houses was a rose: white for York and red for Lancaster. It finally ended in 1487 when Henry Tudor from the House of Lancaster married Elizabeth from the House of York. Though the wrangle was resolved more than 600 years ago, the inhabitants of both counties still espouse an intense loyalty.

Lancashire was always smaller, and did not have the moors of its neighbour, Yorkshire, but was nevertheless just as notable. During the Industrial Revolution and Victorian times, it evolved into the powerhouse of the many new technical developments of that time, and the port of Liverpool became the centre of an international trade route. Many of the small towns burgeoned into huge industrial complexes producing all manner of goods and dominating global trade. By the 1830s, Lancashire was THE centre of cotton production, manufacturing about 85 per cent of all cotton. To transport these goods, a series of canals was built; the first was the Bridgewater Canal that ran from Runcorn to Leigh via Manchester. This was completed in 1761 and was an amazing feat as it did not follow an existing water course. It was so named after its owner, the third Duke of Bridgewater. Over the following years many more canals were built, including the Lancaster, Rochdale, and Ashton. Another feat of engineering was the construction of the Leeds and Liverpool Canal, completed after many years in 1816. This crossed the Pennines, requiring an incredible 91 locks. Feeding into it are several smaller canals.

The Leeds and Liverpool Canal.

Arrival of the railway triggered the decline of the canals, and by the early 20th century, most were derelict. However, in the last 50 years or so a band of volunteers have worked industriously to reinstate most of them, and nowadays the canals are a haven for wildlife and an amazing leisure facility, not only for those with boats but also for walkers and cyclists. It is a wonderful way to see the countryside and the adjacent towns and villages.

The railway not only transported goods more efficiently, but also allowed travel further afield. During holidays, city workers went to the coast where the small towns and villages grew in order to accommodate them. Over time, all kinds of entertainment were also offered, and several of these seaside resorts, such as Blackpool, still attract many visitors.

Easy access is still a necessity for the economy of the county, and these days it is the road network that is important. Lancashire has the distinction of having several motorways running through it, including the M6 that crosses the eastern fringe. This, too, is another first for the county: the section of the M6 near Preston was the very first motorway in the UK.

Wonderful walks from dog-friendly campsites

The reorganization of counties in the 1970s resulted in a significant reduction, geographically, in the size of the county. Many of the populace have refused to accept this, and, in lots of places, a profusion of rose symbols, both red and white, signify their allegiance.

There is much to discover in Lancashire. In addition to learning about the industrial past there are the canals to investigate, wildlife to search out, cities to visit, coast to survey, and the moors and fells of Forest of Bowland, as well as the countryside to explore. The county has a wide range of landscape and a long and interesting history.

CAMPSITE – LOWER GREENHILL CARAVAN PARK

This campsite has all the facilities I like. It is spacious, and well laid out with a modern toilet block and dishwashing facility. The shower is coin-operated requiring one pound sterling (do check it has now been reconfigured to take the new coins). At the time of our visit, the site was undergoing extensive renovations, so several large vehicles of varying kinds were present. When the works are completed it promises to be a lovely site. With all the family seemingly involved in the actual building it could be difficult finding personnel, but this shouldn't be a problem once the reception block is finished. Now that the campsite has an online presence it should be easier to book.

PEARLS OF WISDOM
This campsite was so-so. Before I could have a good run my owner had to take me across a busy road, although, once on the other side, it was wonderful – a long, special, fenced-off path between the fields, so it was easy to ignore the irritating sheep. The path eventually led to a

A spacious and well laid out campsite.

fabulous wide and seemingy unending track; my owner said it was a disused railway line, whatever that is!

Even when we walked along the road to the nearby village it was okay as each side of the tarmac path was a wide, grassy verge, so lots of interesting smells to discover. The path beside the water – a canal, I think – was fun, even though my owner wouldn't let me go in for a dip. A few times we went to a field beside the campsite just for a few throws of my frisbee. I LOVE my frisbee!

SHORT WALK – RAILWAY, ROAD AND CANAL
Distance: 5.5ml (8.8km)
Duration: 3hr

Terrain: Fields, footpaths, track, towpath and roads with some gates and stiles. Very, very wet along rail track. Mostly flat; some short hills.
The disused railway track is easy to follow but it is very wet and muddy. In places the huge puddles can be elbow (half-leg) deep on a Labrador. To complete the entire length of the rail track wellingtons are a necessity. This walk diverts around the worst part of the track

Section 1: 0.75ml (1.2km)
- Exit campsite via entrance, and cross B6382 to go through gate onto footpath opposite
- Continue straight ahead along footpath
- Turn right at footpath junction and go through kissing gate
- Continue along footpath with fence on right and stream on left, through gate, across gated bridge, along edge of field, and through another gate onto disused railway

Section 2: 0.75ml (1.2km)
- Turn right and then right again at the bottom of the steps
- Follow the rail track under a bridge (very wet), and through gate onto grassy path
- Continue along rail track to pair of large gates
- Turn left towards buildings
- Bear left at top of slope through farmyard; then turn right
- Continue straight ahead towards road
- Keep to right at car park

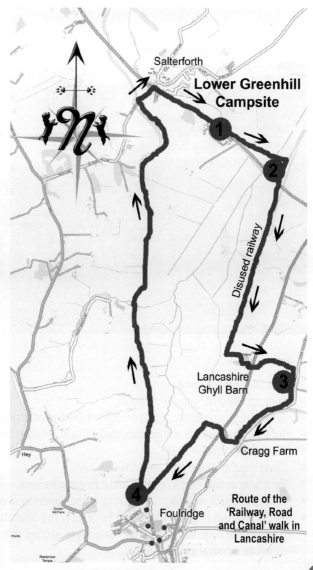

and follow the wall on right to a stony track
- Continue along stony track and through gate to A56
- Bear left and cross road to shed opposite, and go through gate into field
- Bearing right, cross field and over stile
- Turn right immediately and cross bridge leading to path, bearing slightly left up across field and though small gate onto minor road

Part of the disused rail line that is not under water.

Section 3: 1.5ml (2.4km)
- Turn right and continue along road
- Take third signposted footpath on right at Cragg Farm, going through gate onto drive
- Turn immediately left and go through 2nd gate, wooden onto stony track
- Follow track down to A56
- Cross road and over stile opposite into field
- Bear right across field to corner, and through gate back onto disused railway
- Turn left and immediately left again up embankment to avoid deep, muddy puddles
- Follow footpath close to wall on left for 30yd (27m), then descend embankment
- Turn left and continue along track, weaving in and out of trees keeping as close to wall on left as possible for 50yd (45m)

- Cross to other side of track and continue onto a nice, pleasant grassy footpath to canal and cafe (this is Foulridge; a lovely place to stop for refreshments because dogs are welcome, and to explore the village)

Section 4: 2.5ml (4km)
- Turn right onto tow path; left to café
- Follow towpath under several bridges, and go through narrow gate out onto road beside Anchor Pub on right
- Turn right and continue along road to B6382
- Turn right and follow B6382 to campsite entrance

LONG WALK – UP AND DOWN; UP AND DOWN
Details: Distance 8ml (12.8km)
Duration: 5hr
Terrain: Fields, footpaths, tracks roads with some gates and stiles. Several hills: some long and some steep

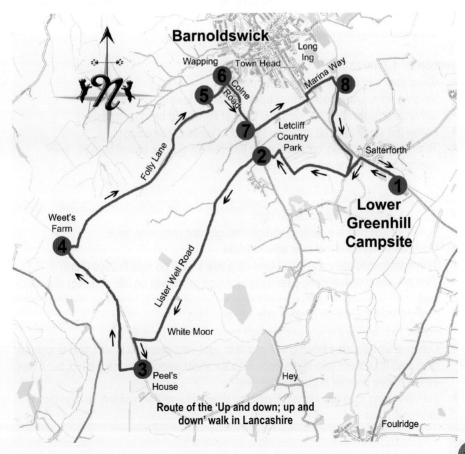

Route of the 'Up and down; up and down' walk in Lancashire

Wonderful walks from dog-friendly campsites

Section 1: 1.25ml (2km)
- Exit campsite via entrance onto B6383
- Turn left along the road to war memorial
- Turn left along Park View Terrace, past pub on left and over bridge
- Turn right along stony track towards houses
- Follow track, keeping buildings on left and going slightly downhill towards fields. Go through large gate into field
- Straight across field and over stile, across stream, and through gate into another field
- Climb up and over stile into field
- Go straight ahead to wall and continue on, keeping wall on right, and over stone step-stile in corner
- Turn right, keeping close to wall on right
- Turn right and go through gate in wall on right
- Bear left to stone wall corner, and continue along path beside wall now on left; then through gate in corner (very narrow: some dogs will have trouble here)
- Continue straight ahead and through gate opposite onto grassy path
- Follow path over stile, then round to left past stable block on left and up to tarmac driveway
- Continue along driveway, over cattle-grid to road

Section 2: 1.75ml (2.8km)
- Cross road and bear left to small car park
- Keeping right, follow wide tarmac track ,climbing steadily
- Continue straight ahead along stony track at right hand bend (signposted)
- Follow the stony track up and over the moor (views are amazing)
- Through gate into field, continue along path, keeping close to wall on right, then through another gate onto road

Section 3: 1.25ml (2km)
- Turn left, passing white house on right
- Turn right just past the garden, and go through gate onto wide track
- Continue along track and over stile into field
- Turn right immediately and over stone-step stile in wall on right in 20yd (18m)
- Turn left and continue along path, keeping close to the wall on left, and over stile into field
- Straight ahead and over another stile into next field
- Follow path beside the wall and through small gate into large field
- Continue along path, following wall round to right, and over stile in wall next to signpost onto road (this stone stile had a large wooden sheet wedged across the top, but it was easy to move in order to go over the stile)
- Turn left along road and climb up, passing Weets House Farm on left, and go through gate onto moor

*Amazing views from one
of the stony tracks.*

Section 4: 1.25ml (2km)
- Turn right immediately along Pendle Way, keeping close to wall on right, and over three stiles

Section 5: 0.25ml (0.4km)
- Through gate in wall on right onto concrete track
- Turn left and follow track as it zig-zags downhill out to Moorgate Road

Section 6: 0.5ml (0.8km)
- Straight ahead and take third right along Colne Road, passing mill on right
- Go uphill to B6251
- Bear right at junction and continue along road
- Turn left onto wide driveway in 50yd (45m) signposted 'Letcliffe Country Park'

Section 7: 0.75ml (1.2km)
- Continue straight ahead past houses on right, and through car park
- Bear right over grass and through small gate in wall into field
- Bear slightly right and cross field; go through gate opposite
- Follow stony track, bearing right downhill and through gate to B6383
- Turn left along road in 30yd (27m)
- Turn right onto Marina Way, and continue straight ahead towards marina car park
- Turn right along a stony track (signposted) just before car park (café at marina on left)
- Turn left and go through gate to cross bridge over canal

Section 8: 1ml (1.6km)
- Turn right and follow towpath under a bridge and through metal barrier.
- Turn left immediately and follow tarmac path past playing fields, and through gap in low wall out onto road
- Turn left along road to B6383
- Turn right and follow road to campsite

IN THE LOCALITY
CYCLING
With few major roads and the towpath beside the canal, many places are easily accessible by bike.

SALTERFORTH
This is a charming small village primarily on the north side of the B6383. The Leeds-Liverpool Canal passes close by on the south side of the road, resulting in a finger of mostly recreational development connecting the canal with the village.

FOULRIDGE
This delightful village has a long history stretching back to Anglo-Saxon times, from

The canals now provide a wonderful leisure facility

whence it derives its name: fola (foal) hyred (ridge). Like many places in Lancashire, its heyday was during the Industrial Revolution. In 1815 a wharf and warehouse were built because the village was situated at one end of the 5000ft (1500m) long tunnel on the Leeds-Liverpool Canal. .These days, the canal wharf is again a hive of activity. The warehouse has been converted into a lovely, popular café, and boat trips – most of which welcome dogs – sail along the canal. Some boats go through the tunnel but usually only on Sundays.

Pendle witches

During the unrest of the early 1600s witchcraft trials were commonplace. The Pendle witches of Lancashire were infamous as so many were accused: 12 women in total. One defendant died whilst in custody; ten were found guilty and executed; one was found not guilty. In addition to the charge of witchcraft, the defendants were also accused of causing madness and laming, as well as many unexplained deaths over several years. Most of the evidence was unsubstantiated hearsay, based on recollection and superstition.

The subsequent trial was recorded in great detail at the time by a London clerk, Thomas Potts, which is why so much is known about these particular 'witches.' Potts' account was then used as a guide to finding evidence against witches all over the country, and he capitalized on his status. In 1613, he wrote a book about these events entitled *The Wonderfull Discoverie of Witches in the Countie of Lancaster*, and, bizarrely, dedicated it to the man who arrested Guy Fawkes in 1605. More information about this can be found at the Pendle Heritage Centre Barrowford, just 5 miles (8km) from the campsite.

Barnoldswick

Like so many places in this area, during the Industrial Revolution Barnoldswick changed from a quiet, sleepy village to a buzzing mill town, with both canal and railway passing through it. In this new technological age the town has changed again. Though there is only one working mill (which is now a tourist attraction), various other concerns are based in the town, and the vibrant town square is full of small independent shops. Known locally as 'Barlick,' this is a fascinating place to visit.

The walks: Central England
(Cambridgeshire, Derbyshire, Shropshire, Staffordshire)

Cambridgeshire — Skies, spires and water
OS Maps Explorer 225 Huntingdon and St Ives

Cambridgeshire is adjacent to Norfolk and Lincolnshire, so much of the county is flat. This makes for easy walking, although the intricate network of streams and rivers creates barriers, and only at specific points can these be traversed, consequently affecting many walking routes.

Sprinkled across the county are numerous hamlets, villages, and small towns. Most of the ancient byways and bridle paths are well marked, with easy-to-negotiate kissing gates. Some trails have been converted into cyclepaths so are tarmac. Without doubt, this makes the walking less strenuous, but the proliferation of cyclists requires consideration, especially if, like me, you are accompanied by a dog. The popularity of many of the routes provides an opportunity for us all to appreciate the countryside.

Exploring some of the villages and even the towns is interesting and informative. The passage of time has left an indelible imprint on the community. Some of the buildings – especially the houses – are remarkable examples of times past, and certainly of interest to anyone with an appreciation of architecture or history; either way, they are intriguing and enchanting to look at. Lofty, slender church spires pierce the sky wherever you look, dwarfing trees and dominating the landscape. Each place possesses a unique quality, and and time quickly passes whilst absorbing the atmosphere

The region is renowned for being the birthplace of Oliver Cromwell. Prior to his involvement in the English Civil War, Cromwell lived in this area until in his forties. Born and educated in Huntingdon, with property in St Ives, he was MP first for Huntingdon and then Cambridge. Of course, this all changed in

Church spire piercing the sky.

1642 when he gathered troops to secure Cambridgeshire for Parliament. Because of his remarkable leadership and military successes, Cromwell quickly gained promotion, eventually becoming Lord General of the army in 1650. Then, of course, in 1653 he became Lord Protector (King in all but name) until his death in 1658.

He is a significant historical figure. The grammar school Oliver Cromwell attended in Huntingdon is now the Cromwell Museum, and contains many exhibits unique to him and his family, and frequently hosts special exhibitions. Huntingdon has a town trail of engraved stones that chronicle his life. As Cromwell's association with St Ives is more transient, there is little commemoration of the time he spent there. Instead, the Norris Museum on the river bank houses artefacts that chart the history of Huntingdonshire, many of which were collected by Herbert Norris. The museum also organizes special shows during the year.

With the river running through the middle of the town, St Ives is a charming place to visit. Of particular note is the remarkable and unique chapel in the middle of the bridge on Bridge Street. This is a delightful area in which to spend time, as there is plenty to see and do whatever your interests, including numerous walking routes and places at which to exercise dogs. In addition, the scenery is inspiring: the uniformity of it being somehow soothing and relaxing.

CAMPSITE – WATERCLOSE MEADOW CAMPSITE, NATIONAL TRUST, HOUGHTON MILL
The location of this campsite is idyllic; a convenient starting point from which to explore the area. On the edge of Houghton village, a delightful place full of character, with a shop and several pubs.

At the entrance to the campsite is the historic Houghton Mill, still working, and cakes and bread are made from flour produced by the mill and sold in the Mill café. The River Great Ouse flows alongside the site, and there are several enjoyable river walks, as well as wonderful places to sit and watch the birds and boats. In addition, footpaths pass each side of the site, leading to a network of routes across fields and meadows, from which the diversity of wildlife can be experienced.

Though the campsite is now run by the National Trust, until the beginning of 2015 it was a Caravan and Motohome Club site, and the facilities are of the same high standard as those on club sites. There are 54 pitches on level grass, with one facilities block housing heated toilets, showers, laundry, and waste points. There is a field for tents but no play area. It is peaceful and relaxing, yet there is much to do and see, and plenty of places to walk.

PEARLS OF WISDOM 🐾
Well, what a fabulous place this is, even though there isn't an exercise area specifically for my kind. There are so many places nearby for me to stretch my legs, however, and particularly intriguing was the large grassy area adjacent to the mill ... an overflow car park, I believe. During the early morning or late evening, this was ideal for chasing my Frisbee or for short walks.

Then there is the large field next door. Yipee! How thrilling: rabbits galore – I didn't

Wonderful walks from dog-friendly campsites

Looking through the mill to the campsite.

know which way to go first. Whenever we set off it was an adventure; I was never sure where we would be going as there are so many paths. It was great fun meeting oodles of dogs. Playing with some of them was terrific.

Route of the 'As I was going to St Ives' walk in Cambridgeshire

SHORT WALK – AS I WAS GOING TO ST IVES ...
Distance: 5ml (8km)
Duration: 3hr
Terrain: Cyclepaths, roads, bridges, meadows and footpaths, with mostly kissing gates. Flat, easy walking

Section 1: 1.5ml (2.4km)
- Leave campsite on north side, and go through kissing gate leading to Ouse Valley Way (tarmac path)
- Turn right away from church
- Continue along path to T-junction
- Turn right and then left onto top of ridge, which is a flood defence

- Continue along top of bank as it turns left, and then right to tarmac path
- Turn right and cross small car park towards signpost
- Turn immediately right to cross bridge, and continue along cyclepath
- Turn left up steps at information board about 'The Thicket,' and follow path into woods
- Turn right along footpath that runs alongside hill, over bridge, and down back to cyclepath
- Turn left and continue along cyclepath
- At fork by Scout Hut turn right (easy to miss)

Section 2: 0.75ml (1.2km)
- Continue along cyclepath towards church, keeping fence on right
- Straight on through gate into churchyard
- Turn right and follow path, keeping church on left, to tall black iron gates
- Continue straight ahead through gates and along pavement
- Bear right onto river walkway. (This walkway is most pleasant and, with plenty of seats, an ideal place to stop and enjoy the river)
- At museum bear left back onto road
- Continue along street into town centre. (St Ives is an interesting place to visit, especially on market days, so continue on past Bridge Street. Retrace steps to Bridge Street)
- Turn down Bridge Street. (At the bridge there is a delightful teashop where you can enjoy refreshments sitting by the river)
- Cross bridge (this is the bridge with a chapel in the middle of it. A notice on the chapel door gives information about how to gain access)
- Turn right onto footpath just past Dolphin Hotel into car park (signposted)
- Continue straight ahead through square arch in building to field beyond

The path beside by the river.

Section 3: 1.25ml (2km)
- Through kissing gate into Hemingford Grey Meadow
- Bear left and follow path across meadow toward trees
- Continue straight ahead along path with streamon left, and through kissing gate onto track
- Contuinue straight ahead
- Turn right at Meadow Close just before right-hand bend (signposted)
- Through gate (with yellow

waymarker) at top of close onto footpath
- Continue along footpath and turn left at road
- Continue along road to footpath (signposted)
- Turn right onto footpath and head towards church
- At road turn right heading towards gates of church
- Turn left at gates onto riverside footpath

Section 4: 1.5ml (2.4km)
- Continue along riverside path, and bear right onto road, then immediately left around hedge back onto path beside river
- Continue along path and through gate, still following riverside path
- Through second gate and across meadow, moving away from river
- Through another gate onto tarmac path between houses
- Turn right at road, and continue on past Hemingford Abbots village hall and pub
- Continue straight ahead at junction along Common Lane
- Turn right at Meadow Lane along road
- Cross bridge and go through kissing gate onto cyclepath, then across meadow to mill and campsite beside it

LONG WALK – DISCOVERING OLIVER CROMWELL
Distance: 8.5ml (13.6km)
Duration: 5.5hr
Terrain: Cyclepaths, roads, bridges, meadows and footpaths, with mostly kissing gates. Flat, easy walking

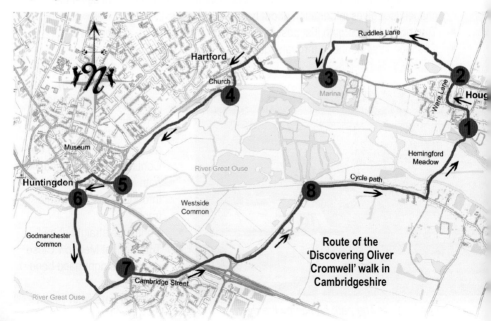

Route of the 'Discovering Oliver Cromwell' walk in Cambridgeshire

Section 1: 0.5ml (0.8km)
- Leave campsite on north side via kissing gate onto Ouse Valley Way
- Turn left and head towards church
- Turn right at road and continue to clock tower
- Bear left to Post Office
- Turn right and follow Huntingdon Road around left-hand bend to Three Jolly Butchers pub
- Turn right at green and along Ware Lane to main road

Section 2: 1ml (1.6km)
- Cross busy road and bear left to footpath opposite (signposted)
- Continue along footpath
- Take left fork at Y-junction onto grassy track
- Continue along track to road
- Continue straight ahead along Ruddles Lane, past Manor Farm on right
- Follow track around left-hand bend to road
- Turn right and cross busy road into the marina (pub restaurant and toilets are available here)

Section 3: 0.75ml (1.2km)
- Go through marina gates and turn sharp right onto cyclepath parallel to road
- Continue straight ahead at right-hand bend of road onto cyclepath beside bus lane
- Follow cyclepath round to right out onto main road
- Turn left along road
- Turn left again at The Hollow opposite Barley Mow pub
- Continue down road to river (a beautiful, secluded spot to pause by the church and admire the view)
- Turn right and follow footpath, keeping church on right; around hut on left to lane

Section 4: 1.25ml (2km)
- Go straight ahead, passing car park on left and row of cottages (possible to follow the river for part of this section)
- Continue ahead to footpath and into copse
- Bear left over two wooden bridges
- Continue through copse over another bridge, and out onto common with river on left
- Follow tarmac path as it winds across common, and over several bridges to Huntingdon Boat Club
- Continue along cyclepath as it winds around play area on left, then back beside the river heading towards the large stone bridge crossing River Great Ouse

Section 5: 0.5ml (0.8km)
- Turn right at main road
- Cross at traffic lights and continue straight ahead along High Street to town centre,

shopping precinct, and Cromwell Museum
- Retrace steps to St Mary's Church on the High Street
- Turn right down St Mary's Street
- Cross over busy road and continue straight ahead along lane, keeping car park on right
- Turn right at T-junction; then left

Section 6: 1ml (1.6km)
- Continue along road, under flyover, and straight ahead to Godmanchester Common
- Go straight ahead across common
- Cross river via lock bridge
- Turn left and, with river on right, follow path to white bridge
- Cross bridge and continue straight ahead to busy road junction

Section 7: 1.75ml (2.8km)
- Cross road and continue straight ahead along Cambridge Street
- Pass under flyover and around long, sweeping, right-hand bend
- Turn left off the bend just before roundabout
- Continue along road past sewage works on right
- Climb over gate on right (a little further on is a kissing gate on right that leads directly onto the cyclepath. Turn right onto cyclepath)
- Bear left across common to tarmac cyclepath

Section 8: 1.75ml (2.8km)
- Turn right and follow cyclepath through kissing gate onto road
- Continue straight ahead
- Turn left into Meadow Lane.
- Cross bridge and go through kissing gate into meadow
- Follow cyclepath to mill and campsite

IN THE LOCALITY

BIRDWATCHING

There is a constant cacophony of birdsong, and I met many bird watchers with the inevitable binoculars slung round their necks. Though there aren't any hides plenty of seats are dotted about.

FISHING

It is permitted to fish in the rivers, and the necessary permits can be obtained from Houghton Post Office. Considering the abundance of water, there was a notable absence of anglers.

WATERSPORTS AND BOAT TRIPS

There are several marinas along the river, as well as boating and sailing clubs. At Purvis

Marine just outside Huntingdon, boats are available for hire by the hour or day. St Ives Electric Riverboat Company runs guided boat trips on the river from the town of St Ives. Crafts of all shapes and sizes use the water.

CYCLING

An ideal area for cycling as it is very flat, and there are many cyclepaths and cycle routes.

HOUGHTON MILL

This is the last working water mill on the River Great Ouse. There has been a watermill at Houghton since before the Norman Conquest, but this one dates from the 18th century, with additions in the 19th and 20th centuries.

In 1930, the mill was decommissioned. Local residents bought the building and gave it to the National Trust. Initially, it was used as a Youth Hostel, but later restored as a mill and, in 1999, new millstones were installed. Now, it is possible to visit and experience the sound and atmosphere of a traditional working mill, and even try your hand at making flour!

HOUGHTON

A picturesque village, in the centre of which is an interesting thatched clock tower, affectionately known as 'the green,' although there is no grass; only a traditional old water pump and red phonebox. Nearby is a statue of Potto Brown, who owned and expanded the mill. There are a number of houses of interest around the village, as well as some shops, two pubs, a school, and playing field.

ST IVES

In medieval times St Ives was famous for its international fairs, at which a whole host of produce was bought and sold, including livestock. Today, it is a quiet market town, but still has fairs on Mondays and Fridays. On every Bank Holiday Monday the market swells to fill almost the entire town, with traders coming from far and wide. In addition, on alternate Saturdays there is an excellent farmers' market. The statue of Oliver Cromwell in the centre of the Market Place presides over all this activity. There are plenty of delightful places to linger ,especially beside the river.

HEMINGFORD ABBOTS

This is another enchanting village on the other bank of the River Great Ouse, that contains many thatched 16th and 17th century buildings, including the village pub. The fine spire of the church is an Ouse valley landmark for miles around Much of the village is in a conservation area. In July, the Hemingford Regatta is fiercely contested by local residents.

HUNTINGDON

An attractive town with busy market days every Wednesday and Saturday. Situated in the centre of town opposite the church is the Cromwell Museum: an attractive building that is at least 400 years old.

Wonderful walks from dog-friendly campsites

CAMBRIDGE

The city is only a few miles away, and is easy to reach from the campsite as a bus runs to it every hour from Houghton Clock Tower.

A market in Huntingdon.

Derbyshire — Tolkien in the Peaks
OS MAPS EXPLORER OL24
THE PEAK DISTRICT

Derbyshire county is synonymous with the Peak District, although, in fact, it spreads over several East Midland counties. The first area in the UK in 1951 to be designated a National Park, of the 500sq miles (1300sq km) it embraces, three quarters lie in northern Derbyshire.

Surprisingly there are few peaks: the landscape is more rounded hills and sharp edges of escarpments, in-between which are valleys or, as they are called in Derbyshire, dales. These long, deep valleys have been carved out of the limestone rock by crystal-clear rivers, the longest and most well-known of which are the rivers Derwent and Dove. Some of the smaller rivers have subsequently dried up, leaving the characteristic dales.

Besides the long, distant trails, the county is criss-crossed with footpaths, possibly due to the actions of numerous people who, over 80 years ago, participated in the mass trespass walk to Kinder Scout, in support of the right to walk over the hills and moorlands. In 1932, this protest was inflammatory, but undeniably instrumental in the establishment of National Parks, and the various 'right to roam' acts subsequently passed. Undoubtedly, it is because of these people that we can now enjoy so much of the countryside, and appreciate the variety and beauty of the UK. We should respect this hard-won right by adhering to the Country Code.

With the lowest point in the Peak District a mere 89ft (27m) and the highest an impressive 2087ft (637m), the range is a staggering 2000ft (610m). Because Alsop-en-le-Dale and Ashbourne are on the edge of the Peak District, at some point a climb is inevitable ... and it can be steep.

One of Derbyshire's finest and popular dales is Dovedale. The tiny hamlet of Milldale at the northern end of Dovedale is a popular tourist attraction, despite the fact that the mill was last used in 1870. The National Trust has set up an information barn in the old mill buildings, and conveniently situated beside the barn are some toilets. An enterprising resident has set up Polly's Pantry in her house – a shop-cum-café. A stable door fronts her house, and she serves the many visitors through the open top half. With a car park nearby, many visitors come and sit on the grassy banks of the river whilst having their lunch, and watch the water as it surges past the stones.

A Derbyshire dale – a long, steep valley.

Other interesting features are the villages of Derbyshire, some of which have notable traditions. At Parwich the local pub doubles as a shop, post office, and information centre, and is an intriguing building. Tissington is renowned for the well dressing ceremony that takes place in May, and is extremely popular with visitors.

With improved access to various National Trust properties, Derbyshire can be very busy, especially at weekends. However, routes across the fields to and from places are frequently much quieter, even on bright, sunny days, as generally they are only used by serious walkers. The views across the Dales are amazing. As well as sheep, lots of the farms in the county have cattle, so take extra care when accompanied by your dog. Derbyshire is a wonderful place to visit, not only for its superb scenery but also for its blend of heritage and history, and rich variety of customs that date back to ages past.

CAMPSITE – RIVENDALE CARAVAN PARK

What a very evocative name! I wondered if it had a special significance connected with the Dales. Undoubtedly, it conjured up images of Tolkien's Middle Earth, an association underlined by the names of various parts of the campsite. The pub is called The Prancing Pony, and the small, intimate, circular sections of this large site are assigned monikers such as 'Willow Bottom' and 'Withywindle.'

Besides 120 pitches for tourers, this large site offers a range of accommodation, ingeniously designed in recurring circles around the single amenities block and play area. The steep walls of the old quarry flanking the outside edge of the circle, and shrubs planted between different areas and some pitches, enhance the feeling of seclusion and intimacy.

Though there is only one amenities block it is well-equipped and easily accessible. There is a huge camping field. This is exactly what it says: a field with limited amenities; just a small toilet and shower block at one end. An ideal opportunity to experience 'real' camping ... not for me, though!

This is an expensive site, especially for the solo traveller, but it does have a convenient shop, nice café, and an excellent pub that welcomes dogs.

PEARLS OF WISDOM 🐾

This was a total let-down! There were a lot of exciting smells but no place for me to run free or chase my Frisbee. I was taken to microscopic spaces in several sections of this

Wonderful walks from dog-friendly campsites

Strategically-placed shrubs create a feeling of privacy and intimacy.

large campsite. It was all rather frustrating being so restricted. My owner was extremely disappointed, especially as she was charged a fee for me; quite a hefty one, too! I thought things were looking up when the only footpath led to a field ... full of cows, though. The same applied to the tarmac track just across a busy road, where it was the many cyclists who impeded my investigations. Once we set out on our rambles, however, matters improved dramatically

SHORT WALK – UP AND DOWN DALE
Distance: 5.5ml (8.8km)
Duration: 3hr
Terrain: Fields, footpaths, tracks, cyclepath and roads, stiles and gates. Several hills to climb and descend; some very, very steep

Section 1: 1ml (1.6km)
- Leave campsite via reception and follow driveway to road
- Turn left and walk along verge for a short distance (take care, as this is a very busy road, and traffic is very fast)
- Cross road and continue straight ahead down minor road signposted 'Biggin'
- Pass under bridge and turn immediate left
- Through gate and up slope onto Tissington Trail
- Continue straight ahead along the trail
- On the right just after bridge is a footpath sign
- Turn right down slope and go through gate
- Cross track, and go through another gate into field
- Straight across field, past yellow waymarker, and through another kissing gate
- Bear right and follow path as it zig-zags downhill to valley, and go through kissing gate in wall

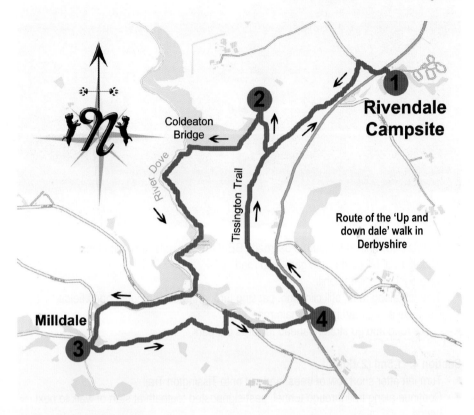

Coldeaton Bridge

Rivendale Campsite

Milldale

Route of the 'Up and down dale' walk in Derbyshire

River Dove

Tissington Trail

Section 2: 2ml (3.2km)
- Turn left and follow path, keeping wall on left, and over a wobbly stile into woods
- Continue straight ahead along valley to Coldeaton Bridge
- Turn left to Milldale (signposted) and over stile
- Follow path along valley with stream on right
- Continue straight ahead over stone stile into wooded area
- Follow path through wood and back into valley
- Path passes close to stream and houses to exit at road and humpback bridge
- Turn right and cross bridge
- Turn immediate left at road junction
- Continue along level road to Milldale with stream now on left (ideal place for refreshments)

Section 3: 1ml (1.6km)
- Cross bridge and go through gate
- Turn left (signposted Tissington), and bear right, ascending steep hill
- Follow zig-zag path uphill, and at brow keep close to wall on left. Over stone step stile
- Follow path along brow of hill, keeping close to wall now on right, even as it turns right twice

Bridge at Milldale.

- Turn left downhill at footpath crossroads BEFORE the gate, now with fence on right
- At bottom of hill go through gate onto road
- Turn right and climb uphill
- Turn left along road, still climbing, passing through trees and out to open fields.
- Continue along road to busy main road
- Cross road and go straight ahead towards car park

Section 4: 1.5ml (2.4km)
- Turn left after short row of trees, and out onto Tissington Trail
- Continue along trail through tunnel, past signposted footpath at start of walk to next bridge
- Turn left off the trail onto footpath just before bridge and out onto road
- Turn right under bridge
- Continue along road to main road
- Cross road and bear left to campsite entrance

LONG WALK – VILLAGE TRAIL
Distance: 8.5ml (13.6)
Duration: 5hr
Terrain: Cyclepath, stony tracks, fields, roads, gates and lots of mostly stone stiles of different kinds. Generally fairly flat but a couple of steep climbs. Cows in some fields. Using TissingtonTrail and Limestone Way

Section 1: 0.75ml (1.2km)
- Exit campsite via reception, and turn left along footpath where driveway bends right
- Over stone stile and straight across field to stone stile opposite
- Continue straight across this field and the next two
- Cross next field, keeping close to wall on right, and over stone stile ahead
- Continue straight on initially with wall on right, then across middle of field and through gate opposite

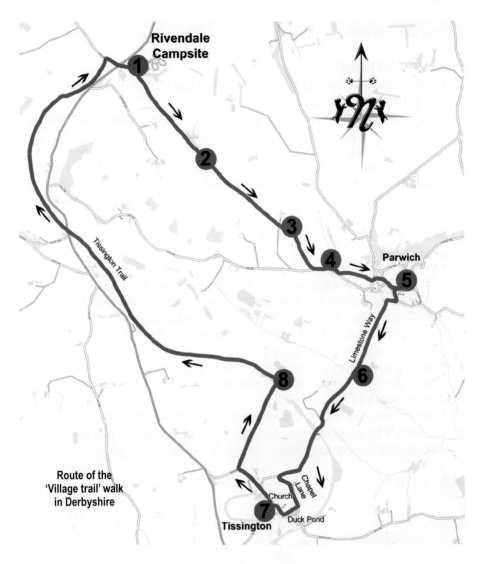

Route of the
'Village trail' walk
in Derbyshire

- Continue ahead across field, and go through gate in corner
- Cross the field and go through gate opposite
- Continue straight ahead across field along small valley

Section 2: 0.75ml (1.2km)

- Bear slightly right and over stone stile to right of gate
- Bear right and go through gap in wall beside yellow waymarker on post
- Bear left, heading for another gap in wall
- Continue straight across top of field and over another stone stile
- Go across field to stone step stile in middle of wall to right of large tree

- Over stile onto farm driveway

Section 3: 0.5ml (0.8km)
- On opposite side of driveway, go over stile under a tree
- Bear left and over stone stile opposite
- Keep bearing left, passing farm buildings on right (can just see tops of gate posts ahead)
- Go through gateway
- Continue straight ahead for about 50 paces to gate on right, which I climbed over as it was difficult to open (Pearl easily squeezed under it)
- Go straight ahead across field and climb gate opposite into next field (as above)
- Bear left and go over brow of hill down to stony track
- Turn left towards road, then left along road

Section 4: 0.5ml (0.8km)
- Opposite Flaxdale Holding warehouse turn left onto stony track with stables on left
- Continue straight ahead onto grass footpath, and over stone stile beside gate
- Bear left across field and over stone stile, wooden bridge, and gate
- Go straight ahead across field through gap in trees opposite
- Continue on and over stone stile by gate
- Bear left towards school
- Over yet another stone stile and gate onto road
- Turn left down hill into Parwich village
- Continue along road and round to left into centre of village and local pub, Sycamore Inn, which is the village communication hub (and a place to stop for refreshments, although dogs have to stay outside)

Looking back to Parwich, where the pub is the communication hub.

Section 5: 1.25ml (2km)
- Exit pub and turn right towards church
- Bear left, keeping village pond on right, and continue onto stony track past cottages and 'Limestone Way' signpost
- Go straight ahead past house towards parking area
- Turn left immediately after house and over stone stile
- Bear right uphill to another stone stile (dogs have to be especially slim to use this)
- Continue uphill and over stone stile in hedge
- Continue straight ahead, keeping close to hedge on right
- Cross another field, still staying close to hedge on right, and over another stile
- Go downhill and cross bridge at bottom

Section 6: 1.25ml (2km)
- Bearing slightly left, proceed uphill and over stile
- Continue uphill and through gate
- Continue ahead to signpost on right by ridge next to stony track
- Turn left onto stony track
- Continue along track and over cattle grid
- Straight ahead along track and over bridge onto tarmac lane (just past the bridge on the left is a footpath to Tissington Trail)
- Follow lane to T-junction with Chapel Lane
- Turn left along Chapel Lane
- Turn right along alleyway, just after red phonebox, towards village duck pond
- Turn right towards the church. (Opposite the church is Herbert's Café which welcomes dogs. It is worth taking time to explore Tissington village, and locate some of the six wells used in the dressing ceremony)

Section 7: 1ml (1.6km)
- Exit café and turn left
- Continue along road through village, past hall and a well until road bends to left
- Take track on right between fields, continue straight ahead and go through gate and into field
- Continue straight ahead, keeping close to wall on left
- Through gate next to stone step stile into field
- Continue straight on, still keeping close to wall on left
- Straight ahead as path goes between two walls, and out into field
- Continue straight on, still close to wall. Again, the path passes between two walls and out into another field
- Bear right towards gate

Section 8: 2.5ml (4km)
- Through gate onto Tissington Trail
- Turn left and continue along Tissington Trail past car park, through tunnel, and past

signposted footpath on left to next bridge
- Turn left off trail just before bridge, and down footpath out onto road
- Turn right and go under bridge
- Continue along road to main road
- Cross main road and bear left to campsite entrance

IN THE LOCALITY
CYCLING
Close to Rivendale campsite is the Tissington Trail, which runs for 13 miles (20.8km) from Ashbourne to Parsley Hay. This intersects with other cycle routes so it is easy to reach other places from it.

DOVEDALE
From Hartingdon in the north, to its confluence with the River Manifold at the picturesque village of Ilam, the River Dove has carved a valley out of the limestone rock. It is only the southern stretch from Milldale that is known as Dovedale – one of the most popular dales in Derbyshire, with its steep sides, spectacular rock formations, and caves. The area is owned by the National Trust, and walkers are able to learn about the environs, find refreshments, and appreciate the remarkable scenery along its riverside paths. At times, it can be very busy.

TISSINGTON
This village, part of Tissington Hall estate, is situated south of Rivendale campsite, close to the Tissington Trail. The present house was built in 1609, and has been in the FitzHerbert family for over 500 years. It is a fascinating building that, although still a family home, is open to the public. The church is also intriguing, situated high up on a mound.

Tissington is a beautiful village with a wide street, duck pond, charming cottages, and also a lovely teashop. However, it is the numerous wells located around the village for which it is renowned.

CARSINGTON WATER
Operated by Severn Trent Water, this reservoir was opened in 1992, and is a popular venue for both visitors and the local population. Besides watersports, it offers a whole range of activities. There's a Visitor Centre where wildlife enthusiasts and birdwatchers can learn about the area, and, to further encourage those interested, there are hides and huts around the lake. Boats are available for anglers to hire.

For the serious angler it is possible to fish in the major rivers, and just 13 miles (20.8km) away in Brailsford is Birch House Lakes, whose eight lakes are open from dawn until dusk.

ASHBOURNE
A charming market town situated at the southern edge of the Peak District, Ashbourne is surrounded by hills, and contains many attractive buildings, several of them listed.

Dominating the skyline is St. Oswald's church, built during the 13th century, and in the town centre is the Tissington Trail.

Ashbourne is infamous for the Shrovetide Football Game (a mass gathering around a ball) that originates from medieval times. The two teams are the Downards – those born south of Henmore Brook – and the Upards – those born north of it. The pitch is the actual town, with goals 3 miles (4.8km) apart. There appear to be no specific rules, tactics or strategy, but the game involves a lot of noise and fun, and frequently injuries.

Ashbourne is also famous for its gingerbread, an unusually-flavoured shortbread, introduced during the Napoleonic Wars by French prisoners.

ILAM (PRONOUNCED EYE-LAMB)

Surrounded by the dramatic hills and upland pastures of the Peak District, there has been a village clustered along the banks of the lower end of the Manifold River since Saxon times. In 1820, the owner of Ilam Hall, Jesse Watts-Russell, moved it to its current location, possibly for more privacy, and had the hall totally rebuilt in what he thought was an alpine style. Hence the church, which has some Saxon stonework, is an unusual distance from the village. The huge, elaborate cross in the centre of the village was also built by Watts-Russell to commemorate his wife, Mary.

Ilam is close to the Dovedale valley and renowned line of stepping stones that cross the River Dove.

Spectacular views everywhere!

Wonderful walks from dog-friendly campsites

Shropshire — Quintessential
OS MAPS EXPLORER 217 LONG MYND & WENLOCK EDGE

Shropshire is ideal as a place to 'escape to the country.' It has only a few towns that are modest in size but with plenty of character and quirkiness, and, curiously, unusual names, such as Clun, which sounds foreign, Craven Arms, which sounds like a pub, and Cleobury Mortimer, which sounds like someone's name. Exploring them is an enchanting experience.

Although most of the roads which criss-cross the county are minor, traffic is sometimes heavier and faster than might be expected. However, this occurs only on a few roads linking the towns, and the remaining roads provide pleasant walking routes.

A neighbour of Shropshire, the mountain foothills of Wales sometimes spill over into the county. There are many hills and, in places, some very steep escarpments, of which Wenlock Edge is the most significant. and has been designated a site of special scientific interest because its geology is exceptional.

With only a few cities and busy roads the views are spectacular, even in the valleys. As you ascend the hills, so the scenery becomes more and more magnificent, and the panorama at the summit is simply breathtaking. From the top of Brown Clee Hill, on a clear day it's possible to see the Welsh mountains on one side and the hills of the Lake District on the other: a distance of over 100 miles (160km). Also on Brown Clee Hill is a memorial that commemorates the 23 Allied and German airmen killed there when their planes crashed into the hillside during World War II.

Memorial on Brown Clee Hill commemorating pilots killed there during WW2.

A number of long-distance trails traverse the county, and the most well-known is the Shropshire Way. These trails are easy to follow – signposted and well-maintained – so are very popular with walkers, including locals. As the paths wind through the fields and up the hills, so, at every twist and turn, the scenery is just incredible.

According to Explorer OS Maps an extensive network of footpaths exists. I found some of these problematic to use as they were difficult to find, often being overgrown. In addition, the preponderance of sheep both on the hills and in the fields resulted in a great many of the stiles being what I call 'sheep-proof'; covered with special, sheep-thwarting fencing. So, unless your dog is small, and/or particularly agile, a measure of strength is required to lift him over some of the stiles, which can be especially awkward when trying to juggle a map, a lead, and backpack at the same time! Sometimes the routes I used resulted in a slightly longer walk because of this.

In this area there are few urban facilities. With the plethora of walking routes giving access to spectacular views of quintessentially English patchwork fields, lots of campsites in the county are convenient for exploring and experiencing the beauty of Shropshire. Because the campsites are located in such a rural setting, it is quiet and peaceful, except for farmyard sounds: bleating of sheep; crowing of cocks; neighing of horses. It is ideal for walkers, but the surrounding hills mean all walks necessitate a climb, and there are few cafés for refreshments or toilet facilities, except in the towns.

Easthope Caravan and Camping Site is close to the Shropshire Way and near the charming hamlet of Easthope. Other footpaths nearby quickly give admittance to the undulating countryside, and reveal the richness of the Shropshire landscape.

CAMPSITE – EASTHOPE CARAVAN AND CAMPING SITE

Although there is no reception area and payment is by cash or cheque only, this small site has all the facilities I like, and welcomes dogs. There are 11 spacious pitches with electric hook-up, and a small adjacent field for tents. Being such a small site it does have only one shower with a toilet, plus an additional toilet, but these are well organized and kept spotlessly clean. On the side of the amenities block is a small area which can be used for dishwashing. Some of the pitches are hardstanding and fairly flat, but levelling blocks are needed. Unfortunately, the phone signal is poor though the free wifi is excellent.

The campsite is part of a working farm, where wheat and barley is grown, breeding ewes are reared, and there is also a livery yard. The friendly owners are only too happy to tell you about the farm, so it is possible to learn a great deal about farming. Staying on working farms is really beneficial for the farming community. Though the campsite is close to the small hamlet of Easthope, it is in a very rural location, and the nearest shop and pub are several miles away.

PEARLS OF WISDOM 🐾

Here, there were some really strange and unusual smells. My owner told me that this was because it is a farm site, whatever that is! There was nowhere special for me as we had only a small space, but that didn't matter: just a short distance away was an interesting trail around some fields (a special farm walk) that passed a pond. Unfortunately, I was not allowed to swim in this because of the fish ... but I don't eat fish! Sometimes I could play with my frisbee as long as the grass space was not cluttered with tents. However, I did have to be careful of all the various animals.

Entrance to the working farm campsite.

SHORT WALK – MAYBE BLUEBELLS
Distance: 5.5ml (8.8km)
Duration: 3hr
Terrain: Fields, woods, footpaths, tracks and roads with gates and stiles. Well defined route but a few quite steep climbs

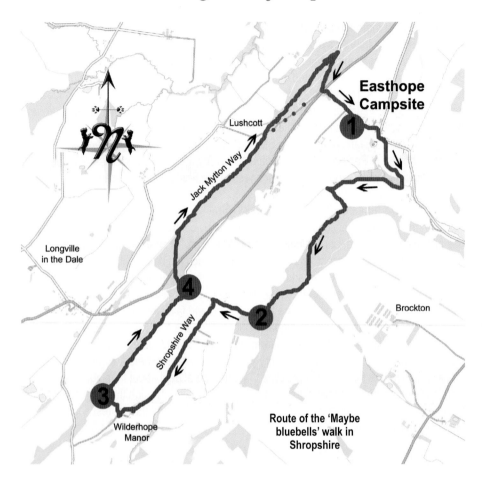

Easthope Campsite

Lushcott

Jack Mytton Way

Longville in the Dale

Shropshire Way

Wilderhope Manor

Brockton

Route of the 'Maybe bluebells' walk in Shropshire

Section 1: 1.5ml (2.4km)

- Leave campsite via entrance
- Turn left along road
- Turn right at junction, and continue on towards church
- Turn immediately left and go through small gate into field (signposted)
- Turn right and follow path around edge of field
- Turn right along wide track snaking between trees
- Turn right at edge of field and follow path, passing pond on right and over stile ahead
- Turn left along edge of field towards trees and over stile (sheep-proof) into woods
- Go up hill to a more clearly defined path, and follow to the right for some distance through the woods, keeping sight of fields through trees on right and ignoring all paths and tracks leading off.

Section 2: 1ml (1.6km)

- Turn right at footpath T-junction along a wide, stony track

Exploring among the bluebells in the wood.

- Continue along track past house on right
- Turn left onto a wide gravel driveway just before tarmac
- Follow track past farm and round to right towards a large, red-brick house
- Continue along track to driveway past magnificent Wilderhope Manor on left (now a youth hostel), and car park on right (there are toilets here but I'm not sure if the caféteria is open to the public)

Section 3: 1.5 ml (2.4km)
- Turn right along driveway
- Bear right up grassy slope at left-hand bend, and go through gate into field
- Cross field, bearing right, and go through gate in top corner
- Continue along edge of field, keeping close to fence on left
- Follow path, ignoring stile on left into wood, and go through gate ahead into another field
- Bear immediately left onto path between trees
- Follow path and go through another gate into another field
- Continue along edge of this field, and go through gate onto road
- Turn sharp left onto a steep track down into the woods, then round to the right
- Take right path at track junction down to the road

Section 4: 1.5ml (2.4km)
- Cross road to footpath opposite
- Continue downhill along path to junction with wide track
- Turn right and follow track (Jack Mytton Trail), crossing bridge over road (can climb down onto road and turn left, then follow road to junction with B4371)

Wonderful walks from dog-friendly campsites

- Continue along trail and go through gate to small car park
- Turn right along road to junction with B4371
- Cross B4371 to road opposite
- Continue along road to campsite on left

LONG WALK – FIELDS TO; RIDGE FROM
Distance: 10.5ml (16.8km)
Duration: 6hr
Terrain: Fields, woods, footpaths, trails, tracks, roads, some gates and several stiles, including 'sheep-proof 'ones. Trails are signposted but route has several hills, some quite steep

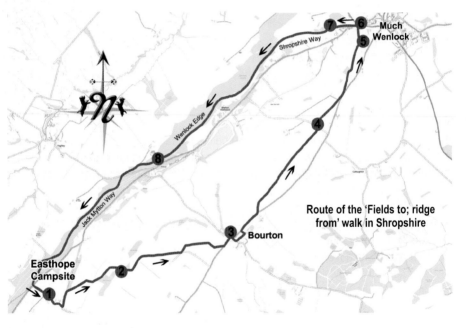

Route of the 'Fields to; ridge from' walk in Shropshire

Section 1: 1ml (1.6km)
- Exit campsite via entrance
- Turn left at road and continue to junction in village
- Turn left along road signposted 'Much Wenlock'
- Turn right along track: Shropshire Way signposted
- Continue straight on past path to left into wood, and go through gate ahead into field (possibly sheep)
- Go along edge of field, keeping close to fence on right, and over stile in corner into next field
- Bear left to left edge of field
- Continue around edge of field, keeping close to copse on right
- Go straight ahead across field at corner of copse (signposted)

- Turn right at hedge opposite, and continue uphill along edge of field, keeping close to hedge on left. Over stile (sheep-proof)
- Over second stile a few yards ahead (sheep-proof)
- Continue along footpath between fields and trees, and over stile at top of climb

One of the many historical buildings in Wenlock.

Section 2: 1.25ml (2km)
- Turn left and cross field uphill towards trees ahead (path through crops)
- Continue on, passing copse on right, and go straight across next field (again, path through crops)
- Cross track and over stile opposite
- Straight ahead along edge of field, keeping close to hedge on left

- Continue straight onto tarmac driveway
- Turn left in a few paces and over stile into field
- Straight on through gap in hedge
- Turn right along edge of field with fence on right
- Turn left into field of crops before next corner and follow path, bearing right towards trees and ignoring all paths leading off
- Follow path through trees and down to road
- Turn left along road into the village of Bourton

Section 3: 1.75ml (2.8km)
- Turn right along minor road beside house ('Dovecote') on right
- Turn left by postbox and cross bridge
- Continue ahead along lane past church, and round left bend to road
- Turn right and continue along road for 500yd (450m)
- Turn left onto wide track, keeping close to hedge on right
- Follow track, ignoring one off to left, and on past mounds of earth to footpath at edge of field
- Through gate in hedge ahead (signposted) into another field
- Continue straight along edge of two fields with hedge now on left (signposted), and across middle of next two fields to road

Section 4: 0.75ml (1.2km)
- Cross road to footpath opposite (signposted)

- Follow path along edge of field, and across two more to B4378 (busy)
- Turn left along road for 500yd (450m), and go through kissing gate in hedge on left just before brown town sign
- Bear right across the field, and go through kissing gate in corner into next field
- Bear right and over stile under tree
- Continue along fenced-off path and over stile on bend into field

Section 5: 0.5ml (0.8km)
- Straight ahead along edge of next two fields with hedge on right, and through kissing gate in right corner into field
- Straight ahead down slope and through gate
- Bear left and go between wooden fences and past buildings; through gate to road

Section 6: 1.25m (2km)
- Cross road to pavement, turn right, and continue straight ahead along High Street to town centre. Partway along High Street is a small car park with a town map information board. Much Wenlock is a very interesting place, ideal for refreshments. On Barrow Street is Tea On the Square café which welcomes dogs. (If exploring Much Wenlock diminishes the desire to walk along Wenlock Ridge a taxi to the campsite costs approximately £12.00)
- Go along Queen Street away from the Priory to A4169 T-junction
- Turn left (cross road to pavement)
- First right along Bridge Street
- First left along Southfields Road and cross A458, bearing right
- Turn sharp left along Stretton Road (B4371)
- Turn first right along tarmac driveway (signposted)
- Continue along tarmac driveway that becomes stony track
- Follow track, ignoring all paths and tracks leading off
- At large footpath junction bear left and go through a wooden kissing gate signposted 'Shropshire Way'

Section 7: 2ml (3.2km)
- Continue along fenced-off footpath towards trees, keeping close to fence on left
- Take right fork at junction along fairly level path
- Follow the path up and down several flights of steps to Presthope car park

Section 8: 2ml (3.2km)
- Keeping right, cross car park and go through gate onto Jack Mytton Way – a wide stony track (signposted)
- Continue straight ahead, keeping large wooden post labelled 'Easthope Wood' on right
- Turn right down a narrow, steep path
- Follow path round to right just past steps
- Turn left at wide track

- Continue along track and through gate onto pebbled driveway
- Go along driveway and cross minor road to footpath opposite
- Follow the footpath up a steep climb, and turn right at top onto wide track
- Follow track, ignoring all routes leading off
- Cross bridge; go through gate into small car park
- Bear left along minor road, and follow to junction with B4371
- Cross B4371 to road opposite
- Continue along road to campsite on left

IN THE LOCALITY

EASTHOPE HAMLET

Close to Wenlock Edge on the south-facing slope, the lovely church is on the edge of the village, separated from the field by a small earth mound. Though now peaceful, often with sheep grazing in the adjacent field, the church has had a turbulent past. The spirit of John Eastwood is said to haunt the church because he was murdered by the serving cleric, Will Germston, in 1333. In addition, two monks who killed each other in a drunken brawl are buried in the graveyard.

WILDERTHORPE MANOR

Built in 1585 for Francis Smallman, in 1734, the family sold the house, which slowly fell into disrepair until 1936, when the W A Cadbury Trust bought it and gave it to the National Trust on condition the building was used as a Youth Hostel. This Grade I listed building is still in use today as a hostel.

MUCH WENLOCK

A typical Shropshire market town, though somewhat off the beaten track, Much Wenlock has several attractive independent shops, cafés and pubs, fascinating buildings, a huge priory ruin, and a museum that documents its long history. Surprisingly, the town is most notable for being the birthplace of the modern Olympics, because it was here that William Penny Brookes was born, whose ambition it was to revive the Olympic Games. Unfortunately, William Penny Brookes did not live to see the culmination of his dream, as the first International Olympic Games was held four months after his death in 1896. However, it all began with the Wenlock Olympic Society arranging the Wenlock Olympic Games, and these have been held annually in July since 1850. A delightful way to see the town is to follow the Olympic Trail.

CHURCH STRETTON

Another delightful Shropshire market town with a long and interesting history, several charming independent shops, a choice of teashops and pubs for refreshments, and, of course, a regular market.

BROWN CLEE HILL

Much of the Eastern slopes of Brown Clee Hill are part of Viscount Boyne's Burwarton

Estate, where, nowadays, sheep graze the upper slopes. But it has not always been so quiet and peaceful. During the Iron Age, there were several hill forts, and coal was mined in medieval times. Then, up until the 1930s, Dolerite or Dhustone was quarried.

It is difficult to imagine such activity taking place. Today, the tops are crowned with various radar masts: because Brown Clee Hill is so high (1770ft (540m), it was a serious hazard for WWII pilots.

Ludlow

According to the poet John Betjeman, Ludlow is "the loveliest town in England." I do not know if it's the loveliest, but it's definitely a charming and attractive town, first established in the 11th century on the confluence of the River Corve and River Teme, and on the hill the Normans built a castle. Despite being in such a pivotal position on the Welsh and English border, much of the medieval town remains.

Ludlow is an architectural treasure trove with almost 500 listed buildings, and also a bustling active community with many small independent shops. There is a market most days in Castle Square, and various events during the year, including an arts festival and a food festival. The impressive ruins of Ludlow Castle occupy the oldest part of the town, and date from Norman times. One of the most interesting castles in the area, it commands an imposing position high above the river Teme. St Laurence's Church, situated close to the castle ruins, is thought to be one of the largest churches in England. The poet A E Housman, best known for his poem *A Shropshire Lad*, is buried there.

Staffordshire — National Memorial Arboretum
OS Maps Explorer 245 The National Forest

Many people I speak to are unaware of the National Memorial Arboretum, probably because it was only recently created. It is a wonderful place; a counterpoint to the hustle and bustle of modern life.

It was the brainchild of David Childs, who, during a visit to Arlington Cemetery in the States, was inspired to create something similar in the UK. With the help and support of Leonard Cheshire VC and then-Prime Minister John Major, and following a lot of hard work, planting began in 1997. However, it wasn't until May 16, 2001 that the National Memorial Arboretum in Central England, Staffordshire, near Lichfield, was officially opened by the Duchess of Kent. It is one of the many registered charities under the auspices of the Royal British Legion.

From the outset, unlike Arlington, the arboretum was not intended as a cemetery, but a place to celebrate and remember the lives of people: the planting of living trees creating an oasis of peace, joy, hope and tranquillity. Also, it was felt that all of those individuals who served our country in so many different ways should be appropriately recognized and honoured: "... this living memorial is to offer families and friends of those who have made the ultimate sacrifice for their country a green and pleasant land to remember their loved ones."

In order for people to feel that the place belonged to them all, pertinent groups and organizations have been encouraged to participate.

A place to remember and celebrate the lives of many different people.

The Remembrance Centre is open all year except Christmas Day. It has been enlarged and refurbished, and the new building was officially opened by the Duke of Cambridge on March 26, 2017. Besides the provision of information, there is more space for exhibitions, a larger restaurant as well as a café, and a delightful outdoor space 'Heroes Square' and 'The Boyes Garden,' where views of the Arboretum can be admired whilst enjoying refreshments. And, of course, there is a shop.

Also to be found in the Centre is The Millennium Chapel of Peace and Forgiveness, created to offer all peoples of whatever faith or persuasion a place of calmness, peace and serenity. Every day at 11am an Act of Remembrance is held in the Chapel.

There is a charge for entry to the Remembrance Centre, although it is free to sit in Heroes Square, visit the shop, café and Chapel, and wander the grounds. Throughout the year a range of events are held both in the Remembrance Centre and the grounds. (Details can be found online.)

The Arboretum covers 150 acres (61 hectares), and more than 50,000 trees have been planted. The Armed Forces Memorial is by far the largest of its kind, and commemorates all those who, since WWII, have been killed whilst on duty or due to terrorist acts. The Queen was in attendance in October 2007 when this memorial was dedicated, and over 330 other memorials honour both military and civilian organizations. One of the newest additions is the Road Peace Memorial dedicated to all those killed on our roads, and many trees have been planted in remembrance of individuals, creating woodlands that now support an ever-increasing diversity of wildlife.

Situated at the confluence of the Rivers Tame and Trent, the National Memorial Arboretum is ideally located, embraced in the arms of both rivers. It offers something for everyone: somewhere to stroll and enjoy the many trees; a place of spirituality and reflection; a place of remembrance; somewhere to increase knowledge and understanding, and now somewhere to admire the natural world with the increase in wildlife,.

Dogs are not allowed in the Remembrance Centre but they are in Heroes Square. Here, seats and refreshments are available. Regrettably, dogs are not permitted onto the many memorials in the Arboretum. However, as there are public footpaths through the Arboretum, a Dog Walk has been established. A Dog Walking Map is available from the Remembrance Centre, and in plastic receptacles on two notice posts nearby. This clearly shows where to go and marks dog bins and 'hitching posts.' The idea is that you can tie your dog's lead to the post whilst you look at a memorial off the path, but do ensure that you can see your animal at all times An excellent idea, although the hitching posts are easily missed. This trail is extensive, and much of it is beside the rivers as well as passing close to many memorials.

CAMPSITE – WILLOWBROOK FARM CAMPSITE
Access to this campsite is very awkward. The entrance is, as the address suggests, on the south side of the A38: a very busy dual carriageway between Burton-on-Trent and Lichfield. If the entrance is missed it is necessary to continue to the next roundabout, go right round it to travel up the north side of the A38 past the campsite, and right round the next roundabout back onto the south side of the A38.

A long and complicated manoeuvre that is well worth the effort, although, as you pull up in front of a large barn to register, it might not appear so. As you proceed between the buildings, however, the whole panorama changes, just like going through the back of the wardrobe into Narnia. A meadow fills the horizon and, taking centre stage, is a large lake bordered by mature trees and shrubs: a stark contrast to the busy road on the other side of the barns.

Though this is a no-frills campsite, there are electric hook-ups, toilets and showers and even a small dishwashing area but no hot water. With grass stretching down to the lake, it's a wonderful place to sit and admire the view, and watch the birds. And what a lot of birds there are!

An amazing, spacious campsite.

PEARLS OF WISDOM 🐾

Oh, look, a lake! And so close! I glanced at my owner thinking, do hurry up, park the vehicle, stop faffing about, and let's explore the lake. I hope it is deep enough for a swim

Eventually we set off, and quickly reached the lake. I just wanted to scramble down the bank to the water, but we began to skirt the lake, and very soon I found more water; flowing, this time (a river, I think). Finally, some distance on was an ideal spot for me to wade into the lake and have a swim.

We continued on round and in a short time were suddenly back at the van. Again, no gates or fences. Very peculiar. The walk around the Arboretum was interesting, but being on the lead was annoying, and so, because it was quite late, my owner let me off along part of the riverside path. What fun, playing hide-and-seek with her in the 'trench' maze!

SHORT WALK – THE ARBORETUM (AN AMAZING PLACE)
Distance: 4.5ml (7.2km)
Duration: 2.5hr (longer to really appreciate the experience)
Terrain: Flat and level. Footpaths (some not always defined), tracks, tarmac paths, rail crossing, kissing gates

A WWI memorial.

Section 1: 0.75ml (1.2km)
- From your unit cross grass towards lake
- Turn left, keeping lake on right
- Continue along path (not always defined) between lake and River Trent
- Follow path around lake, now with railway line on left, and down to lake edge and over brook
- Turn right onto very narrow footpath in 50yd (45m) and cross rail line (take care as notice states)
- Follow the route from rail-line and cross gravel track to footpath opposite (signposted) and into the Arboretum

Section 2: 0.75ml (1.2km)
- Continue straight ahead towards river
- Turn right along gravel path beside River Tame on left
- Following the gravel path, turn right away from river at 'Cheltenham School Memorial' on left
- Continue along path round to left, and then to right and through kissing gate (map available in plastic receptacle here) into small staff car park
- Bear right across green mound beside fir tree and post (maps available in plastic

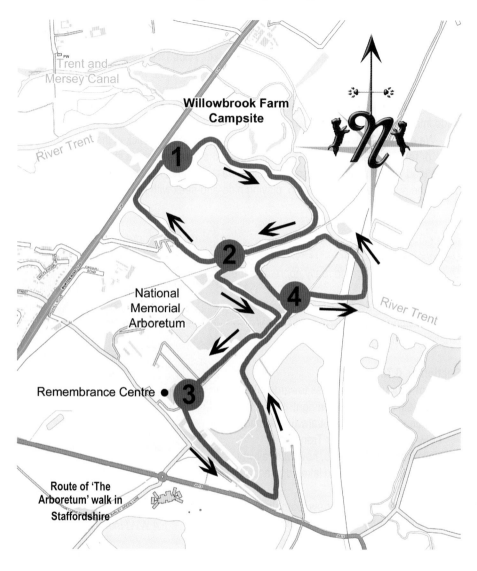

receptacle here). Ahead is large public car park, and to the right is the Remembrance Centre (a good place to stop for refreshments in Heroes Square)

Section 3: 1.5ml (2.4km)
(From here the route is as per the Dog Walking Map)
- Retrace steps to kissing gate
- Continue along path, keeping straight ahead at junction onto earth path (signposted)
- Follow the path with road on right and round to left now beside River Tame
- Continue along riverside path and under railway bridge
- Follow the path now with River Trent on right and under second railway bridge

- Turn left back towards the river (along this path are interesting displays about WWI.

Section 4: 1.5ml (2.4km)
- Turn right along riverside path
- Retrace steps to 'Army Chaplin's Memorial,' and turn right back towards rail line
- Retrace steps over railway track and turn right back round lake to campsite (turning left and following edge of lake back to campsite is shorter. Although it is not a public footpath, it is used by those staying at the campsite)

IN THE LOCALITY
ALREWAS
Just the other side of the A38, which is part of a Roman road, on the south bank of the River Trent, is this charming village, and passing through it is the Trent and Mersey Canal. Its long history is reflected in the main street, where there are many attractive historical buildings; some the typical black-and-white style of the period.

This is an interesting village to explore, and, being just within the National Forest, north of the village are many footpaths, including the recently-created Way for the Millennium Trail.

Visit Hubble and Hattie on the web:
www.hubbleandhattie.com • www.hubbleandhattie.blogspot.co.uk • Details of all books
• Special offers • Newsletter • New book news

137

The walks: South East England
(Buckinghamshire, Essex, West Sussex)

Buckinghamshire — home of an Anglo — Saxon landowner

OS MAPS EXPLORER 181 CHILTERN HILLS NORTH

Buckinghamshire's identity is somewhat eclipsed, not only because it is one of the Home Counties, but also because of its proximity to London. Much of the county is part of the London commuter belt, so has some of the most densely populated areas in the UK. However, in the northern region, near the border with the county of Northamptonshire, transport links to the capital are less efficient. The 'London effect' is less obvious in this part of the county, which, by comparison, is a relative backwater. It is here that the city of Buckingham is situated. As a consequence it is not the capital of the county: that honour goes to Aylesbury.

No doubt the Anglo-Saxon landowner 'Bucca' (whoever he was) would be astonished to learn that part of modern Britain is named after him, and has been for many centuries: Buckinghamshire means 'the district of Bucca's home.'

The notion of escaping from the hassles of London to more rural areas has long been popular, and began in the 1800s when rural communities were decimated by famine and disease – primarily cholera. Those who survived were forced to move to the city, so land in Buckinghamshire became cheap. The newly-rich found the county ideal as a rural getaway; an opinion that still holds sway today, even though property prices have risen. Conurbations along the gentle southern slopes of the Chiltern Hills in the south of the county rapidly grew as London expanded, fuelled by the growth of the railways and advent of speedy transport.

The other half of the county is quite different, where the steeper incline of the Chiltern Hills overlooks the wide, flat Aylesbury Vale, with the River Great Ouse meandering along its northern border. This is very much an agricultural landscape, with typical undulating patchwork fields and farms, and villages sprinkled throughout.

Contrary to expectations, Buckinghamshire is an interesting county to explore, especially for walkers. Besides the River Thames there is also the Grand Union Canal. The Chiltern Hills are designated as an Area of Outstanding Natural Beauty (AONB), and in sharp contrast are the stunning flats of Aylesbury Vale. The network of footpaths and trails across the countryside reflect the rural origins of the county, mostly following the ancient drover routes when animals were herded from one place to another. Many of them have been upgraded to long distance trails, the most well known of which is the Ridgeway. This 87-mile (140km) trail starts at Ivinghoe Beacon in the Chiltern Hills, passes Chequers,

Patchwork fields and farms of the north part of the county.

Trig point on Ivinghoe Beacon.

the Prime Minister's rural getaway, and crosses Buckinghamshire into Wiltshire.

Ivinghoe Beacon is the highest point of Chiltern Hills, and dominates the surrounding countryside, seeming to rise up abruptly and signalling the splendour of the hills. The views from the summit are stupendous. The knoll has a long history, dating back to at least the Iron Age, of being the perfect place for a fort as well as ideal for farming. Marking the top and start of the Ridgeway is a memorial as well as a trig point. Such is the importance of Ivinghoe Beacon the trig point marks the start of two other trails: the Icknield Trail and the Two Ridges Link.

Not only are the views stunning, but, like much of Buckinghamshire, there are many different routes to explore, and so much to see.

Wonderful walks from dog-friendly campsites

CAMPSITE – TOWN FARM CAMPING AND CARAVANNING

Being part of a working farm, the entrance to this campsite is rather unusual. The lovely, wide, tree-lined driveway snakes past several buildings, including an entrance to some dwellings, and on past some holiday cottages, and eventually leads to an open area by two huge grain silos. There are several exits from this area, one of which has a height barrier. Here can be found reception: a large notice board outside an amenities block. Within a few minutes of calling the number listed, a member of staff comes to show you to your pitch.

Two large fields with fabulous views over the vast flats of the Vale of Aylesbury and Ivinghoe Beacon are reserved for campers, part of one being set aside for ball games. Pitches are not demarcated apart from a few that are hardstanding, and others by electric hook-up points. The informal positioning of units creates a casual, relaxed atmosphere. There are two amenities blocks: one has a large indoor laundry and dishwashing facilities specifically for those with tents. By comparison, the toilets and showers are rather cramped, and when the site is full, quickly become congested.

The farmer allows visitors to wander over his fields, and a specially-assigned footpath connects to public ones. Do, however, be considerate of crops and livestock.

Bookings can only be made online so it is necessary to book ahead.

PEARL OF WISDOM 🐾

This has to be one of the biggest campsites we visited. It was HUGE. Though I met lots of doggy companions it was mostly when on the lead. When exploring the edges of the fields I was generally on my own, though I did, on occasion, meet some bothersome sheep. When there was only us and a couple of others I was allowed to run and chase my frisbee closer to our camper.

The walks were hunky-dory: up the hill; along the canal; around the windmill. Occasionally, there were roads: some rather noisy and seemingly large, but generally with grass alongside that I could use.

SHORT WALK – UP AND DOWN
Distance: 5.25ml (8.4km)
Duration: 4hr

Campsite overlooking Aylesbury Vale.

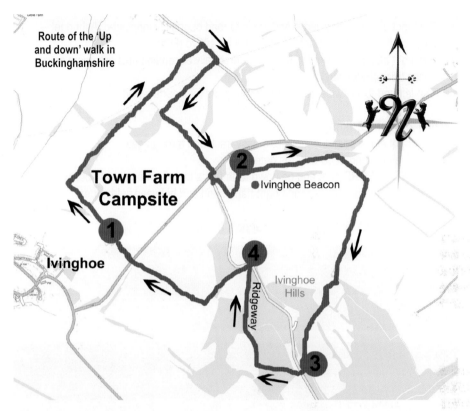

Route of the 'Up and down' walk in Buckinghamshire

Town Farm Campsite

Ivinghoe Beacon

Ivinghoe

Ivinghoe Hills

Ridgeway

Terrain: Fields, footpaths, tracks and roads; some gates and stiles with some very steep ascents and descents

Section 1: 2ml (3.2km)

- Exit campsite opposite entrance to motorhome and caravan field into field via kissing gate
- Go downhill along edge of field with fence on left
- Follow path round right-hand bend, and go through kissing gate on left onto narrow track
- Turn right and follow path
- Take left fork at tarmac driveway and follow toward road
- Turn sharp right BEFORE road along track into field
- Bear left along edge of field, keeping close to hedge on left
- Follow path around corner of field, and through kissing gate on left into next field
- Turn right and go along edge of this large field, keeping close to fence now on right
- Go round corner to left, climb hill, and go through gate gap in fence ahead beside overgrown stile on right
- Continue up along edge of field and through kissing gate onto B489

- Turn right along narrow verge and cross to road opposite signposted 'Ashridge'
- Cross cattle grid and turn left up steep hill for 100yd (90m)
- Turn right along path, skirting hill on left, gradually ascending until emerging onto a wide track (Ridgeway)
- Turn left and follow wide track uphill to trig point (wonderful views)

Section 2: 1.5ml (2.4km)
- Turn right at trig point along wide, grassy track and through gate
- Continue on along ridge towards gate
- Turn right BEFORE gate and go down, with fence on left, through gate below
- Follow the path as it goes round right-hand bend and between fields; then through gate onto a grassy track
- Climb hill and go through gate into car park at top

The grassy track between the fields, close to Ivinghoe Beacon.

Section 3: 0.75ml (1.2km)
- Turn left and go through car park
- BEFORE reaching road continue straight ahead onto path between trees (this is parallel to road)
- Follow the path and go straight on when it emerges from trees across open space to stony patch
- Turn right. Cross road
- Bear slightly right across small parking area to narrow grassy footpath (signposted) and with 'Warning' notice
- Follow path downhill through gate and on to wide stony track (Ridgeway)

- Turn right and continue along Ridgeway, passing gate on right
- Follow path along hillside as it narrows, and go through gate on right signposted 'Ridgeway'
- Ascend hill and continue on to minor road

Section 4: 1ml (1.6km)
- Turn left along road
- Turn left again in 50yd (45m) onto wide, stony track going down
- Go through gate on left at junction (signposted)
- Turn right and follow grassy path beside fence on right
- Turn right and go through gate in fence into field
- Follow the path between the fields, and go through two gates onto B489
- Cross road to campsite main entrance opposite, and up drive to reception

LONG WALK – WIND AND WATER
Distance: 9ml (14.4km)
Duration: 5.5hr
Terrain: Fields, footpaths, tracks, towpath and roads with some gates and stiles. Mostly flat walking; down a hill from campsite

Section 1: 1.25ml (2km)
- Exit campsite into field opposite entrance to motorhome and caravan field via kissing gate
- Go downhill along edge of field with fence on left
- Follow path round right-hand bend,and through kissing gate on left onto narrow track
- Turn left and follow footpath along cul-de-sac
- Turn right at T-junction
- Go along Ladysmith Road, and cross main road to field entrance by bus stop
- Pass through entrance onto footpath on right, keeping close to fence on left
- Turn right at corner, then follow narrow footpath round school grounds and over footbridge
- Turn right and continue along footpath past houses (possibly building works) on left, and over stile into field
- Bear left towards house
- Continue along edge of field with house on left, and over stile in left corner

Section 2: 1.25ml (2km)
- Follow path out to cul-de-sac and onto main road
- Turn right and continue along road for 100yd (90m)
- Turn right, cross road (pavement stops here), and go through kissing gate onto footpath
- Follow footpath through trees to canal

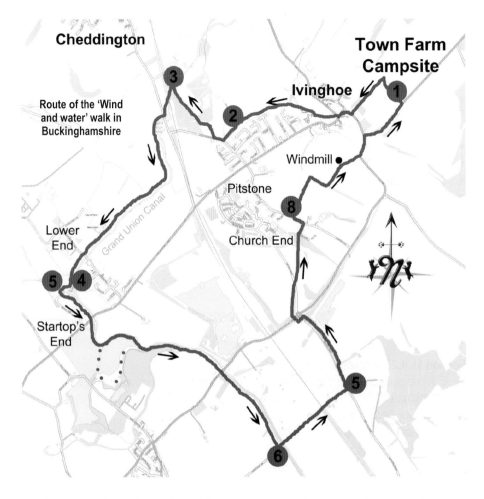

Cheddington

Town Farm Campsite

Route of the 'Wind and water' walk in Buckinghamshire

Ivinghoe

Windmill ●

Pitstone

Church End

Lower End

Grand Union Canal

Startop's End

- Cross canal footbridge and turn left along towpath, going under rail bridge and road bridge

Section 3: 1ml (1.6km)
- Continue along towpath and under bridge at Marsworth, ignoring sign to Red Lion Pub!

Section 4: 0.5ml (0.8km)
- Follow towpath under bridge by canal replenishing centre
- Bear right across square towards houses; then left towards water and locks
- Turn right along footpath with locks on left and cross bridge

Section 5: 1.25ml (2km)
- Turn right back onto towpath and immediately right again under bridge

- Continue along footpath round to the right, passing locks now on left, and up onto bridge
- Cross road to path opposite and back onto towpath (on right are steps to a café: a good place to stop for refreshments)
- Follow along towpath between canal on left and lakes (managed by Wildlife Trust) on right, and on under bridge by a pub (many paths around the lakes lead back to the towpath)

Section 6: 1ml (1.6km)
- Continue along towpath and up onto next bridge
- Turn left and cross bridge
- Continue along tarmac road past buildings onto football pitch
- Go over railway bridge, through farmyard of Park Hill Farm and out to road

Section 7: 1.25ml (2km)
- Turn left along road with footpath on opposite side to layby
- Continue along path and, 30 yards past gate, turn right and go through kissing gate into woods
- Turn immediately left, signposted 'Pitstone'
- Follow footpath through trees parallel to road and over stile on left out to road
- Turn immediately right and take narrow footpath between hedges out to pavement by large roundabout
- Turn left and cross road; turn right and cross road; turn left and, in 30yd (27m) over stile on right onto footpath
- Continue along footpath through trees and out to road
- Cross road and turn left
- Bear right in 30yd (27m) along footpath away from road (signposted) and into large field
- Continue straight across field towards post with waymarker by hedge
- Go on past post on left, keeping close to hedge on left
- Continue straight ahead past all interesting-looking paths and through gate onto road
- Follow road and turn left at main road

Section 8: 1.5ml (2.4km)
- Turn right in 50yd (45m) and go through gate into field
- Cross field heading towards church spire
- Turn right at footpath junction with windmill on left
- Continue along path and turn left at next footpath junction, heading towards windmill
- Follow path past windmill (now on right), and through gate into car park
- Turn left along road to junction (take care: busy, but there is a narrow verge on opposite side)

- Turn right and follow road to campsite entrance

IN THE LOCALITY
BIRDWATCHING
Tring Reservoir Nature Reserve is a site of Special Scientific Interest. Though the primary purpose is to feed the Grand Union Canal, it has, over the years, become a haven for wildlife, and is managed by the Wildlife Trust. It is a popular location with birdwatchers because of the variety of birds to be seen, and the many paths that connect the lakes and so allow easy access.

FISHING
These lakes are also popular with anglers as there's a variety of fish, some of which are quite large.

IVINGHOE
Nestling in the Chiltern Hills is this small but charming Buckinghamshire town, situated near the borders of Bedfordshire and Hertfordshire, close to the Grand Union Canal. It has several interesting timber-framed buildings, especially the Kings Head pub that overlooks the impressive village green. Opposite is the imposing 13th century St Mary of the Virgin church, whose interior is just as magnificent with its Tudor brasses, amazing angel ceiling, and mediaeval bench ends. Visitors are welcome to not only admire the magnificence but also to experience the calm and stillness there.

PITSTONE WINDMILL
In one of the fields just outside Ivinghoe is this fine example of a 'post' mill, now owned by the National Trust. This type of mill can be moved about via a tail pole to face the wind. The exact age of the mill is unknown but, of all the dates inscribed in the woodwork, 1627 is the earliest.

This windmill served the community for hundreds of years, milling locally-grown grain into flour. Then, in 1902, a terrible storm caused substantial damage and it was subsequently abandoned. In 1963, volunteers set up a committee to raise funds to restore the windmill, and in 1970 it again milled flour. In theory, it could still do so today but the structure is too unstable for prolonged use.

GRAND UNION CANAL
This canal was built during the late 1700s and early 1800s to improve transport between London and the Midlands. At 137 miles (220km)

The Pitstone Windmill in the field.

long, and with 166 locks, it is the longest of all the canals, passing through both rural and urban landscape.

Competition from the railways was intense, especially during the early 20th century. The canals did adapt but were unable to maintain commercial viability after WWII. Nowadays, the canal is again teeming with activity, with walkers and boats of all kinds taking full advantage of the area, where wildlife has found a peaceful refuge.

FORD END WATERMILL

This is situated on the outskirts of Ivinghoe. Despite being originally built in the 1700s, it is still operational today due to the efforts of volunteers. Flour is available for purchase on Sundays and bank holidays between May and September, when the mill is open.

WHIPSNADE ZOO

Only 5 miles (8km) from the campsite is the largest zoo and safari park in the UK: home to over 3500 animals, many of which are endangered. Several of the animals actually roam freely around the park, though most are kept in large enclosures. The protection of animals and their habitat is a vital aspect of the zoo's work, and it is one of Europe's largest wildlife conservation parks.

Essex — Island in the estuary
OS MAPS EXPLORER 184 COLCHESTER

The TV programme *The Only Way Is Essex*, which reinforces the idea that people from Essex are 'a few sandwiches short of a picnic,' is responsible for a huge misconception. The programme exploits the pejorative 'Essex Girl' belief that has its origins in the 1980s and 90s. The phrase has so permeated cultural consciousness that there is even a dictionary entry. As a result, many Essex people and visitors are hesitant about making known their location. As with most generalizations and stereotypes the reality is far more complex.

Contrary to expectations, Essex is an extraordinary county, but, because it is so close to London, it is easy to forget that it is part of the East Anglia region. The UK capital hugely influences the county, and many of the towns and villages along the Thames Estuary border in the south are bedroom communities for London. As a consequence, these areas are prosperous, and property prices are high. Fortunately, the Metropolitan Green Belt and Epping Forest have so far prevented the London conurbation from spreading into other areas of the county.

Essex is north east of London, and extends some distance north of the River Thames to Suffolk and Cambridgeshire in the north, and Hertfordshire in the west. Astonishingly, the county has some 350 miles (563km) of coastline along the Thames Estuary and northwards along the North Sea. Dotted along this stretch are islands, one of which is Mersea Island.

Along this coastal part of Essex on the eastern side of the UK lie several harbours, ports, and seaside towns. At one time, fishing was an important industry, and the ports here contributed hugely to the economy. The seaside towns became popular holiday destinations, partly due to the plethora of beaches, and because this area is one of the driest in the country. However, with the advent of cheap foreign travel, the influx of holidaymakers declined, and the allure of a trip to the beach waned. Simultaneously, the fishing industry collapsed, and containerization made the small ports redundant, so the area gradually deteriorated and now east Essex is one of the poorest regions in the UK.

The variety of transport located within the Essex borders is quite unusual. There are several important rail networks, mostly along the south of the county, which serve the many commuters who live there. The port of Tilbury, on the Thames Estuary, has grown over the years, and is now one of the UK's major container ports. Then there is the international port of Harwich situated on the North Sea, with links to Scandinavian countries. In the north west of the country is Stansted International airport, often considered London's third airport. With regard to motorways, however, there are only a couple, and these are mostly in the extreme west and south, with the infamous M25 and Dartford Tunnel that crosses the River Thames skirting the western border.

Like much of the UK, Essex has a long and interesting past. The Romans settled in the area, with the city of Colchester being an important place, its significance such that, during the Celtic uprising led by Boudicca, it was ransacked. Then, during Anglo-Saxon times, even though little is known of this period as there are few surviving written records, Essex was one of the seven kingdoms that eventually united to form the Kingdom of England, and many interesting and historical buildings can be found in its towns and villages.

With industry and large settlements mostly confined to southern areas of the county, much of the land is actually used for agriculture. The wildlife in the county is plentiful and varied due to the long coastline and odd pockets of ancient woodlands dating from mediaeval times. There are many places to walk and so discover the 'hidden' Essex.

The long coastline of Essex.

Illustrative of this is Mersea Island just off the coast in the North Sea but only 9 miles (14.4km) from the city of Colchester.

CAMPSITE – FEN FARM CARAVAN SITE

This is located on the eastern tip of Mersea Island, close to the beach: a large campsite with 85 static vans and 70 pitches for tourers that has been in the Lord family since 1918, with the first tents being pitched in 1923. The site is divided into small interconnecting sections with static vans clustered together off to one side. Facilities are comprehensive, and include an interesting play area and substantial shop, but no bar or entertainment.

The campsite close to the beach.

The amenities block is well appointed. The Lord family is environmentally aware, and, over the years, the site – which is relaxed, tranquil and friendly – has won many awards.

PEARLS OF WISDOM 🐾
Wow, what a wonderful place! Not only is there the usual small exercise area at the edge of the campsite, but a gap in the hedge meant that the path extends all along a large field where, if it wasn't occupied, I could also chase my frisbee. Then there is the tree-lined area, which was very exciting to explore. It's a shame we didn't find these places sooner but, as my owner remarked, they're not noted on the campsite diagram.

And then there's the beach with some fascinating smells along the special route through the campsite to it. Arriving there was exciting as sometimes there was a chance to have a swim. Very mysteriously, on occasion, the water disappeared! I don't know where it went, it simply vanished! And this was the strangest water I had ever seen because it moved, coming towards me and then running away! Anyway, this wasn't very important because once I was swimming, it was just like all the other water I've seen.

Just a little way along the beach is a fantastic park where I met up with doggy companions. Great fun!

PS Apparently, the council has decided to allow dogs on the beach ALL year in the expectation that they are under control, and any mess they make is cleared up. Please, everyone, if you go there, make sure this happens!

SHORT WALK – AROUND THE BAY
Distance: 4.75ml (7.6km)
Duration: 2.5hr
Terrain: Beach, fields, footpaths, roads, tracks, embankments; some gates and stiles.
Beach can be difficult as there are pebbles in several areas

Section 1: 1.25m (2km)
- Exit campsite to beach via footpath by reception
- Turn right around back of reception, then left as signposted
- Follow stony track to beach, keeping caravan park on left
- Turn left along beach

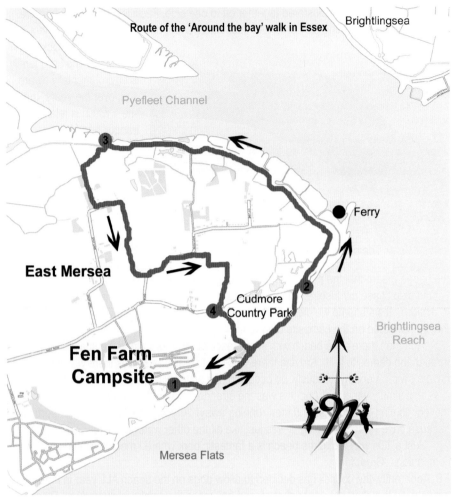

Route of the 'Around the bay' walk in Essex

Brightlingsea

Pyefleet Channel

East Mersea

Ferry

Cudmore
Country Park

Brightlingsea
Reach

Fen Farm
Campsite

Mersea Flats

Path along the top of the embankment.

- Continue along beach to left-hand bend

Section 2: 1ml (1.6km)
- Bear left up ramp on to top of embankment
- Continue along top of embankment as it winds along the river mouth with a small channel on left
- Go through a gate and bear right; cross track and back on to top of embankment

- Go through another gate
- Turn left down steps and bear right to kissing gate and into field

Section 3: 1.5ml (2.4km)
- Cross field, bearing slightly right
- Cross plank bridge into copse
- Turn left and ascend steps ahead
- Cross mound and descend steps other side
- Continue straight along footpath and through kissing gate
- Follow path round to right , then left
- Turn left at T-junction along wide track
- Continue straight ahead, over 'sheep-proof' stile
- Turn right and walk round edge of field
- Turn right and go through small gap in hedge just past corner
- Turn left and continue along edge of field, with hedge now on left, and past footpath on right
- Turn left into copse at yellow waymarker, and follow path to road
- Turn left along road
- Turn right onto grassy track from road at third bend
- Turn right at corner of field
- Turn left in about 50yd (45m), and right again just past stables
- Continue along path past stables and fields
- Turn left at yellow waymarker just past bend

Section 4: 1ml (1.6km)
- Cross bridge to road
- Turn left along road, then immediate left along stony track (this is Cudmore Grove Country Park: a delightful place to explore. There is a bird hide, café, and plenty of space to throw a ball. It is popular with dog walkers so is a good place to meet other dogs)
- Turn right onto grass, heading towards car park
- Continue straight ahead, keeping car park on right
- Turn right along wide grassy track towards café
- Turn left, still on grassy track
- Follow path to left, then right into a copse and out to a green
- Bear left across green and drop down to the beach where possible
- Turn right along beach
- Turn right by wooden bench onto campsite footpath

LONG WALK – BEACH, BOATS AND HUT
Distance: 11ml (17.7km)
Duration: 6hr
Terrain: Flat, mostly stony beach, some fields, footpaths, tracks; quiet residential roads

Wonderful walks from dog-friendly campsites

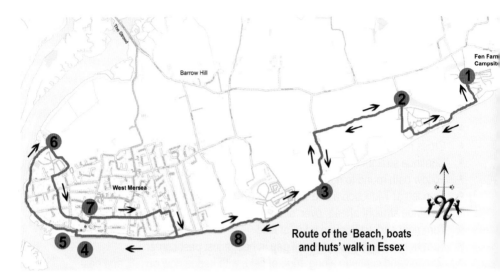

Route of the 'Beach, boats and huts' walk in Essex

Section 1: 1ml (1.6km)
- Exit campsite to beach via footpath by reception
- Turn right around back of reception; then left as signposted
- Follow stony track to beach, keeping caravan park on left
- On beach, turn right towards another caravan park
- Bear right towards gate, but turn left onto a tarmac path between sea and static vans
- Continue along tarmac path to end of sea wall
- Turn right into caravan park along narrow path
- Turn left at junction and follow tarmac path past swimming pool and shop to play area
- Turn right and continue along path past play area and football pitch on left

Section 2: 1.25ml (2km)
- Exit caravan park and turn left onto footpath opposite East Mersea church, and cross three fields to road

Huts along the beach in West Mersea.

- Continue straight along road around left-hand bend
- Follow road past vineyard and café on right (a nice place to stop for refreshments); through gates of outdoor centre
- Bear right to a green through another set of gates (signposted yellow waymarker)
- Official route is straight ahead along edge of green to corner, and then left to brow of slope. Unofficial route is to bear right diagonally across green to brow)
- Turn left, keeping close to fence on left, then right at corner, following fence round to left
- Continue straight along path, and down steps to beach

Section 3: 2.25ml (3.6km)
- Turn right and along the beach, past typical, brightly-coloured beach huts for about 2 miles (3.2km)

Section 4: 0.25ml (0.4km)
- Turn right off beach and follow wall on right to the 'Monkey Steps' (signposted)
- Up steps to road
- Turn right and follow road round to the left to church, shops and cafés (a good place to stop for refreshments). St Peter and St Paul's church in the Centre of West Mersea is 4.5 miles (7.2km) from the campsite. If, at this point, you wish to return to the campsite, jump to Section 7. Having come this far, though, it's a shame not to experience the 'Old City' of West Mersea (Sections 5 and 6) – boats; sailing businesses; oyster farm, etc – which is very different to the beach area

Section 5: 1ml (1.6km)
- Retrace route to Monkey Steps and descend steps
- Turn right along plank walkway signposted 'St Peter's Well'
- Go up a few steps and continue along footpath parallel to beach and road
- Continue along wide grassy path past steps to road, then boardwalk to beach on left

- Continue along the road signposted 'Old City' past several pubs, cafés restaurants, and a great many boats, and the 'Lady Grace Boat Trip' jetty
- Straight ahead to narrow lane between buildings, passing 'Dabchicks Sailing Club' on left
- Turn left at back of sailing club building and towards beach through small car park
- Turn right along concrete path (signposted) onto a sandy path parallel to beach
- Continue along path past caravan park on right

Section 6: 1ml (1.6km)
- Turn right off path immediately after caravan park
- Follow path along edge of field, and round left- then right-hand bend
- Continue straight ahead along narrow path close to hedge on right
- Turn right at T-junction
- Follow path, keeping close to wooden fence on left
- Turn left at road (top of The Lane)
- Continue ahead and cross road, bearing slightly left to go along Rosebank Road
- Cross over road at T-junction and go along lane opposite
- Cross road and continue on along lane opposite to Church Road
- Go along Church Road to the junction by church and café
- Turn left along High Street to Yorick Road on right

Section 7: 1.75ml (2.8km)
- Turn right along Yorick Road
- Straight ahead along Prince Albert Road over crossroads
- Turn right at T-junction into Oakwood Avenue; then left into King Charles Road
- Turn right into Alexandra Avenue and continue along this road, which becomes a stony track to road (Victoria Esplanade)
- Cross road and green opposite, going towards refreshment hut on beach
- Turn left along beach
- Turn left at last beach hut and climb small concrete mound onto footpath
- Turn right and follow footpath parallel to beach into a copse and across green
- Bear slightly left and go through gap in hedge
- Bear right and go through gate
- Turn right along wide track back towards beach
- Turn left along coastal footpath and down steps to small car park

Section 8: 2.5ml (4km)
- Straight ahead along path at edge of field, keeping close to mound on right
- Turn left at corner by steps down to beach
- Continue straight ahead towards hedge and beside fence on right
- Follow fence round to right and then left
- Bear right down green towards track and gates

- Turn right onto stony track, then onto road through two sets of gates
- Follow road past Mersea Vineyard to large barn
- Turn right along road and continue straight ahead at bend onto footpath (signposted)
- Follow path across three fields towards church
- Turn right into caravan park and follow route to play area
- Turn left, then right just past buildings on right
- Turn left along concrete walkway through caravan park
- Continue along beach to campsite footpath on left

IN THE LOCALITY
BIRDWATCHING
There's an incredible variety of birds because Mersea is an island. The tidal range of the North Sea is enormous: at low tide the extensive mud flats are home to all kinds of wading birds, and the area is also a pit stop for migratory birds.

MERSEA ISLAND.
Situated on the periphery of the North Sea in the estuary of the rivers Blackwater and Colne, Mersea Island is the most easterly inhabited island of the UK, yet is freely and easily accessible. The B1025 connects the island to the mainland, and the stretch of road that actually crosses the estuary is known as 'The Strood,' that, because of the vast tidal range, floods twice every day at high tide. In order not to become stranded, journeys to and from the island are carefully scheduled, which is a hot topic of conversation for both locals and visitors.

This small island covers only 7sq ml (18sq km). East Mersea, where the campsite is, is mostly farmland, so is much quieter apart for all the visitors to Cudmore Country Park.

On the other end of the island is the bustling village of West Mersea. Beside the charming village centre with its shops and cafés, there is also the old town with its many boats and associated industries, especially oyster harvesting. Then, on the south side of the village, is the beach with its array of brightly-coloured huts.

Just as in Roman times tourism is important. There are a number of large, static caravan parks ... perhaps a few too many. Nevertheless, there is plenty to see and do: the dramatic sea scenery; the West Mersea Island Museum; a vineyard; some interesting buildings, including churches; the remains of WWII defences; possible smuggler hideouts, and, of course, the boats. There's even a cookery school. Mersea Week is held every summer, usually in August: a boat festival involving many activities.

CUDMORE GROVE COUNTRY PARK
The Park is situated right on the eastern tip of Mersea Island, and is a refuge for wildlife. Unusual shells and fossils can be unearthed along the beach at the foot of the cliffs, and grassland meadows surround the remains of WWII gun emplacements and pillboxes, as well as what's left of a 16th century fort. The café not only provides refreshments but also information about the area.

Wonderful walks from dog-friendly campsites

SAILING

From April to October a ferry service for foot passengers only operates across the creek between East Mersea and Brightlingsea, providing quick and easy access for both locals and visitors, the trip taking just nine minutes. Dogs are welcome onboard for a small charge.

LADY GRACE BOAT TRIPS

The Lady Grace offers 20-minute trips around Packing Shed Island, in the mouth of the River Blackwater on the western side of the island. This island was where, in the 1850s, oysters were packed. The boat trip provides an ideal way to see the island and various sailing craft, and also learn about the oyster business. Trip times vary due to the enormous tidal range. There are no specific conditions: simply turn up at the jetty. There is a flat charge for each passenger, and dogs are welcome onboard.

COLCHESTER

Boasting the longest recorded history in Britain, Colchester was originally known as Camulodunum, and was such a significant city that it even had a mint. The city maintained its importance with arrival of the Romans until it was destroyed by Boudicca, when London became the capital of the new Roman province, Britannia. In modern times, oysters, cloth weaving, and flower growing were the mainstay industries, but, nowadays, it is a modern metropolis complete with museums, galleries, a range of shops, cafés and restaurants, and plenty to see and explore. There is a bus service from Mersea Island to Colchester.

West Sussex — trees, hills, and horses
OS MAPS EXPLORER GRAFFHAM CAMPSITE SOUTH DOWNS

(I could not find a ready-made Explorer Map of this area so I ordered a custom-made one, with Graffham Campsite in the middle, for the price of two pre-published maps.)
West Sussex's claim to fame, according to the Met Office, is that it has, on average, 1902 hours of sunlight each year, making it the sunniest county in the UK. This seems feasible, considering it's located in central southern England on the coast of the English Channel, roughly midway between the Atlantic Ocean in the west and the North Sea in the east. The counties surrounding it are Hampshire, Surrey and East Sussex.

Throughout history, many significant events and happenings have occurred in West Sussex, due to its location on this stretch of the English Channel looking towards mainland Europe. In addition to evidence of Stone Age habitation, Roman presence was widespread: not only were there several Roman towns, some palaces and villas, but also a network of Roman roads, as well as thriving commerce and industry. Later, the Anglo-Saxon Chronicles emphasized the importance of the area, referring to Sussex, which means 'South Saxon' in old English, as a 'Kingdom.' As a consequence, there are many fascinating places and several notable historical buildings.

Most of the county is rural, and much of this is protected. Over half of it is designated an Area of Outstanding Natural Beauty (AONB), despite the fact that the huge international Gatwick airport is located in the far north-east corner. The majority of towns and cities and major roads are to be found along the coast or eastern edge of the county, with motorways close to the airport, whilst dotted about the county are quaint and charming villages.

In addition to the usual farming activities, there are stud farms, with many fields occupied by horses rather than cows or sheep. No doubt the close proximity of Goodwood racecourse has influence here, and it wasn't surprising to come across a polo field during one of our walks.

The most significant feature in West Sussex is the long chalk escarpment known as the South Downs, that stretches for over 70 miles (112km) east to west across three counties, though over half of it is in West Sussex. Back in the 1920s when the idea of National Parks was first proposed, West Sussex was considered as important as the other 11 distinctive areas of the UK, and again in 1949 when the National Parks and Access to the Countryside Act was passed. Unfortunately, it was 60 years before the South Downs National Park was established in 2011.

Besides the chalk escarpment, about a quarter of the other noted geographical characteristics, such as the woods and vales of the Weald, are contained within the new National Park. Though it is quite a climb to the top of the Downs, the highest point of the Park is only 919ft (280m).

As with other National Parks there are several long-distance trails, but the South Downs Way is the only one that is wholly within a National Park. A staggering 1500 mile (2500km) web of footpaths and tracks meander across the county, making it possible to explore out-of-the-way places, enjoying the splendour of the countryside and variety of landscape.

CAMPSITE – GRAFFHAM CAMPING AND CARAVANNING CLUB
This is an unusual campsite, situated deep in the woods in the heart of the South Downs National Park. Pitches are dotted about amongst the trees and rhododendron bushes in delightfully secluded glades, which the many footpaths and tracks that snake around

Path along part of South Downs Way in the Chiltern Hills.

the site offer intriguing glimpses of. There is no uniformity of size or arrangement, and, despite being quite a large site with 90 pitches, there is a feeling of privacy and tranquillity. Bluebells in the spring and rhododendrons in early summer ensure a profusion of colour throughout the site, and the amenities block is of the usual high standard routinely expected of club sites.

This is wild camping with mod cons, thanks to Mr Herbert Visick, who bought the land to enjoy the solitude, peace and relaxation of nature. He allowed some of his friends to also use the site, and, because they belonged to the Camping Club (the fledging Camping and Caravanning Club), he bequeathed the land to the club in 1947. In the intervening years the club has gradually developed the site, endeavouring to maintain it as he would have liked.

PEARLS OF WISDOM 🐾

This is a really exciting place because of the intricate network of paths that go this way and that through the trees and bushes, though it was a bit difficult for me to know the difference

between communal paths and pitches. However, if I wagged my tail frantically and allowed people to make a fuss of me, accidental intrusions were forgiven.

With so many paths leading off into the surrounding woods and countryside, I didn't need a dog exercise area, although I did miss playing with my frisbee. Also, my owner was unsure when to allow me to explore off-lead. Most of the walks were along wide tracks – even those between fields – but I had to be careful as some of the fences were electrified. Surprisingly,

Pitches are haphazardly dotted about among the trees and bushes.

some of the sheep were actually curious about what I was doing, although the horses were totally indifferent – what a lot of them there were!

I really enjoyed myself as there were so very many places to explore.

SHORT WALK – TREES, TREES, AND YET MORE TREES!
(I could not find an Explorer Map of this area so I ordered a custom-made one with

Graffham Campsite in the middle, for the price of two pre-published maps)
Distance: 6ml (9.6km)
Duration: 3.5hr
Terrain: Tracks, fields, footpaths, roads, stiles and gates ... muddy in places. This is rather long for a 'short' walk, but there are several easy stretches – and a delightful pub to stop at for refreshments)

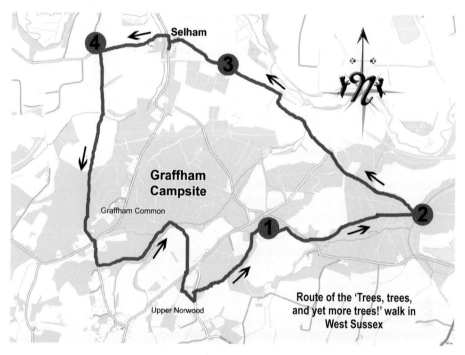

Route of the 'Trees, trees, and yet more trees!' walk in West Sussex

Section 1: 1.5ml (2.4km)

- Exit campsite from toilet block
- Descend wooden steps with toilet block behind signposted 'Wright Way'
- Bear right across pitch to narrow path in undergrowth and continue along path to T junction
- Turn left and follow path to signpost (campsite visible through trees on left), and through gate on right
- Continue straight ahead, crossing wooden planks
- Turn left at first junction (signposted); follow this straight path to fence by road
- Turn right and follow path beside fence, and through gate on right out to road
- Cross road into car park
- Bear right across car park onto path with notice 'Circular Woodland Walk: 20 minutes'
- Turn left at junction
- Continue on path between trees and through zig-zag wooden fence

- Straight on (signposted) and follow path through woods, ignoring all routes off until path emerges onto a wide track with fields just beyond trees

Section 2: 1.5ml (2.4km)
- Turn sharp left then take right fork signposted 'Public Bridleway'
- Follow path as it narrows until emerging at large footpath crossroads
- Continue straight ahead along a wide track opposite
- Follow this track, going straight on at first footpath crossroads.
- At 2nd junction bear slightly right across footpaths towards signpost, passing under tree arch
- Turn immediately right along narrow path between bushes BEFORE signpost
- Continue along path and cross very muddy 'road' to footpath opposite
- Follow narrow footpath between trees with fields just beyond; over stile, then a very muddy patch
- Turn left and cross footbridge
- Turn right and over stile (signposted)
- Follow narrow footpath round to right and over stile into field
- Continue along edge of field straight ahead towards building, and climb gate onto track (your dog can go underneath)
- Turn right and go through two gates
- Follow wide track round right-hand bend; through gate and onto disused rail line

Section 3: 1.5ml (2.4km)
- Turn left and continue along rail line, ignoring temporary barrier for cows; past farm on left and down slope through gate onto wide track
- Turn right and continue along very wide track between fields
- Go through farmyard to road
- Turn left to pub 'Three Moles' (refreshments areaavailable)
- Exit pub and turn right back past Hurlands Farm
- Turn left along road signposted 'To Selham Church'
- Continue on past church and priory on left
- Turn left down tarmac driveway (signposted), past house and over bridge

Section 4: 1.5ml (2.4km)
- Continue along tarmac onto stony track
- Bear left at right-hand bend onto track between fields
- Continue straight across footpath junction and follow path through gate into woods
- Go along path between fences to T-junction
- Turn left and follow path round right-hand bend going down to road
- Turn left then immediately right along road signposted 'Graffham'
- Turn left at brow of hill through gate of first building

- Keeping building on left, continue straight ahead onto footpath
- Take right fork, then turn left at T-junction
- Continue straight ahead through strangely-shaped trees, and follow path to stream
- Turn left (signposted), along bank, and cross footbridge on right
- Follow path uphill (steep but with rails to help), through trees and through gate
- Continue along path to road between hedge on left and fence on right
- Cross road, bearing slightly right, to footpath opposite
- Pass gate on right and go through kissing gate into woods
- Follow path and over stile
- Turn left onto narrow footpath at end of wooden fencing
- Continue to road along path between fencing
- Turn left, then right along 2nd footpath (signposted) opposite large iron gates
- Continue along path and turn left at footpath with large moss-covered stone in ditch
- Follow path up to campsite toilet block

LONG WALK – UP AND UP; DOWN AND DOWN
(I could not find an Explorer Map of this area so I ordered a custom-made one with Graffham Campsite in the middle, for the price of two pre-published maps)
Distance: 7.5ml (12km)
Duration: 5hr
Terrain: Tracks, fields, footpaths, roads, stiles and gates. Very steep climb onto South Down Way, and long, steep descent. Diversion to see Graffham village extends the walk

Some of the many trees, bushes, and ferns.

Wonderful walks from dog-friendly campsites

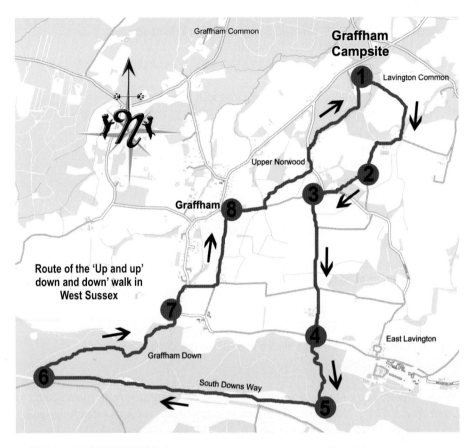

Section 1: 1ml (1.6km)
- Exit campsite from toilet block
- Descend wooden steps with toilet block behind signposted 'Wright Way'
- Bear right across pitch to narrow path in undergrowth
- Turn left and follow path to signpost (campsite visible through trees on left), and through gate on right
- Continue ahead, crossing wooden planks, and past track off to left and on through kissing gate
- Turn right, go through gate, and continue straight ahead along wide, stony track between fields
- Turn right onto narrow footpath immediately after passing hedge and BEFORE house on right (signposted)

Section 2: 0.5ml (0.8km)
- Continue along footpath past wooden fence into wood, and over stile onto road (can be muddy)
- Turn right and continue along road for 50yd (45m) to sharp right-hand bend

- Turn left off road and continue straight ahead onto wide, stony track
- Turn left immediately past two houses, and over stile onto narrow, grassy path

Section 3: 0.75ml (1.2km)
- Follow path left and right, and over two footbridges and a stile
- Bear right onto a stony track
- Continue straight ahead along track past large footpath junction onto a tarmac driveway
- Follow driveway past buildings on right to minor road

Section 4: 0.75ml (1.2km)
- Cross road to footpath opposite, into woods
- Continue along path as it first climbs then levels off to signposted footpath crossroads (very, very steep)
- Turn right, going uphill for 200yd (180m)
- Turn left at T-junction onto wide track, climbing steeply
- Turn right at next crossroads, still climbing out of woods
- Continue straight ahead across field to South Downs Way

View from South Downs Way between the many trees and hedges.

Section 5: 1.5ml (2.4km)
- Turn right along wide, stony track
- Follow the track signposted 'Cocking' past Graffham Down Wildlife Reserve (interesting information boards along this part of route)

Section 6: 1ml (1.6km)
- Turn right down wide track at 2nd information board (path has a road sign prohibiting cars)

- Follow track as it winds downhill, ignoring all paths and tracks leading off, and go through kissing gate onto road (difficult because of the ruts and stones)

Section 7: 1ml (1.6km)
- Turn left and continue along road to village
- Turn right onto tarmac driveway by green, and sign 'Lavington Stud,' and through automatic gate
- Turn left onto grass just before buildings, keeping close to fence on left, and over stile
- Continue straight ahead, keeping close to another fence on left
- Bear right towards hedge, and through gap into playing area
- Turn left towards pavilion
- Follow path beside hedge on left behind pavilion, and out onto driveway and entrance to playing fields

Section 8: 1ml (1.6km)
- Turn left along wide, stony track, past playing fields and small car park into trees. Graffham village can be reached by turning right along stony track. Then retrace steps to playing fields and small car park
- Turn left and over stile beside gate into field
- Bear slightly right across field to stile opposite
- Turn right BEFORE stile, and go along edge of field for 50yd (45m) to another stile on left
- Over stile and follow path round to right, over another stile onto a narrow footpath between hedge and fence
- Follow path and over stile (sheep-proof) onto tarmac driveway
- Continue along driveway and turn left at road
- Turn right along 2nd footpath (signposted)
- Follow footpath to narrow path on right with large moss-covered stone in ditch that leads to wooden steps of campsite

IN THE LOCALITY

SELHAM

This quiet village is remarkable for its pub, 'The Three Moles,' which is probably the smallest pub in England, let alone Sussex. Not to be eclipsed, the village church of St James has remained largely unaltered since it was built in the 11th century.

PETWORTH HOUSE AND GARDENS

Situated on the north west edge of Petworth town is the magnificent Petworth House and Gardens, now managed by the National Trust, though the family does live in the west wing. Both town and house have a long and interesting history, so there is plenty to see. Petworth town actually has an entry in the Domesday Book of 1086, but nowadays is notable for arts and crafts, and its several antique shops.

The house and gardens first gained prominence during the reign of Henry I (1100 -1135), when they were given as a gift, and then, via marriage, passed into the possession of the Percy family – an important, powerful, northern family whose main residence from 1309 was Alnwick Castle in Northumberland (the estate was, in fact, the family's summer residence). Over the centuries, Petworth House was decorated, updated, and refurbished by various distant descendents of the Percy family upon inheritance. Consequently, the house is full of architectural gems and other treasures, including landscape paintings by Turner.

The magnificent gardens were first landscaped by Capability Brown, which took several years. Dogs are not allowed in the house but are welcome to have fun and investigate the 700 acres of parkland. Owners need to be aware of the large deer herd that roams the grounds.

GRAFFHAM

A typical West Sussex village situated on the northern slope of the South Downs, Graffham is just a short walk across the fields from the campsite, and has two very historical pubs: 'The Forester's Arms' and 'The White Horse.' Unfortunately, as is often the case with many pubs, when I visited they were both closed, although The White Horse was due to re-open shortly. However, the village does have an infant school, and large recreation area, as well as a busy shop-cum-café that is extremely useful and whose staff are very friendly and obliging. Though there is no Post Office, a mobile service now operates twice a week from the village hall. Graffham is a delightful place to spend some time.

GOODWOOD

On the southern slopes of the South Downs is the large Goodwood Estate, where the infamous 'Glorious Goodwood' racing is held every year, which may explain the many horses in the fields around Graffham. On the other side of the estate is the Goodwood motor racing track that holds various events throughout the year, such as Speed Week and the Goodwood Revival.

BIGNOR ROMAN VILLA

It was in 1811 that farmer George Tupper's plough struck a stone that led to the discovery of the remains of a large Roman settlement, including some incredible mosaic floors. The site first opened to visitors in 1814, with thatched huts erected to protect the artefacts. Despite the many visitors to Bignor since the discovery, the farm is still owned by the Tupper family.

SINGLETON MUSEUM

This is a most unusual museum. Scattered over the 40-acre site are some 50 buildings, most built from bricks gathered from various locations, charting 950 years of history. The many volunteers in period costume who people the museum bring it to life. With a variety of events also on offer, it is a unique experience.

The walks:
South West England
(Cornwall, Somerset and Wiltshire)

Cornwall — Kilkhampton on 'Atlantic Highway'

OS MAP EXPLORER 126 CLOVELLY & HARTLAND

Cornwall is renowned for its long coastline and wonderful beaches. Though the sea is always nearby, there are many charming places to explore inland, and one such is near the Devon border around the village of Kilkhampton, a few miles north west of Bude seaside resort. Few visitors stop to enjoy this lovely village, as the owner of Annie's Coffee Shop in Kilkhampton remarked, which is a shame, as this is a delightful area with several walks over rolling hills, along valleys, and around lakes.

The route to the centre of 'Kilk' as it is referred to by the locals, is a pleasant experience, being just an access route for local residents, and to the leisure centre. However, the A39, or 'Atlantic Highway' through the village, is, on the contrary, very busy, especially during the holiday season. Nevertheless 'Kilk' has a strong community spirit, with many local activities and a surprising range of businesses, including a framing shop and toy shop. Refreshments are available from the two pubs, as well as a café that welcomes dogs.

Kilkhampton has a long history, and is even mentioned in the Domesday Book. It must have been important to the invading Normans, because sometime during the 11th and 12th centuries they built a 'Motte and Bailey' castle (a fortification with a wooden or stone keep situated on a raised earthwork called a motte, accompanied by an enclosed courtyard, or bailey, surrounded by a protective ditch and palisade) sometimes known as Penstowe Castle. This is to the west of present-day Kilkhampton on an elongated knoll of land with steep-sided valleys falling away, affording extensive views over surrounding countryside. Today, all that remains of the castle, which is owned by the National Trust, are earthworks. These can be explored as the site is criss-crossed with many tracks winding through the trees, easily accessed from the campsite via the footpath.

Also on the outskirts of the village is Kilkhampton Common, which has very recently undergone significant upgrading to improve several diverse habitats with the aim of increasing wildlife. The number of routes across the common has been increased, and from some the views of the Cornish countryside are stunning. Information boards have also been erected. This is a delightful place to spend some time, whether walking your dog, birdwatching, or just enjoying the outdoors.

A visit to the village would not be complete without at least a walk through the grounds of the Parish Church of St James the Great, which, like many village churches, is very imposing. It is at least 450 years old, with a magnificent south door and lynch gate. Inside the church is an imposing monument to Sir Bevil Grenville – MP for Cornwall – who, at the outbreak of the Civil War, joined the Royalists, and, supported by local Cornishmen, won many skirmishes. Unfortunately, Grenvillle was mortally wounded at the Battle of Lansdown in Somerset. His body was carried home by his Cornish soldiers, who refused to fight under any other leader.

Cornwall has a long coastline with many wonderful sea views.

Inside the church is a fine series of wonderfully-carved bench ends depicting a variety of scenes, including fanciful arabesque ornamental fringes, heraldic shields, Biblical symbols, and heads of various sorts.

Just three miles to the East of Kilkhampton on the Devon/Cornwall border lie the Tamar Lakes, and around the shores of both are many footpaths. The larger Upper Tamar Lake was opened in 1977 to supply water to surrounding towns and villages, which is a busy place in summer with a Watersports and Activity Centre and café. The smaller Lower Tamar Lake was built much earlier when the Bude Canal was an important route. Now managed as a nature reserve, it is a quieter, more serene place with several bird hides around the lake, from which it is possible to see a variety of common British birds – up-close and personal, too, when the feeders are filled. A pleasant place to spend some time.

CAMPSITE – PENTIRE HAVEN HOLIDAY PARK
Situated on the outskirts of Kilkhamton, Pentire Haven Holiday Park is an ideal base from which to explore, as a footpath passes right through the campsite. It is a large site, over 200 level pitches, with a wide range of facilities: shop; adventure park; heated pool in

summer; free Wifi; three heated modern facilities blocks which are especially welcome in winter; a variety of pitches and a rally field. There is also the option to use the adjacent Penstowe Leisure Park, where you will find a choice of bars, restaurants, entertainment, and various sporting activities, including an indoor pool.

The campsite is set in 25 acres of carefully-tended parkland with banks and hedgerows, so feels very spacious. It has far-reaching views over both countryside and sea. Only a few minutes walk away is Kilkhampton Village.

PEARLS OF WISDOM 🐾
There's a lovely designated exercise area here where I can be free to search out interesting smells, and chase a ball or my frisbee. It's not very big but big enough for me to stretch my legs in preparation for longer excursions, or before I settle down for the night.

Far reaching views from Pentire Haven campsite.

It is a very large campsite, and there seem to be special paths that lead to some fields. From here it is not very far to a most exciting place where I can investigate amongst lots of bushes and trees, and even have a dip in a stream! It is just a wonderful place! There are some roads, which are boring, especially the busy ones, but not many.

SHORT WALK – EXPLORING THE COMMON
Distance: 4ml (6.4km)
Duration: 2hr
Terrain: Fields, footpaths, tracks and roads, with many gates and some stiles. Easy walking but hilly and, in places, very wet

Section 1: 0.75ml (1.2km)
- Take grass footpath that passes through the campsite, going away from reception and road
- Follow as it turns left ,and continue to stile in corner of campsite field
- Over stile into field; turn right to cross field
- Bear left down slope to gate and stile
- Over stile and continue straight ahead up a slope across field
- Through gate and straight on, as yellow arrow indicates
- Over stile and bear left down very steep slope to gate in bottom left corner of field (another rather muddy path)
- Over stile into marshy field (coarse grass ideal for cleaning boots!)

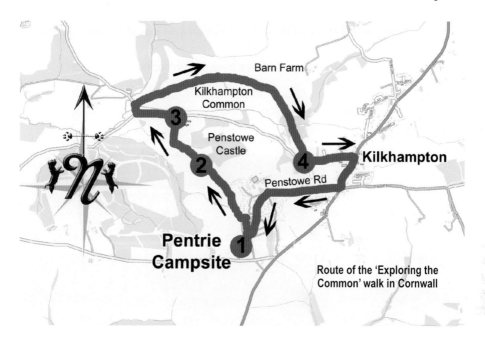

Route of the 'Exploring the Common' walk in Cornwall

Section 2: 0.75ml (1.2km)
- Straight ahead to gate opposite
- Go through gate (this is very difficult as it is usually extremely wet)
- Continue straight across the field to two gates opposite (to your left the 'Motte and Bailey' earthworks stretch up to the sky. A post indicating a footpath around the earthworks is visible halfway up the slope. Now is a good opportunity to detour and explore this ancient remain). Retrace steps to gates

Section 3: 1.5ml (2.4km)
- Through two gates onto road
- Turn left and continue along this quiet road, past white-painted house to T-junction
- Take road to right
- Immediately after crossing stone bridge, take driveway on right (signposted)
- Continue along driveway past Cross Cottage and through gate onto stony track
- Continue on track, going uphill
- When wide track turns left into a field, bear right onto single stony track
- Continue uphill to junction of footpaths by a gate (now on Kilkhampton Common. All of the routes lead across the Common, and eventually to the village. There are several information boards to help you decide which route to follow)
- Path on the right goes down into the valley and follows the stream across the Common. Path on extreme left skirts the Common and connects with other footpaths. The middle path goes across top of Kilkhampton Common, with some amazing views

Wonderful walks from dog-friendly campsites

- To leave Kilkhampton Common head for car park on west side of Common, as shown on information boards
- Cross stream via wooden bridge, and take track on right, going uphill to gate

Path across Kilkhampton Common towards the village.

Section 4: 1ml (1.6km)
- Go through gate onto road
- Turn left and follow road past church and houses to T-junction with A39 at village centre
- Turn right and along A39 to Annie's Café on left (this is a lovely café that welcomes dogs, offering a range of homemade food)
- Exit Annie's Café and turn left
- Continue along A39 past church, car park and public toilets to crossroads (take care on this busy road)
- Turn right down Penstowe Road
- Continue along road through two stone pillars
- Keep to path with swimming pool on right and the 'Stables Inn' pub on left
- Continue through car park to a large wooden gate
- Through gate into campsite

Long walk – Lakes and canals

Distance: 8.5ml (13.6km)
Duration: 5hr
Terrain: Fields, footpaths, footbridges, tracks and roads, with many gates and stiles. Easy walking but some hills, and very wet in places. Some footpaths are difficult due to fencing

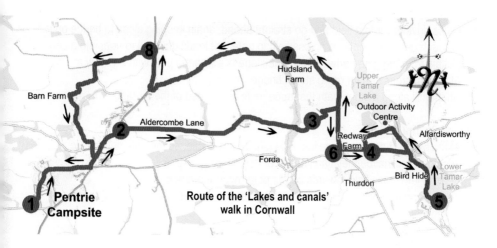

Route of the 'Lakes and canals' walk in Cornwall

Section 1: 1.25ml (2km)
- Leave campsite near swimming pool
- Cross gravel car park and continue up drive to Leisure Centre entrance on Penstowe Road
- Along Penstowe Road to crossroads on main A39
- Turn left along A39 towards church
- Continue on through the village to Aldercombe Lane (first road on right and signposted as a footpath)
- Turn right into Aldercombe Lane and continue on past houses and businesses (road gradually becomes stony track, then grassy one, and is extremely muddy in places)

Section 2: 1ml (1.6km)
- Stay on track and, at stile, cross onto grass footpath
- Over another stile, then through gate into field
- Continue straight ahead across field, bearing slightly right towards large clump of prickly bushes
- Follow path through bushes and down to stream
- Over wooden bridge and stile to emerge onto road
- Turn left and follow road through Aldercombe and Barton farmyard
- At cowshed take path to the left around back
- Just past cowshed bear right to gate on left that leads to a track
- Continue along track to kissing-type gate
- Through gate into field and straight ahead, keeping close to hedge on left (there was a fence across this field so you might have to scramble under it. Take care because it may be electrified)
- Through gate in left corner of field and continue straight ahead, again keeping close to hedge on left
- Path crosses a tarmac driveway, which has a stile on both sides

Wonderful walks from dog-friendly campsites

- Cross driveway into a field and go straight ahead, again keeping close to hedge on left
- Through gate and continue across field to gate that leads downhill to right into a copse (visible from the gate partway down the slope is a wooden post with a yellow arrow)
- At bottom cross stream using stone 'bridge'
- Up the hill along a stony path that appears to be the bed of the stream

Section 3: 1ml (1.6km)
- At top bear left and over stile into field (sheep-proof stile, so the only option is to lift dogs over, or maybe they can jump over this very large stile)
- Bearing left, cross field towards corner of farmyard entrance
- Keep farmyard entrance and hedge on left; continue straight ahead along tarmac driveway
- At T-junction turn left
- At next T-junction turn right
- Right again at next T-junction
- Continue along road to Redway Farm
- Turn left onto track immediately after farm
- Through two gates onto grassy track, and follow to solid kissing gate on right just past barn

Section 4: 0.75ml (1.2km)
- Through kissing gate into field
- Through middle of field, heading towards opposite side where wooden step gate makes it possible to go over wall into next field
- Bear right to the gate in the corner of field and road
- Turn right and cross access road to signposted footpath on opposite side
- Through kissing gate onto footpath that runs along edge of lake to bird hide on left (if the feeders have just been filled there will be plenty of birds to see. They are obviously used to the building, and frequently come very close. You can also continue on along the path to the southern tip of Lower Tamar Lake and car park and toilets, cross the weir, and walk for a short while beside Bude Canal)

Section 5: 1ml (1.6km)
- Retrace steps to footpath beside lake and kissing gate that leads onto access road
- Cross access road and take road opposite to

Bird hide on the shores of lower Tamar Lake.

Tamar Lake Water Sports Centre, car park and café (another good place to stop for refreshments and enjoy the surroundings)
- Behind the café is a field, and a gate close to the building gives access to it
- Through gate and continue straight ahead, keeping close to buildings on right
- In right-hand corner is a stile: go over this and turn immediately left to cross bridge
- Walk across field, bearing left to gate in top left corner
- Turn left and go through gate
- Walk towards stone barn ahead and skirt round it
- On reaching track turn sharp right and continue, with barn now on right
- Continue along track through two gates to road

Section 6: 1ml (1.6km)
- Turn right and follow road over cattle grid to Hudsland Farm
- Pass house on right and farm entrance on left
- Through gate at next track on left
- Follow track to sharp right-hand bend
- Straight ahead over stile onto grass footpath
- Follow footpath down slope to wooden bridge over a stream on left. (It is very wet here, being the bed of the stream. I left the designated footpath and found a drier route to the wooden bridge)

Section 7: 1.25ml (2km)
- Cross bridge and continue along path; over another stile
- Bear right uphill towards wind turbine, and over stile into field
- Continue straight across field to a combination of three stiles
- Bearing slightly right, cross field to gate in middle of hedge opposite
- Through gate; straight on to another gate
- Through this gate and along edge of field, keeping hedge on left
- Over stile and continue, following hedge
- Over stile onto main A39
- Cross road and turn right (a busy road but there is a wide tarmac and grass verge. It is easier walking here than on some minor roads)
- At brow of hill opposite turning on right for Bradworthy, turn left and through gate onto track

Section 8: 1.25ml (2km)
- Continue along track. Pass turning to Heatham on right
- At next junction turn left to Herdacott Farm
- Turn immediate right along road labelled Barn Farm
- Follow road until it ends at gate into field
- Into field and bear left to stile
- Over stile onto footpath with steps going down into valley
- Use wooden planks to cross stream

- Over stile and bear right
- At access road bear left and take path around gasworks
- Cross wooden bridge and over stile; then up the hill
- Follow designated footpath around paddock on right
- Over step stile and turn left along lane
- Follow lane as it turns right onto West Street, Kilkhampton
- Cross West Street and continue straight ahead to footpath through churchyard
- At main A39, continue on away from village to crossroads
- Turn right along Penstowe Road, back to campsite

IN THE LOCALITY
BIRDWATCHING
Though there aren't any hides on Kilkhampton Common, there are many seats which are useful for birdwatching. Lower Tamar Lake is the ideal birdwatching venue, with an ever-changing variety of migrants visiting throughout the year, as well as an interesting range of resident birds. During the winter, the lake is an excellent place to spot wildfowl, and is one of the best water bodies in Devon for Goosander, with more than 40 present in some winters. A bird hide is situated on the west bank, in front of which a wetland area has recently been created with an expanse of mud and scrapes. A feeding station providing nuts, seeds and fat has been established near the hide, and regularly attracts Willow Tits, as well as a wide range of other birds.

FISHING
Lower Tamar Lake is more popular with local anglers because it is in beautiful surroundings, and is much quieter. However, it is possible to fish in both lakes. Coarse anglers will enjoy the Upper Tamar, and day permits are available from the fishing kiosk on-site.

WATERSPORTS
The Outdoor + Activity Centre at Upper Tamar offers sailing, windsurfing and kayaking for individuals, families, and groups. Visitors can benefit from tuition from qualified instructors, hire equipment, or launch their own craft. The Centre is open seasonally, April to September, as is the recently-renovated café, which serves a large selection of food.

BUDE CANAL AND AQUEDUCT
This runs south from Lower Tamar Lake for approximately 5 miles (8km) to Burmsdon. A unique canal, it's well worth extending the walk from Tamar Lakes to see it, if time permits.

DUCKPOOL
A wild and romantic cove with a small, west-facing beach. The wooded Coombe Valley (a very pleasant place to walk) meets the sea. The spectacular peak of Steeple Point Cliff, over 330ft (100m) high, dominates the beach, which is beautiful, though not suitable for swimming, as currents are extremely dangerous, and lifeguard cover is not provided.

RONALD DUNCAN HUT

Seven miles (11.2km) north of Kilkhampton beside the South West Coastal Path in Welcombe, the hut is often unlocked, and visitors are encouraged to go inside and learn about Ronald Duncan's life and literary works. Duncan is probably best known for his poem *The Horse* (https://thereadphonebox.wordpress.com/2014/11/26/the-horse-poem-by-ronald-duncan/). The Ronald Duncan Literary Foundation, a charitable trust, encourages creative excellence, particularly the writing and performing of poetry.

BUDE

This popular seaside resort is just 6 miles (9.6km) south west of Kilkhampton.

Somerset — unassuming Exmoor

OS MAPS EXPLORER OL9 EXMOOR

The county of Somerset is probably most associated with the famous Glastonbury Festival held at Worthy Farm, Pilton, just outside the village of Glastonbury, although is, of course, just one of the many different facets of this diverse county. The allure of the festival and distinctive mystery of Glastonbury with its tower on top of the tor dominating the landscape is but one aspect, and there are many other significant landmarks, some quite well-known, but each with very different distinct characteristics. This is, indeed, a county of contrasts.

Besides the urban sprawl of towns such as Taunton and Bridgwater, Somerset is home to the amazing Mendip Hills, which has several impressive dry gorges, the largest being at Cheddar. Contrasting sharply with the gorges are the Somerset Levels, probably best-known due to extensive flooding that occurred there a few years ago.

Then there are the many beaches – some quite large and sandy – that can be found all along the 40-mile (64km) coast of the Bristol Channel from Weston-super-Mare to Porlock. Despite such variety, however, surrounding counties still appear to overshadow Somerset.

Two-thirds of the National Park that is Exmoor falls within the boundaries of Somerset, with only a third stretching into Devon. As a consequence, it is quite possible to camp in one county and walk in the other.

Many, many years ago, Exmoor was a Royal Forest and Hunting Ground, that, in 1954, was designated a National Park that now comprises 267 square miles (690sq km) of what is generally referred to as 'semi-natural' landscape, as it has been influenced by people for many hundreds of years.

The charm of Exmoor, like the county of Somerset, is its infinite variety. Besides cultivated farmland there are high, rolling moorlands of both heather and grass; ancient woodlands where a variety of native trees can still be found in the 'combes' (steep-sided valleys), and many rivers and streams, including the River Exe after which the moor is named. The 34-mile (55km) northern border is a rugged coastline with numerous sheer cliffs, and the A39 coastal road is equally as precipitous. Just past Minehead around Porlock, the road is unsuitable for caravans and many motorhomes. A few years ago, I unknowingly drove my motorhome along this section of the A39, somehow missing all the warning notices. It was a most terrifying experience, and, on many occasions, I wondered if I was going to actually reach the top of the hills. Several times I only just managed the twists and turns in first gear, inching slowly upward. Going down the hills the other side was no easier, as the road is so steep and tortuous I worried that my brakes might fail, and I would hurtle down uncontrollably. I have subsequently avoided this route ...

The coast of Exmoor is so dramatic, with towering cliffs, rocky headlands, waterfalls and ravines, that, in 1991, it was established as a Heritage Coast, and is popular with outdoor activity enthusiasts. The longest National Trail in England, at 630 miles (1014km), starts at Minehead and runs all along the Exmoor coast and on into Devon. Numerous sailing crafts make full use of the many bays and ports.

Exmoor is simply an amazing place: large in size, with panoramic views around every footpath corner, and a profusion of flora, fauna, and wildlife, some of which, like the Exmoor ponies, are unique to the area. Unlike most wildlife, however, the ponies are usually visible, and can often be seen grazing on the moor. Dotted across Exmoor are hamlets, towns, villages and resorts full of character and charm. With over 600 miles of footpaths and bridleways, the Exmoor National Park is an ideal place to explore, and those with a literary interest can visit parts of Exmoor mentioned in *Lorna Doone* by Richard Dodderidge Blackmore.

Wherever you wander, stay alert at all times. You may just catch sight of, and so be able to confirm the existence of, the 'Beast of Exmoor,' who, supposedly, roams the moor, and is popularly thought to be a big cat, such as a Puma.

Exmoor in Somerset.

CAMPSITE 1 – EXE VALLEY CARAVAN PARK

An ideal place from which to explore Exmoor, being situated in the valley of the River Exe, right on its banks and adjacent to the hamlet of Bridgetown, close to the attractive village of Winsford. Next to the campsite is the old Bridgetown Mill House, that dates back to the 17th century, and opposite is the Badger's Holt Inn, that dates back to the 18th century.

With many of the pitches located along the river or close to the mill, the gentle murmuring of water adds to the peace and tranquillity. The river very much dictates the rather unusual layout of the campsite, which is long and thin, with the facilities block at the entrance near the Mill House. As a result, it is a considerable distance from some of the pitches. The block is modern and well-equipped, and behind the reception and shop is an additional small toilet block. Unusually, not only is WiFi free, but long cables are provided to connect up to TV points.

This is a well-appointed, adult-only site in a delightful rural setting.

PEARLS OF WISDOM
What a wonderful campsite! Although the exercise area at the far end was not very big, it was sooo exciting, and I could roam about there, freely investigating all of the interesting smells amongst the trees, bushes, and shrubs; there was even enough room to chase a ball or my Frisbee!

In addition, I could take a paddle in the stream, although it wasn't quite deep

Exe Valley campsite beside the watermill.

enough for me to swim. It was fun, though, splashing about chasing my ball. The huge field on the opposite side of the river was just as amazing to explore, although I was disappointed not to be allowed to chase after all of the irritating pheasants strutting about there.

SHORT WALK – AN EXMOOR VILLAGE
Distance: 5ml (8km)
Duration: 2hr
Terrain: Quiet roads, fields, lanes, footpaths, gates and stiles. Some steep hills

Section 1: 1ml (1.6km)
- Exit campsite via reception
- Turn right at road and over humpback bridge
- Turn right again along footpath (signposted) immediately after bridge

Wonderful walks from dog-friendly campsites

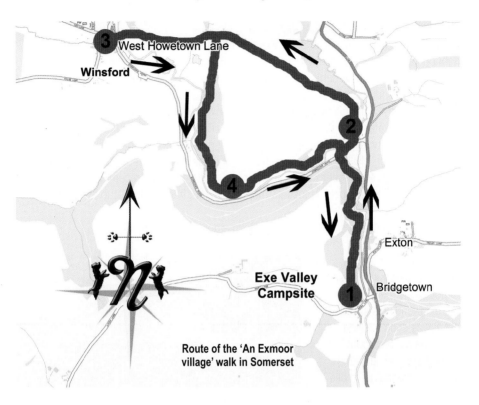

Route of the 'An Exmoor village' walk in Somerset

- Follow path across fields with river on right
- Bear left away from river towards gate with a stile and blue waymarker
- Over stile and continue through wooded area
- Through gate and follow path round to left and out onto road
- Turn right and along road for approximately 200yd (183m)
- Turn left, signposted 'West Howetown,' and along driveway, passing between buildings
- Continue straight ahead towards houses up driveway signposted 'Winsford'
- Continue straight ahead past houses; through gate by signpost onto grassy path

Section 2: 1.25ml (2km)

- Keep left of fence and over stile
- Continue up the hill (very steep) along edge of field beside fence
- Over stile and follow path
- Through a gate into copse

Centre of Winsford with the memorial close to the tearooms.

- Continue straight ahead along the ridge of hill, and into a field through gate on left
- Straight on along edge of field with fence on right
- Through another gate into next field
- Follow stony track along edge of field, and through another gate in right-hand corner, out onto a wide track
- Turn left and follow track (which soon becomes a road 'West Howetown Lane')
- Continue along road into Winsford, passing tennis courts and crossing a bridge
- Turn right at end of road to the centre of the village (where you are spoilt for choice for refreshments. By the ford is the 'Bridge House Tearooms,' whilst opposite along Halse Lane is the stunning-looking 'Royal Oak' pub)

Section 3: 1.25ml (2km)
- Retrace steps and cross bridge to road West Howetown Lane
- Continue along road (which becomes a track) to signpost at top
- Turn right (signposted 'Coppleham,') and through gate into field
- Straight ahead along edge of field with hedge on right
- Through gate in corner onto footpath
- Follow footpath into wooded area and through another gate.
- Continue along path, going downhill
- Take left fork
- Continue along path, through trees high above the river
- Turn right immediately after gate signposted 'bridleway'
- Continue along track and through gate into field.
- Bear right down to the river

Section 4: 1.5ml (2.4km)
- Cross field, keeping close to fence on left, and go through another gate.
- Follow path as it winds beside river, and through another gate into field
- Continue along path around field, keeping close to fence on left and with river on right
- Continue straight ahead and through gate
- Bear right up a slope to gate between gorse bushes
- Through gate onto footpath
- Continue straight ahead through another gate onto track
- Cross track and go through gate opposite, back onto footpath
- Continue straight on to signposted fork
- Take right fork and go through gate
- Continue straight ahead past stables on right
- Cross driveway and go through small gate opposite
- Follow path towards another stable block
- Turn right at the driveway
- Follow driveway out to the road
- Turn right and continue along road for 200yd (182m)
- Turn left along track, signposted 'Bridleway'

- Continue straight ahead, and follow path through trees beside river
- Through gate on left
- Turn right and out into the field
- Straight ahead across field, keeping near river on left, onto lane beside river with campsite on opposite bank
- At road turn left
- Cross bridge and turn left again into campsite

LONG WALK – ACROSS EXMOOR
Distance: 9ml (14.4km)
Duration: 5hr
Terrain: Mostly clearly defined wide tracks across moorland. Some quiet roads, fields, gates and stiles. A few short steep hills

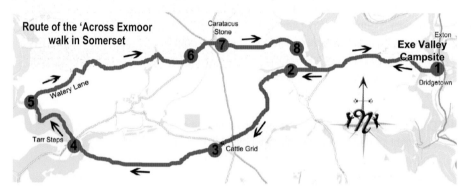

Section 1: 1.5ml (2.4km)
- Leave campsite via reception
- Cross humpback bridge and continue along road uphill (Weeks Lane)
- Turn right at the gate AFTER a signposted footpath to Edbrooke Hill Gate
- Walk along edge of field, keeping fence on the right (the slurry patch at the gate entrance requires careful negotiation)
- Continue across field, bearing right towards wooden gate and fence

Section 2: 1ml (1.6km)
- Turn left after gate along footpath signposted 'Tarr Steps Clapper Bridge' keeping close to fence now on left
- On left is a wooden gate: go through onto stony track
- Turn right and continue along track around a left-hand bend.
- Continue straight ahead onto grass footpath, still keeping close to hedge/wall on left
- A gap in the wall is boarded up by a wooden fence. Just a few yards further on is a wooden gate. Between these a footpath bears off to the right (the junction is not very obvious). In a short while the path becomes obvious
- Continue straight ahead towards the road (signposted)

The Bridge Tar steps across the river.

- Cross to road opposite, signposted 'Tarr Steps Clapper Bridge'
- Continue along road and cross cattle grid

Section 3: 1.5ml (2.4km)
- Continue straight ahead along track that bears left
- In a few yards take right fork and continue along path
- Through gate and follow path, bearing slightly left (take care as it is often muddy)
- Straight ahead, following path as it goes downhill to footpath X-junction
- Continue straight, still going downhill
- Follow track round to right and, at fence, through wooden gate
- Continue along stony track going downhill

Section 4: 1ml (1.6km)
- Turn right at T-junction by wooden gate heading towards car park
- Cross bridge on right (the Tarr Steps Clapper Bridge is on the left. Refreshments are available at the Tarr Farm Inn on the right. The views from the garden are delightful)
- With Tarr Steps bridge and River Barle on the left, continue straight ahead along riverside path
- Cross wooden bridge and go through gate
- Turn immediately right up a hill ('Watery Lane')

Section 5: 1.5ml (2.4km)
- Continue along stony path up the hill through two gates and into a farmyard

Wonderful walks from dog-friendly campsites

- Continue along track signposted 'Winsford Hill,' passing footpath on left to Tarr Steps
- Follow track around right-hand bend and left-hand bend (signposted 'Higher Knaplock')
- Take right fork and continue along driveway-cum-track
- Cross cattle grid after right-hand bend

Section 6: 0.5ml (0.8km)
- Continue along track to road
- Straight ahead along minor road to main road
- Straight across at crossroads
- Take footpath on right through bracken to Caratacus Stone where road bends left

Section 7: 1ml (1.6km)
- With Caratacus Stone behind, take wide footpath straight ahead
- Follow path as it bears round to the right, keeping close to hedge and fence on left
- Continue along path when it becomes a stony track, still keeping close to fence on left
- Turn left and through a gate
- Turn immediately right

Section 8: 1ml (1.6km)
- Through gate on right by a signpost
- Turn left and cross field, keeping near fence on left
- Pass two gates on left
- Continue straight ahead to gate that leads to road
- Turn left and follow road downhill to campsite

CAMPSITE 2 – BURROWHAYES FARM CARAVAN AND CAMPING SITE
This campsite is also situated beside a stream, though on this occasion the notable feature is the stone packhorse bridge over Horner Water at the campsite entrance. Footpaths run right past the rear of the campsite over Exmoor, as well as to the dramatic headlands and beaches. In addition, it is only a short walk to the delightful coastal village of Porlock. There is a large, sloping field for tents, that gives the impression of spaciousness. The touring pitches with electric hook-up, etc, are beside the stream and near the entrance where it is flatter. Also here are the facilities blocks and reception, which also houses a well-stocked shop selling a range of interesting goods, including maps of the area and local walks. Phone signal is patchy but the wifi, which is free, is good, though only near the reception block.

This is a delightful campsite with very good facilities, and so very many walking routes direct from the campsite. However, what sets it apart from other sites are the onsite riding stables that offer an opportunity of discovering Exmoor on horseback as well as on foot.

PEARLS OF WISDOM 🐎
Although it was quite a long walk through the campsite to the gate into the woods, once we

182

Burrowhayes campsite and the horses.

got to them there were so many tantalizing smells everywhere that I did not know where to start! It seemed every time we entered the woods we went a different way, and there was always something new to discover. Sometimes, we stayed for just a short time, but other times we seemed to go on and on. Just occasionally we went over the stone bridge to the other side of the stream. Though this was interesting it was just a short path, and didn't seem to lead anywhere.

My owner always gave me a vigorous going-over after every outing because I attracted so many ticks.

Pearl having fun on Exmoor.

Wonderful walks from dog-friendly campsites

Distance: 4ml (6.4km)
Duration: 2hr
Terrain: Mostly clearly defined wide tracks across moorland. A quiet road and some gates. Some long, steady climbs

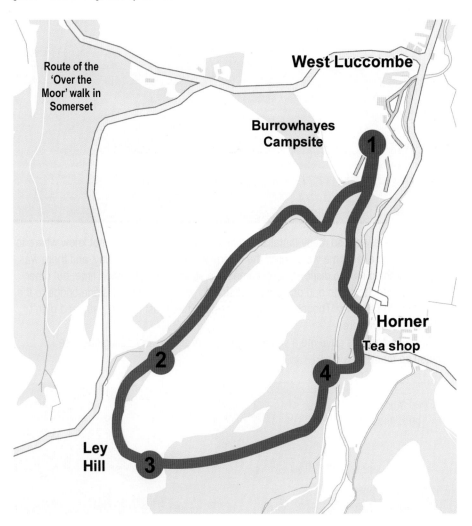

Route of the
'Over the
Moor' walk in
Somerset

West Luccombe

**Burrowhayes
Campsite**

1

Horner
Tea shop

2

4

**Ley
Hill**

3

Section 1: 1ml (1.6km)

- Exit at rear of campsite, up slope by the woods
- Through gate onto track in the woods
- Turn right (signposted 'Porlock')
- Take left fork along wide track

- Turn sharp left at junction with road, and continue along wide track signposted 'Granny's Ride'
- Follow track as it climbs through trees to open moor
- Straight ahead at footpath X-junction
- Continue along path as it narrows and descends to a stream
- Follow path across stream, round to left and back onto open moor
- Turn right at footpath X-junction signposted 'Ley Hill'

Section 2: 1ml (1.6km)
- Continue up hill along path
- Turn left along wide, grassy track at wide X-junction of footpaths. This is 'Flora's Ride'
- Follow path and, at next X-junction, turn left again
- Turn left at T-junction, and immediately after take right fork
- Follow the path along the hillside (magnificent views), and down into the woods
- Take 2nd path on left at a big junction
- Just ahead, take left fork signposted 'Horner Water'

Section 3: 1ml (1.6km)
- Follow single-track footpath through the woods going downhill joining 'Granny's Ride' (signposted) to a wide track (Lord Ebrington's Path)
- Turn left and follow path downhill to a riverside path
- Turn left along a wide path with river on right
- Continue along stony path passing a footbridge on right
- Turn left and take left fork, still on riverside path but with river now on left

Section 4: 1ml (1.6km)
- Follow path to road
- Turn left and follow road to 'Horner's Tea Gardens'
- Exit teashop and turn right; continue along road around a right-hand bend
- Turn left just past the green, and cross stone bridge onto footpath
- Follow path up a hill with river on right, and through a gate
- Continue straight ahead
- Turn right through gate into campsite

Long walk – Headland Lookout
Distance: 6.5ml (10.4km)
Duration: 3.5hr
Terrain: Fields, footpaths, headland, beach, gates. Many clearly-defined paths, and some long, steady climbs

Section 1: 1ml (1.6km)
- Exit campsite via reception
- Follow the road to a left-hand bend

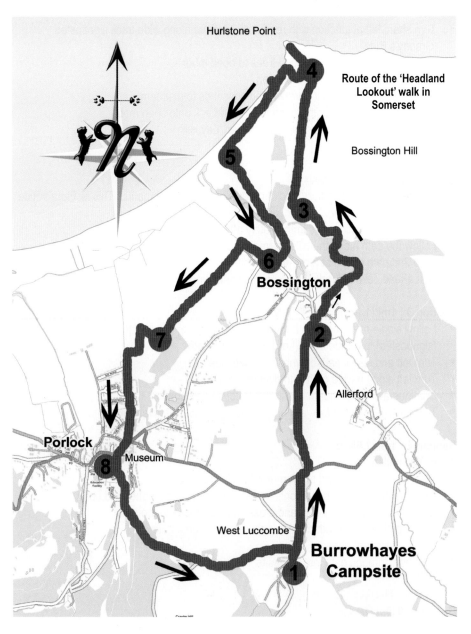

Hurlstone Point

Route of the 'Headland Lookout' walk in Somerset

Bossington Hill

Bossington

Allerford

Porlock

Museum

West Luccombe

Burrowhayes Campsite

- Continue straight ahead to wide entrance leading onto a track signposted 'West Lynch'
- Through gate ahead (take care: may be sheep in field)
- Bear left across field towards gate opposite leading out onto A39 (be very careful as this is a busy road, and very narrow, too, especially over the bridge)
- Turn right and cross narrow bridge
- Turn left immediately after bridge and through kissing gate into field

- Continue straight ahead, keeping stream on left, and through gate in opposite corner onto a footpath through trees
- Follow footpath and go through kissing gate into field
- Bear left to gap in hedge and through gate in gap
- Continue straight ahead and through another gap in corner of hedge
- Turn right and follow hedge through kissing gate onto road
- Turn left and follow road towards the village of Bossington (the outskirts of this village are delightful to explore, with a very interesting church, bird of prey centre, another riding centre, and a café)

Section 2: 0.75ml (1.2km)
- Turn right and cross Lynch Bridge onto a bridleway (signposted)
- Continue along track, between buildings with interesting roofs
- Follow path around to left and up the hill
- Cross a small stream and head towards gate
- Turn right, signposted 'Selworthy Beacon,' and continue climbing
- Through gate into National Trust area, and continue along bridleway, still climbing
- Turn left at footpath junction signposted 'Hurlstone Point,' and through another gate, keeping left
- Continue along path as it follows the contour of the hill

Section 3: 0.75ml (1.2km)
- Keep right at fork signposted 'Hurlstone Point' (path emerges suddenly from trees to spectacular view of the bay)
- Continue straight ahead to Hurlstone Point where there is an old coastguard lookout shelter
- Retrace steps along coastal path

Section 4: 0.75ml (1.2km)
- Bear right at fork, going downhill towards beach
- Turn left and over stile, still descending
- Follow path as it winds down hillside to stony beach
- Turn left and walk along beach with Hurlstone Point now behind
- From water's edge go up the beach to the hedge on the left
- Turn left off beach through gap between two

Coastguard tower at Hurlstone Point.

bushes, and down a slight slope towards a makeshift fence
- Immediately beside fence, over a makeshift stile into field

Section 5: 0.75ml (1.2km)
- Bear left across field, heading towards hill, and through gate opposite
- Continue straight ahead to footpath
- Turn right onto coastal path and follow
- Turn right across bridge into Bossington car park
- Continue straight on across car park to entrance, passing public toilets on right
- Turn right along road to 'Kitnor Tea Rooms' on right (an ideal place for refreshments The teashop serves lovely food, and has a delightful garden)

Section 6: 0.75ml (1.2km)
- Exit teashop and turn left
- Follow road towards car park
- Keep left with car park on right, and continue along road over bridge
- Keep straight ahead into cul-de-sac, which then becomes a stony track and is signposted 'To the Beach'
- Turn left along a footpath just before a gate (signposted)
- Continue along footpath and through gate
- Straight ahead along path between hedges

Section 7: 0.75ml (1.2km)
- Turn right and then sharp left, and along edge of field
- Continue along edge of field towards Porlock (signposted) with hedge on left
- Straight ahead into a road (cul-de-sac)
- Straight on and up steps ahead out onto A39 (take care: this is a narrow, busy road though there is a pavement).
- Continue along main A39 towards village centre

Section 8: 1ml (1.6km)
- Turn left at Doverhay, with Dovery Manor Museum on corner (to explore the village of Porlock continue along the High Street (A39), where there are several pubs and cafés, and some interesting shops. Retrace steps to museum and Doverhay)
- Along road up the hill past some lovely thatched houses
- Straight ahead at brow of hill
- Bear right onto a track branching away from the road and into trees
- Keep left at fork, going slightly downhill
- Turn left and through a gate into campsite

IN THE LOCALITY
BIRD/WILDLLIFE WATCHING
The calm and serenity of both campsites and close proximity of the river attract a variety

of wildlife. Many different birds visit, including the less-seen Kingfishers, Dippers and Herons. Early in the mornings, on occasion red deer can be seen drinking from the river, and, if you are really still (difficult with a dog, sometimes) and observant, you may be fortunate enough to see an Otter. The fish in the river are mostly Grayling and some Brown Trout, but in late summer and early autumn, Salmon and Trout can be seen near the weir, leaping up-river to spawn.

FISHING

With several fish farms in the vicinity, two reservoirs and rivers as well, there are plenty of opportunities to fish.

TARR STEPS CLAPPER BRIDGE

This bridge across the River Barle is constructed of 17 huge, unmortared stone slabs, and is a fine example of a 'clapper' bridge (an ancient form of bridge usually found on the moors of Devon and in other upland areas of the United Kingdom including Snowdonia and Anglesey, Cumbria, Yorkshire and Lancashire), and is the longest in the country. During the last hundred years or so, the river has silted up, so now, unfortunately, during periods of sustained rain, the river flows over the stone slabs. Though there is mention of the bridge during Tudor times, it is thought to be much older.

CARACTACUS STONE

This standing stone is believed to date from the sixth century. The Latin inscription 'Caraaci Nepus' roughly translates as 'Kinsman of Caratacus.' It is thought someone who was related to Caratacus, a chieftain of a tribe in Britain that rebelled against the Romans, erected the stone as a memorial. To protect this ancient standing stone, a shelter was built in 1906, but it was not until 1925 that it was classified as a scheduled monument. It is situated on Exmoor just off the B3223.

WINSFORD

One of the many charming villages to be found on Exmoor, Winsford is situated at the confluence of the River Exe and several small streams and brooks. As a result, there are, in all, eight bridges in the village, including a packhorse bridge believed to have medieval origins.

In the centre of the village is a ford across Winn Brook, from which the village derives its name. With its small park, village green, shop, garage and post office, Winsford is a delightful place in which to spend time. One of its most impressive buildings – dating from around the 12th century – is the local pub, the 'Royal Oak,' which also serves food. Close to the ford are the Bridge Cottage Tea Rooms, a typical teashop that welcomes dogs.

WIMBLEBALL LAKE

A large, man-made reservoir in Exmoor, which has something for everyone, has an outdoor activity centre that offers a range of things to do, not only the usual water-based activities, but also land-based ones such as climbing and archery.

Wonderful walks from dog-friendly campsites

The trout fishery offers tuition as well as providing fishing opportunities from the bank or a boat, and there are walking and cycling routes, a children's play area, and a café for refreshments. In addition, this is an ideal place for birdwatching, with a bird hide near Bessom Bridge.

However, Wimbleball Lake is probably not the best place to take dogs, especially Labradors like Pearl, as they must be kept on a lead, and are not allowed in the water.

DULVERTON

This market town lies on the southern edge of Exmoor, between the rivers Exe and Barle, and is known as the 'Gateway to Exmoor.' Mentioned in the Domesday Book, in the Middle Ages when its waters were used to wash fleeces, it became an important wool town.

Nowadays, with its many shops – several of which are small, interesting, independent establishments – and various pubs, cafés and restaurants, Dulverton is an enchanting place to visit. In Exmoor House on the western edge of town are the headquarters of the Exmoor National Park Authority.

HURLSTONE POINT

Jutting out into the Bristol Channel, this headland offers extensive views of the water, and, in 1900, a coastguard station was built there. A large, solid two-storey building, the station was manned until the late 1940s. The outer shell of the building remains on the point.

PORLOCK

There has been a settlement on this site for many years. Nowadays, it's a typical Exmoor village with many attractive buildings, several with traditional thatched roofs. The High Street has many shops, pubs, and cafés, and is a delightful place to explore.

Besides the Visitor Centre situated at one end of the High Street that contains a wealth of local information, there's also the Dovey Manor Museum, housed in a 15th century Manor House. Even today it is an impressive building, with stone fireplaces, oak-beamed ceilings, and intricate windows. In addition to containing memorabilia, it hosts various exhibitions during the year.

Just two miles (3.2km) further west at Porlock Weir is the Boat Shed Museum. As its name suggests, the artefacts here are all connected with the sea.

Wiltshire — mysterious tracks and byways
OS MAPS EXPLORER 130 SALISBURY & STONEHENGE

Wiltshire is another county of contrasts, renowned for its countryside, market towns, and villages.

Slashing across the northern edge of the county is the M4 motorway, and close to it are several national and international businesses. This 'corridor effect' of the M4 significantly benefits Wiltshire's economy, but also divides the county.

It's the same with the landscape. The Cotswold hills and the distinctive characteristics of this region spill over into the north of the county; likewise, the sandy soil

Tracks between the fields stretching off into the distance.

of the New Forest and the foliage that thrives in such conditions stretches up to the south east corner of Wiltshire.

Sandwiched between are broad valleys, enclosed by high downlands of chalk and limestone. Salisbury Plain is the largest of the downs, and much of it is used by the MoD for training the UK's armed forces. Elsewhere, the geological nature of the rock of these downs has resulted in enormous figures being etched on several hillsides. Most commonly, these are horses, startlingly white against the green backdrop, and at Cerne Abbas in Dorset a giant man lies in naked splendour on the hillside.

There are many iconic sites in Wiltshire, of which Stonehenge and Avebury are the most well-known. There are a number of other ancient monuments and long barrows, though, as well as numerous large houses such as Longleat with its various attractions; Stourhead with its beautiful gardens, Philipps House, and Wilton House. In addition, besides the magnificent Salisbury Cathedral, many similarly remarkable churches are dotted around the county.

And then there's the village of Lacock, which is unique for its many charming buildings, and the fact that practically the entire village is owned by the National Trust.

Imposing Salisbury Cathedral.

Wonderful walks from dog-friendly campsites

With almost half of the county a designated Area of Outstanding Natural Beauty, it's hardly surprising that Wiltshire is a popular destination. There are numerous long-distance walking routes, the best-known of which is the Ridgeway, and the Kennet and Avon Canal Walk. These trails are merely the tip of the iceberg, though, and, with over 8200 footpaths throughout the county, whether it's a gentle stroll or a more challenging hike that's required, there's something for everyone in the county's glorious countryside, showing rural England at its very best.

With so many footpaths the choice is somewhat overwhelming, of course. The paths to the south of the county allow you to explore huge swathes of the Wiltshire countryside, but, with only a few hamlets and the odd village, there is little opportunity for a refreshment stop. Many of the routes incorporate wide, stony tracks stretching off into the distance, and, mostly, they are clear and easy to follow with only a few returning to grass. Several of them interconnect so it is easy to find circular walks of varying lengths. Fields border these tracks so few stiles and gates are encountered.

The downs are characteristised by sweeping, rolling hills, and though there are several, the gradient is gentle. With such clearly-defined paths, the miles quietly slip by.

CAMPSITE – SUMMERLANDS CARAVAN PARK

Situated just south of Salisbury, the campsite, in a quiet secluded place on the edge of the rolling Wiltshire downs, is sited in a designated Area of Outstanding Natural Beauty. It is a small, with 20 pitches spread over a very flat field in a way I found somewhat unusual. Perhaps this was to provide some space for tents.

The facilities block is well appointed: modern and clean with laundry and dishwashing facilities, as well as a useful information area.

On approaching the campsite, the house on the right is first to be reached. Just inside the gate there is a new reception hut, with a bell to ring to announce your arrival, whereupon someone comes to book you in.

Being situated on one of the highest points around, the views from the campsite are extensive, and because this is one of the secluded pockets of the county, some distance from busy roads and with few other walkers, it exudes a sense of peace and tranquillity. To the north of the campsite are several villages, some quite large, such as Coombe Bissett, as well as the beautiful city of Salisbury with its magnificent cathedral.

PEARLS OF WISDOM 🐾

I liked this campsite because there are so many places to explore ... which is just as well as the designated dog walking area is a short section of footpath that runs along the length of the campsite (and really only suitable for a leg-stretch). There's nowhere for me to chase a ball, though there are rabbits to see off!

I really enjoyed the longer trail that encircles the campsite, especially when we happened to meet up with some doggy companions from nearby houses. I was amazed at the large number of paths and bridleways helpfully fenced off from neighbouring fields so that I did not have to worry about leaping over large stiles, or other animals. There were some delightful smells along these tracks!

The flat field of Summerlands campsite.

S HORT WALK – A VILLAGE FOUND!
Distance: 4.5ml (7.2km)
Duration: 2hr
Terrain: Mainly clearly-defined wide tracks and quiet roads. Some footpaths, fields, gates, and stiles. Mostly level but with some gentle inclines

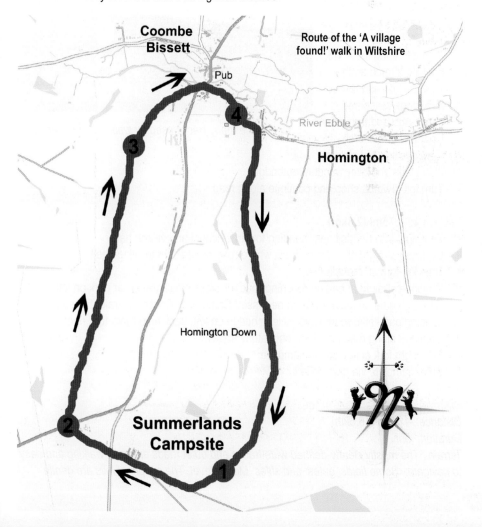

Route of the 'A village found!' walk in Wiltshire

Wonderful walks from dog-friendly campsites

Section 1: 0.75ml (1.2km)
- Exit campsite via dog walk gate
- Turn left along track, passing campsite and house
- At T-junction turn right towards riding school.
- Continue along track to road
- Cross road and continue along track opposite to A354

Section 2: 1ml (1.6km)
- Cross A354 to path opposite
- Follow track along edge of three fields, then around first a right-hand and then a left-hand bend (Coombe Bissett can be glimpsed on the right)

Section 3: 1ml (1.6km)
- Track becomes tarmac road that goes downhill into village and busy A345
- Turn left along the A345, passing church on the right, to 'Fox and Goose' pub (dogs welcome)
- Leave pub and turn left back towards church
- Continue straight ahead along lane and over wooden footbridge
- Turn left towards shop and continue along road

One of the many tracks used by walkers and riders.

Section 4: 1.75ml (2.8km)
- Turn right into Shutts Lane, heading towards school and village hall
- Continue straight ahead onto track where road bends right to village hall
- Take left fork at Y-junction
- Continue straight ahead on reaching road, or cross small gravel car park on left. (Through gate on left onto Coombe Bissett Common.) Continue straight ahead, keeping parallel to road. Over stile in hedge on left, back onto road; turn right
- Continue along road past farm onto stony track
- Take right fork at junction to campsite
- Enter campsite via gate on left

LONG WALK – TALLEST SPIRE IN THE LAND
Distance: 11.5ml (18.5km)
Duration: 5hr
Terrain: The mostly clearly-defined wide tracks and quiet roads are easy walking and easy to navigate. Some fields, gates. and stiles. Mostly level. The couple of hills are gentle

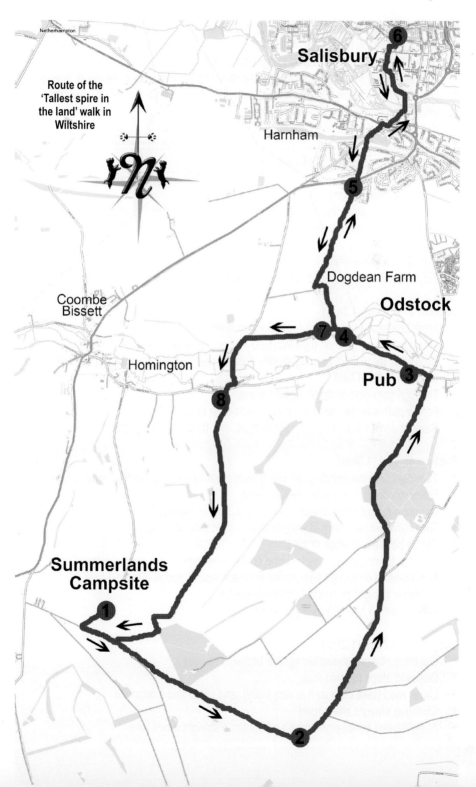

Route of the
'Tallest spire in
the land' walk in
Wiltshire

Wonderful walks from dog-friendly campsites

Section 1: 1.5ml (2.4km)
- Exit campsite via reception
- Straight ahead along driveway to right-hand bend
- Turn left (away from riding school) along stony track, which soon becomes grassy
- Continue along track that passes footpath off to the left and, further on, one off to right which then meets footpath intersection
- Straight ahead, passing footpath off to right and then left
- Continue along footpath that passes between trees, then out into open fields on right
- Continue along grassy track to crossroads junction

Section 2: 2.5ml (3.6km)
- Turn left along stony track and continue on past Yew Farm on right, where track becomes tarmac driveway into Oddstock Village
- On approach to main road of village, the 'Yew Tree Inn' is on the left (a good place to stop for refreshments)
- Turn left at crossroads and continue along main road

Section 3: 0.75ml (1.2km)
- Straight ahead at sharp left-hand bend in road
- Through kissing gate on right into field signposted 'Avon Valley Path'
- Cross this large field, bearing slightly right, to kissing gate on right, opposite telegraph pole in middle of field
- Through gate onto footpath beside stream
- Follow path over two wooden bridges and over stile into field
- Straight across field, bearing slightly right, and through kissing gate beside a gate

Section 4: 1ml (1.6km)
- Turn right and immediately left along wide track heading towards Dogdean Farm
- Follow track as it bends left around farm
- Continue straight ahead along stony track through farmyard
- Turn right just past farm at waymarker on right side of track.
- Follow path along edge of field
- Through kissing gate in hedge, and continue straight along path at edge of next field
- At right-hand corner go through kissing gate also in hedge into next field
- Continue straight across field towards houses
- Follow path to a lane, passing houses on right

Section 5: 0.75ml (1.2km)
- Continue straight ahead along lane between houses
- Descend steps to main road
- Cross road (take care as it is very busy), and climb steps opposite.
- Continue straight along road
- At right-hand bend, cross road and continue straight down lane

- Down steps to another road
- Continue straight along pavement to main road
- Turn right
- Cross road and turn left at traffic lights along Harnham Road North
- Follow road past 'Rose and Crown' pub
- Turn left again at traffic lights
- Cross bridge (lovely views)
- Continue straight along road towards large house with white front door
- Turn left just before the house, along road signposted 'The Cathedral'
- Under arch and turn right
- Follow pavement through Cathedral grounds and past Cathedral (during summer months there is a café just outside main entrance: a good place to stop for refreshments)
- Continue straight under another arch to High Street where there are shops, several cafés, and pubs ('The Boston Tea Party' partway down the High Street welcomes dogs inside and out)

Section 6: 2ml (3.2km)
- Retrace steps to Dogdean Farm (go through arch and along road into Cathedral grounds with Cathedral on left. At corner, turn left and go under the arch. Next corner, turn right
- Cross bridge and turn right along Harnham Road North. At T-junction traffic lights turn right and first left along Old Blandford Road
- Climb steps on left pavement. Continue along lane, across road, and continue straight to another lane.
- Descend steps and cross busy road. Up steps opposite, along lane and into field; straight across field and along edge of next two fields to waymarker
- Turn left and along path round Dogdean Farm to the next corner)

Section 7: 1ml (1.6km)
- Turn right and keep straight on, passing kissing gate and gate on left into field (we came through this on the way to Salisbury)
- Take footpath straight ahead (this is narrow as only occasionally used)
- Continue along footpath to Homington Road
- Turn left; cross bridge
- Turn right at crossroads towards wooden bus shelter
- Follow road round to left and up to main road
- Cross main road

Section 8: 2ml (3.2km)
- Continue straight ahead along road opposite
- At Down Barn, road becomes stony track
- Turn left at T-junction

Wonderful walks from dog-friendly campsites

- Take next right marked with wooden signpost
- Turn right at T-junction
- Right again into campsite

IN THE LOCALITY
CYCLING
Though there is a network of bridleways across the countryside, these seem to me, an occasional cyclist, rather too rough and stony for cycling on.

BIRDWATCHING
The wide open sky of the Wiltshire downs is an ideal place for spotting birds, and the location of the campsite at one of the highest points of the downs makes it especially suitable.

GREAT YEWS ANCIENT SAXON WOODLANDS
Just to the SW of the campsite, adjacent to one of the many bridleways, are the remains of an ancient Saxon Woodlands called 'Great Yews.' The trees are very old and gnarled; reminiscent of Tolkien's woods. Though there are many footpaths through these woods, and despite the fact that, deep in the woods is a building run by the Scouts, this is, in fact, private property.

SALISBURY
Nestled in the chalk downs on the banks of the River Avon, at the confluence of the Rivers Bourne and Nadder, is the city of Salisbury with its majestic Cathedral, whose 404ft spire not only dominates the surrounding countryside, but is the tallest in the UK. The medieval Cathedral Close, grounds and Chapter House are surrounded by a sturdy outer wall, and access is via arches with gates (apparently, these are locked at night). Going under one of these arches is like passing through a time warp. It is, however, the contents of the Chapter House that are truly exceptional: one of the original Magna Carta manuscripts dating from 1251 is housed there.

Work began on the Cathedral in 1221, and for more than a thousand years Salisbury has been an important provincial city. Consequently, its streets comprise some fascinating buildings from all eras. Nevertheless, today it is a modern town with shops, pubs and cafés, and a vibrant theatre. Besides the regular weekly markets held on Tuesdays and Saturdays, various festivals and events are held throughout the year.

MUSEUMS
There are several museums in Salisbury: the Rifles Military Museum, Salisbury Museum, the Museum of Army Flying, Arundell (the home of Edward Heath who was Prime Minster from 1970-1974), and in Cathedral Close is Mompesson House, often referred to as 'The House in The Close,' and owned and managed by the National Trust. Built for Charles Mompesson in 1701, this is an excellent example of Queen Anne architecture, which was

used in the 1995 film *Sense and Sensibility*.

COOMBE BISSETT

Just south of Salisbury is Coombe Bissett, informally known as 'Crumbly Biscuit.' This charming Wiltshire village, with the River Ebble running through it, comprisrs a delightful pub, 'The Fox and Goose' that welcomes dogs inside; a shop and Post Office, and an imposing church, St Michael and All Angels, plus attractive housing.

To the south of the village, Coombe Bissett Down Nature reserve is a Site of Scientific Interest, where the Wildlife Trust aims to restore wildflowers to the chalk grasslands using sheep and cattle to control the grass. Not only are the views fantastic from the reserve, but the landscape variations reflect the different seasons.

ROCKBOURNE ROMAN VILLA

At Rockbourne, 5 miles (8km) south of the campsite, in the centre of what was once a large farming estate, are the remains of a Roman Villa, including bath houses, workshops, living quarters, and mosaics. In the surrounding grounds there's a museum that houses artefacts found on-site, and information about the villa; an activity centre for children, and a café and picnic area.

BREAMORE HOUSE AND MUSEUM

A few miles south of Salisbury on the edge of the New Forest in Breamore village, is the imposing Elizabethan Breamore House that overlooks the Avon Valley. Completed in 1583, this is the family home of the Hulses, who have lived there since 1748. Besides an interesting collection of works of art and furniture there's also a museum that houses various farming machinery.

There's also a gift shop, and refreshments are available from a Tea Barn.

Visit Hubble and Hattie on the web:
www.hubbleandhattie.com • www.hubbleandhattie.blogspot.co.uk • Details of all books
• Special offers • Newsletter • New book news

199

The walks: Scotland
(Borders, Highlands and Moray)

Rights of Access in Scotland are slightly different to the rest of the UK. The 2003 Scotland Land Reform Act established a "statutory right of responsible access over most areas of land and inland water," which means that, as long as we respect the countryside and behave responsibly, it is permitted to access practically all Scottish countryside (Appendix i). As a consequence, it is only long-distance footpaths, such as the West Highland Way, that are shown on OS Maps in the customary green dashes.

Most of these routes are linear. They are well signposted, and popular with walkers of all abilities, so are busy during the long summer days, even in inclement weather. Once having reached the correct path, it is possible to walk many, many miles before the need to check location. (However, it is always prudent to refer to the map at regular intervals to ensure you are on the right path). It is interesting talking to the walkers, who come from all over the world. Some aim to complete a whole trail, whilst others enjoy a short climb for the spectacular views.

I was surprised to discover on the Ordnance Survey Maps of Scotland that few tracks or paths appear to intersect these well known routes, and finding circular walks was problematic without local knowledge. Most circular walks usually involve the busy popular routes as well as tracks generally only used by locals. It is possible, therefore, to experience the beauty of Scotland in the company of others, and also appreciate the remoteness and vastness of the country in solitude.

Whenever and wherever walking in Scotland, always check weather conditions, as these can suddenly become inclement, making navigation even more difficult: because of the landscape and lack of human habitation, it is easy to become lost.

Borders (Melrose) — The place of a hundred walks
OS Maps Explorer 339 Galashields, Selkirk & Melrose

During a search of campsites close to walking trails, I stumbled across the description "lots of walks" and "Melrose," and decided this required authentication. Hence, I checked into the Caravan and Motorhome Club Campsite at Melrose. Immediately, I realized that this could be a special place when I saw for sale on the counter an expertly-produced booklet entitled *Paths around Melrose*. I bought a copy, and it has turned out to be one of the best walking manuals I have encountered in a long time, essential for all those wishing to walk in this area. Melrose prides itself on being especially friendly to walkers, promoting walks of all types, and has become the first town in the Scottish Borders to be awarded, in August 2010, 'Walkers are Welcome' status – and deservedly so.

The town is a bustling hive of activity. There is a fantastic abbey ruin; the view from the top must be spectacular if you can manage the climb. There are two gardens – Harmony and Priorwood Gardens – and even a mill factory shop which has a café, where you can ponder about what to purchase over a cup of tea.

Surprisingly, there is a large Roman presence, which contradicts the common belief that the Roman invasion of Britain stopped at Hadrian's Wall. Information about the occupation of this region and all-things Roman can be found at the local Roman museum. During the summer, Roman discovery walks are organized, on which dogs are welcome.

The many small independent shops in the town centre are delightful and charming, offering a whole range of different products. (Surprisingly, there were no empty units, which might reflect the vitality of the town). Of special note is the local ironmonger 'Kennedy's Country Store' at which an eclectic mix of goods is available, including a range of dog toys and treats. It is like stepping back in time, and the proprietor is a larger-than-life character: I was reminded of the TV comedy *Open All Hours*. At the other end of town, near the library, appropriately enough, is a secondhand book shop – 'Bookends' – with a huge stock of books. Interspersed amongst the shops and as equally diverse are pubs, cafés, and restaurants. As if this is not sufficient, the Market Square is also the venue for open-air events, weather permitting.

Then there is the walking. It takes only a few minutes to reach the surrounding countryside – the routes in *Paths around Melrose* have been carefully researched – and these are well sign posted and are easy to follow. There are a variety of walks, so something for everyone: amblers and ramblers; historians (Romans), and literary fans (Sir Walter Scott). The paths around Melrose have been thoroughly catalogued in the booklet. Parts of several different walks have been cobbled together to try and give a flavour of the area in just two walks.

The town is a truly delightful place to spend several days with plenty to see and do for everyone. Throughout the year there are various events: for example, the Rugby Sevens Tournament is in April, with the Borders Book Festival and Melrose Festival Week taking place in June.

The countryside around Melrose.

Wonderful walks from dog-friendly campsites

CAMPSITE – MELROSE GIBSON PARK CARAVAN AND MOTORHOME CLUB

Situated in the centre of the town, next to the site is Gibson Park; hence its name. In the corner of the park beside the campsite entrance is Melrose Tennis Club, and across the road is the Rugby Club. A few minutes' walk away is the High Street with its shops, pubs, and restaurants, so the campsite is in a prime position from which to explore the town, as well as the surrounding countryside.

The facilities are of the usual comprehensive and high standard of Club sites, and it is quiet and well-ordered, and efficiently run, with wardens who are friendly and helpful. As well as the 59 pitches there's a separate field for tents. The site is open to both members and non members, which might explain why it is busy, and advance booking is advisable. The views of the town and hills are captivating; access to the network of footpaths is easy.

Melrose campsite in the centre of the town.

PEARLS OF WISDOM 🐾

Each time we set out it was an adventure to discover where we were going, even for those quick 'leg-stretching' outings. There is a short route between the trees on one side of the campsite, and immediately outside the gates is the park for chasing balls and frisbees. Wonderful!

We did seem to spend a lot of time on roads and pavements, though this was interspersed with places where I was free to roam and explore. Stopping at all the shops was boring, though, occasionally, some had very intriguing smells. The longer walks beside the river, or up a very steep hill where it was very, very windy, were fabulous!

SHORT WALK – TOWN AND COUNTRY

Distance: 4ml (6.4km)
Duration: 2hr (longer, if enticed by the town)
Terrain: Fields, footpaths, track, roads, kissing gates

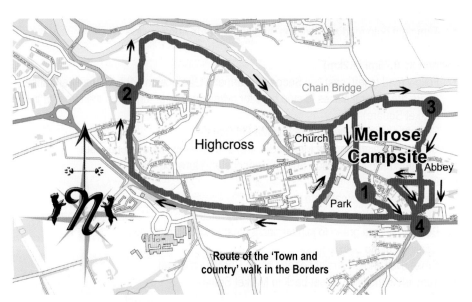

Route of the 'Town and
country' walk in the Borders

Section 1: 1.25ml (2km)

- Exit campsite via reception
- Turn right immediately at zebra crossing into car park
- Bear left across car park.
- Proceed along street signposted 'Melrose Station'
- Turn right signposted 'Melrose Station'
- Continue along street and up steps on left
- Turn right along footpath at top
- Follow footpath to road by cemetery
- Turn left and up slope
- Turn right onto cycle path parallel to main road
- Continue along cycle path over road by flyover
- Turn right at T-junction
- Continue along lane to road
- Take second turning left with a bus stop on left and Memorial Hall on right
- Continue along road and cross over A6091 (take care: busy road!)

Section 2: 1.25ml (2.km)

- Straight ahead through large brown gates to left of Waverley Court Hotel
- Continue along path past white house onto grassy track down to river
- Turn right along river walkway
- Continue beside river and through kissing gate onto road (signposted)
- Bear left along road and through kissing gate on left in 50yd (45m), back onto riverside path (signposted)
- Continue along path past enormous Melrose Parish Church and 'The Chain Bridge,' onto path signposted 'Borders Abbey Way'

- Turn right onto road at T-junction, heading towards Abbey ruin

Section 3: 0.75ml (1.2km)
- Follow road to left, past Mill Shop and Harmony Gardens on right, to Abbey entrance (there are several places to stop here for refreshments, or further up the street at the Market Square)
- Straight ahead to town centre and Market Square
- Continue straight on past Market Square, and take left fork at roundabout
- Turn left down lane beside Ship Inn signposted 'Nutwood'
- Cross bridge.
- Turn left along footpath into wood
- Cross bridge into open green beside abbey ruins
- Bear left across green to join tarmac footpath parallel to railings
- Continue along path to road
- Cross over and go straight ahead along Buccleuch Street
- Turn left along High Street back to Market Square
- Keeping right, continue past museum and library towards flyover

Section 4: 0.75ml (1.2km)
- Turn right to Melrose Station (signposted)
- Continue straight ahead through car park
- Bear right and take grass footpath straight ahead with fence on right
- Continue along footpath, passing campsite dog exercise area on left

Melrose town centre and Market Square.

- Turn right along road past cemetery and school
- Continue straight ahead
- Cross road at junction towards Melrose Parish Church
- Take path with church on right ,and go straight ahead to footpath by two benches
- Turn right and follow riverside footpath down to River Tweed
- Turn right to town centre (signposted)
- Continue straight ahead and cross road into park
- Cross road ahead and bear left towards tennis courts and campsite

LONG WALK – THE ROMANS WERE HERE
Distance: 7ml (11.2km)

Duration: 4hr
Terrain: Fields, footpaths, tracks, roads, stiles, kissing gates, some steep climbs. Hill climb is taxing

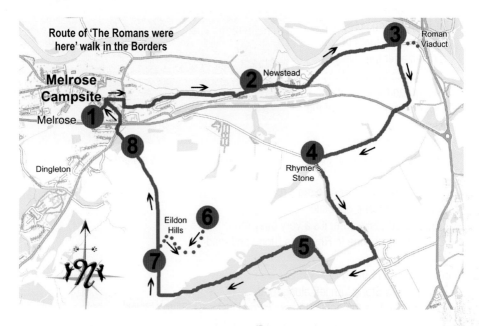

Section 1: 1ml (1.6km)
- Leave campsite via reception and go straight ahead to main road
- Cross road and turn right
- Follow road round to left into Buccleuch Street
- At T-junction, cross Abbey Street and turn right
- Turn first left along Priors Walk (lane beside Abbey ruins)
- Cross park and footbridge ahead
- Turn left, keeping close to stream on left
- Straight ahead and along road to rank of garages
- Turn left after last one
- Through kissing gate onto stony path
- Continue along path to road, then turn left and continue to T-junction

Section 2: 1ml (1.6km)
- Turn right along Main Street and follow road through village
- Turn left by Millennium Stone towards NHS Clinic and through gate
- Follow road under viaduct to bridge across River Tweed (surprisingly, the Romans established an extensive fort in this area, and made full use of the resources there to maintain it. There are information boards and view points along the road)
- Retrace steps back up slope and under viaduct

Wonderful walks from dog-friendly campsites

Section 3: 1ml (1.6km)

- Turn left up steps in hedge signposted 'Broomhill,' and through gate into field
- In 100yd (90m) cross stile on left onto a footpath (if you turn left after the stile you can walk to the top of the viaduct, and also climb a tower for a better view of the Roman fort)

The Roman Viaduct: still a magnificent structure.

- Turn right and continue along footpath through trees
- Bear right onto stony track (signposted), and follow to main road
- Cross road to lane opposite (signposted): take care: it's a very busy road)
- Continue along lane to Rhymer's Stone and road

Section 4: 1ml (1.6km)

- At Rhymer's Stone turn left along road
- Continue and go through gate across road just past 'Eildon Mains'
- Turn right onto footpath into wood signposted 'Eildon Hills'
- Turn right, continuing up through trees, and follow path round to left to gate and two wooden seats with spectacular views down to viaduct (this a good place to stop for lunch)

Section 5: 1ml (1.6km)

- Continue along path through wood
- Take path to right at left-hand bend, and go through gate
- Turn left and follow path around Eildon Hill North on right, and wood on left
- Turn right uphill at T-junction with wide track
- Continue climbing to a footpath crossroads

Section 6: 0.5ml (0.8km) (feels more like 1ml (1.6km)

(If you want to climb to the fort at top of Eildon Hill North, turn right up the hill and follow path to the top. The views are absolutely amazing, but little remains of the Roman fort. It can be very windy)

- Retrace steps down hill to footpath junction and now turn right

Section 7: 1ml (1.6km)

- Straight ahead and follow signposts downhill towards Melrose for 'St Cuthbert's Way.'

(In order to prevent serious erosion, St Cuthbert's Trail down the hill is re-routed during the year. It is well signposted so follow these)

- Turn left at foot of hill, descend steps and through gate

Section 8: 0.5ml (0.8km)

- Follow path straight ahead and through another gate
- Cross track and through gate opposite
- Follow path along edge of fields, and down very long flight of steps
- Turn right at street towards flyover and Melrose Market Square
- Bear left at Market Square and continue along High Street to Rugby Club and campsite opposite

IN THE LOCALITY
BIRDWATCHING

Out in the countryside the numbers and varieties of birds increase. Amongst the heather are red grouse, although hearing their characteristic 'goback, goback' call is much more likely than seeing them.

FISHING

Anglers come from all over the world to fish in the River Tweed, and, although there are all kinds of fish, the river is renowned for salmon and trout. The months between April and September are trout season. Regulations for fishing in the River Tweed and permits can be obtained from the local Spar store in Melrose.

GOLF

A mile to the south of the campsite, at the foot of the Eildon Hills, is Melrose Golf Club, which has a pay and play policy, so visitors are welcome, irrespective of ability.

GARDENING

For the keen gardener, Melrose offers not one but two gardens to visit. Though both are walled gardens, they are very different. Harmony Gardens is located around a fine example of an early 19th century house built by Robert Vaughan, a local joiner. He called it Harmony after the plantation in Jamaica where he made his fortune. In addition to flower borders, vegetable, and fruit plots, the garden has a small croquet lawn. It is aptly named as it is a serene, restful place.

The beds at Priorwood Gardens are especially interesting. The flowers cultivated here are used to make wonderful dried flower arrangements, which are then sold in the gift shop. The entire process of drying the flowers and assembling the different posies takes place on the premises.

Both gardens are managed by National Trust for Scotland.

MELROSE ABBEY

Since its founding in 1136 by King David I, Melrose Abbey has had a turbulent history. As each successive wave of English invaders passed through, so the abbey was damaged and had to be repaired. In 1385, under Richard II the destruction was severe but the abbey was rebuilt. In 1544, during the reformation, Henry VIII not only destroyed the abbey but also any desire to restore it. In 1610, a parish church was instigated in part of the ruins, and used for the next 200 years until a new building was erected.

The abbey must have been a magnificent building because the present ruins are themselves remarkable, dominating the town. The abbey is also famous because it is here that the heart of Robert the Bruce is reputed to be buried.

THREE HILLS ROMAN HERITAGE CENTRE

Located right in the centre of Melrose, opposite Market Square, the centre houses the 'Trimontium' exhibition that documents the Roman heritage of the area. Trimontium was the name of the Roman settlement discovered at the village of Newstead, a mile east of Melrose; so-called because it was overshadowed by the three Eildon Hills – north, mid, and west Eildon. This Roman settlement was important as it guarded the crossing of the River Tweed, and was the largest one north of Hadrian's Wall, as well as comprising many important buildings, and regarded as the capital of Scotland. There are many interesting artefacts.

ABBOTSFORD

In this village, located about two miles (3.2km) west of Melrose, is the house that the author Sir Walter Scott lived in until his death in 1832. The house and gardens are open to the public, and there is a Visitors Centre and café.

RHYMER'S STONE

This monument is situated at a viewpoint on the Eildon Hills near Melrose. Thomas Rhymer, after whom it is named, was a 13th century Scottish laird, who was supposedly able to predict the future after a meeting at that spot with the Faerie Queen. The views from the stone are stunning.

Highlands — in the shadow of Ben Nevis
OS MAPS EXPLORER 392 BEN NEVIS & FORT WILLIAM

The Highlands of Scotland are renowned for impressive mountains, spectacular valleys, and truly amazing scenery that is breathtaking; the varying light from changeable weather merely enhancing its splendour. Whatever the weather, though, the mountains are a constant reminder of man's insignificance. One can only stand and stare.

This is the least inhabited region of the UK, so access can be tricky, though some quite secluded places are busy with visitors.

In Scotland, the names of some of the geographical features are different. The term 'Glen' is one such example, and denotes a valley, so Glen Nevis is the valley of the River Nevis. All the way along it to the source of the River Nevis, numerous streams and brooks tumble down the mountains and through the verdant foliage, with countless waterfalls cascading over rocks, some gouging vast gullies down mountainsides. The River Nevis winds its way along the valley floor, becoming deeper and wider, until it eventually spills out into Loch Linnhe at Fort William on its way to the sea.

All around, mountains tower imposingly, with occasional glimpses of more distant mountains behind them. The impression the mountains portray seem to vary with the weather. On bright, sunny days they appear benign, inviting exploration; should high cloud mask the sun they appear aloof and bored; swirling wisps of mist, through which peaks can occasionally be seen, make them seem mysterious and challenging, and cloud thick enough to shroud the mountains gives the impression of menace and threat.

Spectacular mountains and river valleys.

Glen Nevis is both physically and metaphorically dominated by Ben Nevis, the highest mountain in the UK, which is situated quite close to the mouth of the Glen near the town of Fort William. It captures the imagination because it is the first obvious-looking mountain in the valley; yet it does not exude a feeling of inaccessibility, a consequence of which is that very many people regard climbing it as essential, but this is not an easy undertaking.

'Ben Nevis' means 'venomous,' and locally this is taken seriously. It is a mountain, after all, and although the lower slopes are not especially difficult, it becomes challenging further up. If the weather is less than perfect it becomes a dangerous expedition, even for those with experience, who have good navigation skills, the proper equipment, and are physically fit (many underestimate the level of fitness required).

To ensure a safe and successful climb a large Visitor Centre is located in Glen Nevis, and contains maps, equipment, information, and advice. Even so, the mountain rescue team is regularly called out, and, on the few occasions I have been camping by Ben Nevis, I have witnessed a search-and-rescue helicopter in action, and also some lost climbers.

Wonderful walks from dog-friendly campsites

Fortunately, this latter expedition had powerful torches, which meant that, as it got dark, their progress down the mountain could be tracked. (I did not learn the outcome of either incident but assume all ended well as I did not hear otherwise.)

The West Highland Way, which starts at Fort William on its way over the mountains towards Glasgow, passes very close to the campsite, and offers a true 'mountain' experience. Also just outside Fort William is a gondola that takes sightseers to the summit of Aonach Mor, and a spectacular view of the Nevis range. In addition, Fort William is an interesting town to visit, and is close enough to replenish supplies.

Climbing the highest mountain in the UK may not be on your agenda, but the area still has much to offer. Basking in the shadow of Ben Nevis is in itself a special experience.

CAMPSITE – GLEN NEVIS CARAVAN AND CAMPING PARK

A large site with over 300 pitches, being spread over several smaller, enclosed fields contributes to an impression of privacy and intimacy, as does the generous amount of space allocated to each pitch. Ample watering points and amenity blocks are dotted about, so everything is to hand, although reception and the shop are slightly further away at the entrance. An adjacent bar and restaurant are only a few minutes' walk away. Even though the campsite is busy it is clean, and staff are pleasant and polite.

Surrounded by mountains and with footpaths close by, it is ideally located to watch the many climbers of Ben Nevis; maybe become one of their number, or just experience being outdoors in the mountains.

PEARLS OF WISDOM 🐾

Here, I had a *choice* of exercise areas, as there was one at each end of the campsite!

Glen Nevis campsite nestling in the lee of Ben Nevis.

These were okay – big enough to chase a ball or my frisbee, but otherwise a bit dull. I particularly liked the one with the path going through it, and sometimes there were lots of people to meet and greet.

I enjoyed the different walks we went on, although the water wasn't really deep enough for a swim. There were only a couple of really hairy cows (behind a fence, luckily), and I could have done with fewer tarmac routes. All-in-all, though, an agreeable jaunt.

SHORT WALK – UP AND OVER TO FORT WILLIAM
Distance: 4.5ml (7.2km)
Duration: 2hr (longer if visiting Fort William)
Terrain: Footpaths, tracks, hills, roads, kissing gates. Some steep climbs

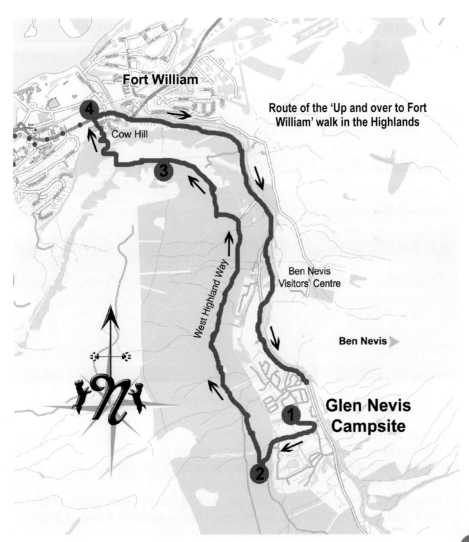

Route of the 'Up and over to Fort William' walk in the Highlands

Wonderful walks from dog-friendly campsites

Section 1: 0.25ml (0.4km)
- Leave campsite via dog exercise area near to bar and restaurant
- Turn right at restaurant driveway and follow road between houses and garages
- Bear right towards large shed and through gates into wooded area
- Continue along path to T-junction

Section 2: 1.75ml (2.8km)
- Turn right along wide, stony track (signposted)
- Continue straight ahead (in a few yards the track joins the West Highland Way)
- Continue on, ignoring other paths until West Highland Way descends towards car park and road
- Turn left just before reaching main car park
- Continue up steep path signposted 'Cow Hill and Town Centre' to seat on hillock (from here there are lovely views of Fort William)

Fort William on Loch Linnhe.

Section 3: 0.5ml (0.8km)
- Continue along path signposted 'Town Centre' towards church spire
- Straight ahead at next footpath junction (signposted)
- Follow path downhill, through gate and out to car park
- Straight ahead across car park to main road, passing Leisure Centre on left. (This is the outskirts of Fort William: to visit the town, which is well worth it, turn left at the

main road, pass the hospital on the left, and bear left through gardens to the church and shopping precinct. This is a good place to stop for refreshments as there are several pubs and cafés. To return to the campsite, retrace route to the Leisure Centre)

Section 4: 2ml (3.2km)
- Turn right and follow road to roundabout
- Continue straight across roundabout (2nd exit) onto much quieter road (if you decide not to go into the town refreshments are available at a restaurant near the roundabout)
- Continue along road
- Turn left into car park of Ben Nevis Visitor Centre
- Straight ahead through car park to riverside path
- Turn right and follow path beside river to Visitor Centre on right (this is an interesting place: the information about the area is useful and instructive, especially if you are contemplating climbing Ben Nevis)
- Exit Visitor Centre and turn right
- Turn right at corner of building with the river on left
- Continue along side of building onto footpath, and up steps back to road
- Turn left and continue along road to campsite entrance

LONG WALK – UP THE VALLEY TO PADDY'S BRIDGE
Distance: 8.5ml (13.6km)
Duration: 5hr
Terrain: Footpaths, tracks, hills, roads, kissing gates. Return route beside the river is demanding

This walk is unusual for the Highlands because there is little climbing involved. It follows the contours of the Glen as the River Nevis twists and turns until close to its source. The return route – much of it along the bank of the river – is also quite level, though makes for more difficult walking because, frequently, the path is very narrow, low-hanging branches obstruct progress, and tree roots protruding across the path can trip the unsuspecting walker.

In addition there are many places where the bank has been eroded, and it is necessary to scramble up and down it, or leap across. If, therefore, you elect to return to the campsite via the road, this is physically much easier but do watch the traffic. Though it is a cul-de-sac it is used by a surprising volume of traffic, especially in the summer, en route to and from the car parks at Achriabhach Falls and 'Paddy's Bridge.'

Section 1: 0.25ml (0.4km)
- Leave campsite via dog exercise area near to bar and restaurant
- Turn right at restaurant driveway, and follow road between houses and garages
- Bear right towards large shed, and through gates into wooded area
- Continue along path to T-junction

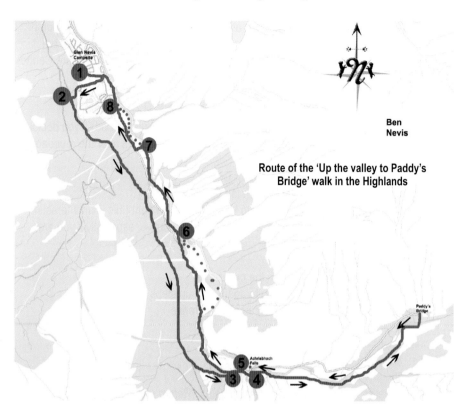

Ben
Nevis

Route of the 'Up the valley to Paddy's
Bridge' walk in the Highlands

Section 2: 2.25ml (3.6km)
- Turn left and continue along logging track for approximately two miles (Ben Nevis dominates views of the surrounding mountains, which are breathtaking)
- Take left path at a Y-junction going down to road

Section 3: 0.25ml (0.4km)
- Turn right at road and cross narrow bridge (take care with the traffic going to the car park. On the right is an interesting information board detailing plans for the area: in addition to land management, it is

Ben Nevis from the logging track.

intended to instigate walking routes in here)
- Continue along road past car park on right, and around left-hand bend to bridge over waterfalls

Section 4: 3.25ml (5.2km)
- Turn right along riverside footpath immediately before bridge (signposted 'Paddy's Bridge'). The 1.5ml (2.4km) footpath is easy to follow as it winds alongside the river. This is an ideal place to stop for lunch as there are several big rocks to sit on and admire the view
- Retrace steps along route to car park at Achriabhach

Section 5: 1ml (1.6km)
- Continue along road with river on right, wood on left, and Ben Nevis ahead. At the first layby a kissing gate leads into a field: go through this and straight ahead is the river. Off to the left is the riverside path. (I did not walk this route but met two people who had)
- At second layby go through gate on left onto a track that bears right down towards the river

Section 6: 1ml (1.6km)
- Continue straight ahead along path by river (the riverside footpath is easy to follow but is not easy walking, and is very, very wet)
- Climb gate and cross field; climb gate opposite back onto riverside path, still staying close to river
- Follow path towards two gates close together
- Turn left before gates, along footpath leading to road
- If you can easily lift your dog over stiles use Section 7; otherwise go to Section 8

Section 7: 0.25ml (0.4km)
- Continue along riverside path until it bears left across a small field to road
- In right-hand corner is a wooden fence
- Climb over fence onto road by Youth Hostel

Section 8: 0.25ml (0.4km)
- Turn right and continue along road to campsite
- Turn left past restaurant along driveway, and bear right into dog exercise area

IN THE LOCALITY
CLIMBING
With Ben Nevis towering over the campsite, and a footpath leading to the route to the top just the other side of the river, the challenge to climb it is compelling, but remember that the frequency at which Mountain Rescue is called out is frightening.

Wonderful walks from **dog-friendly campsites**

WEST HIGHLAND WAY
Easily reached from the campsite, as you climb the trail the views of the Glen and mountains are spectacular. Though it is linear, sections of the Way can be incorporated into a circular route, but these are long and physically demanding. Ideal for a workout with a breathtaking backdrop.

MOUNTAIN BIKING NEVIS RANGE
Mountain Biking is extremely popular, with numerous trails for all abilities. Competitions are held throughout the year, culminating in the World Cup in June. Bikes can be hired at Nevis Cycles in Fort William or two miles (3.2km) north in Torlundy.

FORT WILLIAM
Dominated by mountains, this is the main town in the region, renowned for being at one end of the West Highland Way. The pedestrianised High Street has a range of shops, including specialized outdoor stores, and several restaurants and cafés. St Andrew's Church, with its attractive interior, overlooks Parade Park. Close to the station is The Old Fort and a supermarket. Just to the north of the town are the ruins of Inverlochy Castle.

WEST HIGHLAND MUSEUM
In the centre of Fort William this museum houses an interesting local history collection and Jacobite artefacts.

CRANNOG CRUISES
These depart from the Town Pier in the centre of Fort William. The daytime cruises around Loch Linnhe provide the opportunity to see a range of wildlife. Loch Eil is the destination of the evening cruises, allowing a unique view of Ben Nevis. Dogs are welcome.

JACOBITE STEAM TRAIN
This 84ml (135km) round trip to Glenfinnian can be boarded at Fort William. The train passes through some spectacular scenery, and over the Glenfinnian viaduct, made famous in the Harry Potter films. Dogs are welcome.

BEN NEVIS DISTILLERY
Established in 1825, this distillery, which is 1.5ml (2.4km) north of the town, is one of the oldest licensed distilleries in Scotland. Adjacent is Legend of the Drew Visitor Centre. A visit provides an explanation of the legend, as well as a tour of the distillery – and a sample to taste. Also on site is a shop and café.

MOUNTAIN GONDOLA
At Torlundy, just north of the town ,the gondola climbs 2130ft (650mt) up Aonach Mor, which is in the same mountain range as Ben Nevis. At the top is a Discovery Centre that provides a wealth of information, a restaurant, and details of walks to view points. The

scenery is magnificent, and, on a clear day, it is possible to see the Inner Hebrides. Dogs are welcome.

Moray — sea and sand; sand and sea
OS MAP EXPLORER 423 ELGIN, FORRES & LOSSIEMOUTH

Moray is in the north of Scotland between Aberdeen and Inverness. As the name suggests, it is located along part of the south bank of the Moray Firth, with the Highlands to the west, the Cairngorms Mountains to the south, and Aberdeenshire to the east. Most of the region is strung out along the shoreline, which is dotted with several villages, but its triangular shape does stretch as far as the Cairngorms National Park. This part of Scotland is quite distinctive: due to its numerous beautiful, sandy beaches and the particularly mild climate, it is often referred to as the 'Riviera of the North.'

The Moray region may be somewhat off the beaten track but it's not isolated, and is easily accessible via the two main north/south routes that traverse Scotland. Though there are only a few roads in the area, access to towns and villages is quite straightforward, and bus services are regular and quite frequent, especially in comparison to similar outlying locations. With railway stations at the larger towns of Elgin, Forres and Keith, getting about is not too onerous.

This is a very rural part of Scotland, and, besides the huge swathes of open countryside, woodlands and forests cover a quarter of the area. Much of the woodland is along the coast to prevent sand blowing inland and covering the countryside. When walking through the woods, it is easy to see how effectively the trees trap sand, and in many places a layer coats the earth, with small dunes interspersed amongst them. Patches of sand regularly mark most of the paths through the woods.

Because of the mild climate this area has been populated for many hundreds of years, and there are even remains of Bronze and Iron Age settlements. The outcrop at Burghead was once an important Pictish settlement, with a fort on the headland overlooking the Moray Firth. Nowadays, there is a large and striking, white circular Visitor Centre on the site of the fort. Besides being an information centre, it is also a museum housing many local artefacts, and has two large wildlife viewing galleries: one on the roof, and the other inside the Visitor Centre, sheltered from the elements. This is a very interesting building and its location is extraordinary. The spit of land that the Centre and village occupy, has two coasts. The locals refer to the one on the west side (which is sandy) as the 'front shore,' and the one on the east side (which is pebbly) as the 'back shore.' It's uncanny, standing on the green and seeing a beach to both left and right. Both the Visitor Centre and the village are well worth exploring, for no other reason than to understand why the New Year is celebrated twice in Burghead.

Fallout from many historical upheavals has had minimal impact due to this area's seclusion. In the past it was the natural resources of the area that sustained local communities, and whilst agriculture and forestry are still important, fishing has declined significantly over the past 50 years; this is especially so in Burghead. During the 1700s, with a burgeoning ship-building and fishing industry, a better harbour was needed, and this – together with the accompanying warehouses – was designed by none other than

Thomas Telford in 1807. As a result, for the next hundred or so years Burghead was an important fishing port and the town prospered. Unlike many other such places, Burghead remains an operational port, although only a few fishing boats are based there.

Nowadays, the main industries of this area are tourism and whisky; even in Burghead, where a large, rather ugly, maltings has been built on the outskirts of the town on the 'back shore.' Meandering across Moray is the popular 'whisky trail,' which not only visits many of the distilleries but also includes sampling the produce. However, the largest employer in Moray is the MOD with an army base at Kinloss, and an RAF base at Lossiemouth.

Without doubt the jewel in Moray's crown is the Firth itself with its amazing golden sandy beaches, jutting headlands, distant highland hills on the opposite bank, forest, large expanse of sea, ships that skim across the water, and, of course, abundant wildlife (the possibility of seeing dolphins and whales is indescribably exhilarating). In addition is the changing weather characteristic of the Firth: the rain that obscures all, lowering clouds that churn the sea and make the hills opposite appear menacing, wisps of high cloud gently decorating the summits, and brilliant sun that casts a benign glow over all, encouraging ambles along the beach beside a glassy sea.

CAMPSITE – BURGHEAD BEACH HOLIDAY PARK

This campsite is on the outskirts of Burghead village, squashed between the front shore's amazing sandy beach and the forest. It is deceptively big, and comprised predominantly

Fishing nets drying on Burghead harbourside.

of large, static vans, with just 20 pitches for tourers, squeezed into a small space encircling the modest play area near reception. The cheek-by-jowl positioning of the pitches – especially the ones with hardstanding (there is no room for an awning) – ensures that all comings and goings are obvious. The one isolated pitch is equally open to scrutiny, situated right at the entrance of not only the campsite but also the beach car park. However, it does have magnificent views of the Moray Firth. On the plus side, the staff are very friendly and obliging, and the facilities block is wonderful – large and spacious, and always scrupulously clean.

*Campsite squeezed
between the beach
and the forest.*

PEARLS OF WISDOM 🐾
I LOVED this campsite, even though there was no special exercise area for me and my kind.

First of all, it's just a hop, skip and a jump to the beach and a paddle, or, if the tide is high, an actual swim! The beach is very flat and underpaw is sand, so my owner says. This is strange stuff: sometimes hard and solid and generally damp, and other times dry and shifting, slithering about when I stepped on it. This was very confusing but I soon got used to it. The beach was full of all kinds of things to explore as well as people to greet.

Secondly, just a few minutes' walk away through a gate directly from the campsite is the forest, which has so many paths to choose and intriguing smells.

Thirdly, unusually, I met and greeted lots of doggy friends, and, lastly, there was even space in the forest for me to chase my frisbee!

SHORT WALK – ALONG THE BACK SHORE
Distance: 6.5ml (10.4km)

Wonderful walks from dog-friendly campsites

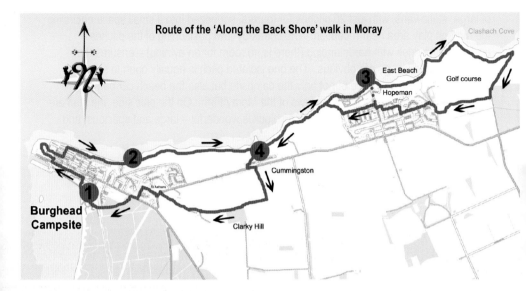

Route of the 'Along the Back Shore' walk in Moray

Duration: 3hr (longer if stopping at the Visitor Centre)
Terrain: Coastal path, some quiet roads, lanes, cyclepaths, footpaths, only a couple of gates and stiles. Steep, rock-hewn steps, and a climb to golf course

Section 1: 0.75ml (1.2km)

- Exit campsite via entrance
- Turn left towards sea and descend to concrete jetty
- Turn right along footpath parallel to coast along top of sea wall
- Bear right at corner and through gap in wall
- Turn left towards headland with sea wall on left
- Turn right at second black safety rails and along street with harbour on left
- Follow harbourside round to left
- Bear right to Shetland Bus Memorial: during WWII, the Norwegian resistance movement operated the 'Shetland Bus' from here. The trips were very successful, carrying agents, wireless operators and military supplies to Norway for the resistance movement, and returning with refugees, recruits for the Free Norwegian Forces, and, in December, Christmas trees for the treeless Shetlands. This is a moving tribute on the waterfront, built with stones from both countries in commemoration of those Norwegians who lost their lives here during WW2
- Continue along the road with harbour still on left
- Turn right up wide steps
- Turn left; through barrier head towards rocky headland
- Bear right up narrow steep steps and follow path around headland to right towards buildings (take care: narrow and steep)
- Turn sharp left before first house up very narrow steps in grass bank onto grassy headland

- Continue ahead towards Visitor Centre (worth a visit)
- Climb steps on left just past Visitor Centre
- Turn right at top along path by another monument
- Continue along top of bank to road with front shore (sandy) on right, and back shore (pebbly) on left
- Turn left along road towards back shore
- Turn right along coastal path, taking left fork to keep close to sea on left
- Follow path past houses and malt factory on right

Looking out to sea.

Section 2: 1.5ml (2.4km)
- Continue along the Moray coastal path past St Aethan's Well on right, Red Craig Rock on left, and under two bridges
- Follow path to top of 3rd bridge
- Turn left and cross bridge
- Follow path round to right, past static vans on right
- Turn left at road junction onto narrow footpath, and down bank to beach
- Turn right along beach towards wooden fence
- Climb path on right and go through gap in wooden fence onto road (this is the main road of Hopeman: turn right for shops and café (unfortunately, dogs are not welcome) It is worth a small detour to see the Ice House on the far side of the play area)

Wonderful walks from dog-friendly campsites

Section 3: 2ml (3.2km)
- Cross road and descend steps opposite
- Follow path along edge of playing fields
- Turn left along road to beach
- Turn right along pavement beside car park onto a narrow, stony footpath
- Take left fork to junction, passing beach huts on right
- Take 2nd exit signposted 'Lossiemouth'
- Continue along narrow footpath through gorse, passing another well on right
- Follow path around headland towards a golf 'green' on right (there is a seat beside the path overlooking the sea: a good place to sit and observe. If you're very lucky you *might* see dolphins ... or even a whale!)
- Bear right along a short, grassy path onto the 'green'
- Skirt 'green' to wide track ahead on right
- Follow track to golf course
- Cross fairway to gorse bushes opposite, and turn right
- Straight ahead past bushes on left, onto a wide, stony track with a 'green' on right
- Follow track to junction, and turn sharp right, then left onto another wide track
- Continue along track towards trees and out onto another 'green'
- Skirt to right of green towards back of large, white sign beside another wide track to right of clubhouse
- Follow track out to the road
- Turn right along road and take left fork
- Turn left along stony track and continue along to Golf Road
- Turn right along School Road (school is ahead)
- Follow School Road round to the left with school on right
- Turn right at T-junction, then left along McPherson Street out to main road
- Turn right then first left along Duff Street to left-hand bend
- Turn left onto cyclepath
- Follow path down to the left onto Moray coastal path

Section 4: 2.25ml (3.6km)
- Follow coastal path to first bridge
- Turn right along footpath before bridge, signposted 'Clarky Hill'
- Turn left in 50yd (45m)
- Follow path over top of bridge and out to road
- Turn left along road, then first right along single lane road (signposted)
- Turn right along wide, grassy track at brow of hill
- Continue along track past track on right and footpath on left, and through gate
- Follow path right and left onto stony track and out onto road
- Turn right along road
- Turn left at T junction opposite cemetery, then first right
- Follow road round to T-junction
- Turn right along main road

- Bear left across football pitch towards seat by centre line of pitch
- Continue ahead into trees onto footpath to right of seat
- Follow path straight ahead through trees
- Bear slightly right up bank to footpath T-junction
- Turn left and then right by waymarker down steps
- Straight ahead past footpath X-junction
- Take right fork by static van, passing kissing gate on right
- Follow path towards signposts
- Turn right at signposts towards campsite entrance

LONG WALK – FOREST AND BEACH

Distance: 8.5ml (13.6km)
Duration: 5.5hr
Terrain: Forest tracks, sandy beach trail, gates and steps

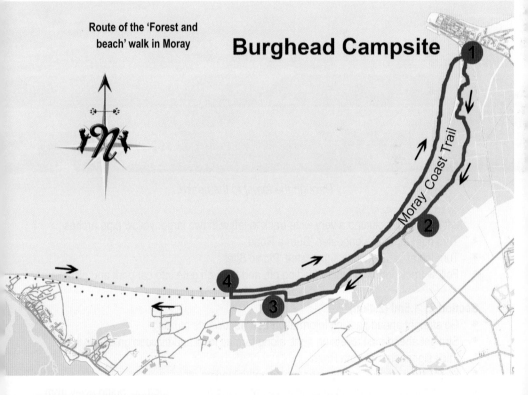

Route of the 'Forest and beach' walk in Moray

Burghead Campsite

Moray Coast Trail

Section 1: 2.25ml (3.6km)

- Exit campsite via path with reception on right, and through gate to woods
- Straight ahead along wide track signposted 'Burma Road'
- Follow track as it twists and turns through woods, ignoring all tracks and paths off to

Through the forest to the beach.

left and right, including a very wide track to left with two large, yellow pipe arches
- Turn right at bend signposted 'Burma Road'
- Turn left at next junction signposted 'Picnic Site'
- Follow track, ignoring others leading off, and through gate into car park and picnic area

Section 2: 1.5ml (2.4km)
- Go straight ahead passing information boards towards building
- Straight ahead past toilets on right, along tarmac road and through gate onto wide track signposted 'Burma Road'
- Keep going straight ahead, ignoring all paths leading off
- At right-hand bend continue straight on onto narrow, sandy footpath going away from trail
- Bear left at footpath junction, then turn left back onto wide, stony track
- Follow wide track, ignoring paths leading off as it turns first right then left towards the beach

Section 3: 0.75ml (1.2km)
- Turn left and follow path along top of dunes
- Take right fork and continue ahead as path narrows and weaves between trees
- Turn right down steps onto sandy beach at edge of wood, and opposite big, locked gate

Section 4: 4ml (6.4km)
- Turn right and walk back along sandy beach to concrete jetty below campsite
- Along jetty and turn right into campsite

Just 2.25ml (3.6km) further on through the sand dunes along the Moray Coast Trail is Findhorn. Keeping right on approach to the village, heading towards a large, low building, leads to the marina. The return route is also along the beach. This is a day-long trek, especially if taking a boat trip or visiting the village. Using buses is feasible but not especially convenient).

IN THE LOCALITY
ELGIN
This, the capital of Moray, is the largest town in the region. Unusually, it is situated inland, having grown up around the cathedral that, nowadays, is just a ruin. Further expansion occurred during the 19th century when bridges were built over the rivers Findhorn in the west and Spey in the east. Situated in the world-famous whisky region, and having several local distilleries, Elgin is now better known as a producer of whisky, and is a vibrant, thriving community full of character.

PLUSCARDEN ABBEY
Situated in the quiet glen of Black Burn, close to a wood just 6 miles (9.6km) southwest of Elgin, is this unique abbey. Alexander II founded the medieval monastery in 1230, since when, and right up until the present day, the Benedictine monks have lived and worshipped at Pluscarden: somehow, the turmoil of the reformation during the 16th century passed them by. Visitors who wish to join the monks are very welcome, especially in prayer and contemplation.

CLARKY HILL
A recent dig just outside Burghead found evidence of Iron Age and Pictish habitation, as well as some Roman artefacts.

KINLOSS
This town is best known for the army base here, especially, as located in the grounds is one of the WWII Commonwealth war graves. There are several interesting buildings, too, as well as an intriguing legend concerning the King of Scotland, Duff MacMalcolm.

Wonderful walks from dog-friendly campsites

Lossiemouth

Another of the villages dotted along the coast of the Moray Firth, this, too, is probably best known for the proximity of the RAF base here. Though the base is important, and has been here for more than 70 years, Lossiemouth has a long history of its own, chiefly as a port for the capital, Elgin, and its fishing industry. The local museum charts the fortunes of the town, and the lighthouse is now run by the community as a tourist attraction.

Findhorn

This coastal village seems to have really embraced modern times, possibly due to the fact that, over the years, it has been buried by sand ... twice! To prevent a repetition of this, during the late 17th century the village was relocated along the banks of the mouth of the River Findhorn, slightly away from the coast and sand dunes. Findhorn Bay is now a site of scientific interest because of the unique ecology of its shingles, saltmarshes, and sand dunes. The marina on the northerly outskirts of the village, where the river feeds into the Firth, provides a wide range of services, and hence it is a hive of activity, with both people and dogs having fun.

Then there is the charming village itself with its narrow streets and small cottages, on the southern edge of which is Findhorn Foundation, whose aims are to promote peace, spirituality, and eco-friendly living. Over the 50 years since its foundation, this community has grown and flourished to international repute. It runs courses and workshops, and holds many events, including concerts. Visitors are always welcome.

North 58 Sea Adventures

This company runs wildlife boating trips around the Moray Firth, and operates out of Findhorn Marina. Uniquely, it will look after your dog whilst you track dolphins.

Appendix i
Countryside codes

UK Government: Rights of Way and Open Access Land

PUBLIC RIGHTS OF WAY

You can walk on all public rights of way.

Some public rights of way are also open to horseriders, cyclists and motorists. You can use –

- footpaths – for walking, running, mobility scooters and powered wheelchairs
- bridleways – for walking, horseriding, bicycles, mobility scooters and powered wheelchairs
- restricted byways – for any transport without a motor and mobility scooters and powered wheelchairs
- byways open to all traffic – for any kind of transport, including cars (but mainly used by walkers, cyclists and horseriders)

Rights of way in England, Wales, and Northern Ireland

Public rights of way are marked with signs or coloured arrows: for example, yellow for footpaths; blue for bridleways

You can find the route of public rights of way –
- on Ordnance Survey and other maps
- on some council websites

RIGHT TO ROAM

You can access some land across England without having to use paths: this land is known as 'open access land' or just 'access land.'

Access land includes privately-owned mountains, moors, heaths and downs, common land registered with the local council, and some land around the England Coast Path. Your right to access this land is called the 'right to roam,' or 'freedom to roam.'

WHAT YOU CAN AND CAN'T DO

You can use access land for walking, running, watching wildlife and climbing. There are certain activities you can't usually do on open access land, including –
- horseriding
- cycling
- camping
- taking animals other than dogs on to the land

- driving a vehicle (except mobility scooters and powered wheelchairs)
- water sports

But you can use access land for horseriding and cycling if –
- the landowner allows it
- public bridleways or byways cross the land – horseriders and cyclists can ride along these
- there are local traditions, or rights, of access

DOGS ON OPEN ACCESS LAND

You must keep your dog on a lead of no more than two metres long on open access land –
- between 1 March and 31 July – to protect ground-nesting birds
- at all times around livestock

On land next to the England Coast Path you must keep your dog under close control. There may be other local or seasonal restrictions, but these don't apply to public rights of way or assistance dogs.

EXCEPTED LAND

On access land some areas remain private ('excepted land'), and you *don't* have the right to access these areas, even if they appear on a map of open access land.
Excepted land includes –
- houses, buildings and the land they're on (such as courtyards)
- land used to grow crops
- building sites and land that's being developed
- parks and gardens
- golf courses and racecourses
- railways and tramways
- working quarries

Use public rights of way to cross excepted land.

PRIVATE LAND

You may be able to access private land if the landowner has agreed to let the public use it: for example, for walking, cycling or horseriding (sometimes known as giving 'permissive access'). Look for signs.

Scotland: Outdoors Access Code 2003

Everyone has a statutory right of access to all land and inland waters, unless specifically excluded. These access rights are for outdoor recreation, and for crossing land and water.
There are some obvious commonsense restrictions, including –
- private houses and gardens
- farm buildings and yards

- farmland that has been planted or has crops growing
- school land and sports or playing fields when in use
- golf courses (but you can cross a golf course provided you don't interfere with any rounds)
- airfields, railways, telecommunication sites, military bases and installations, working quarries and construction sites, and visitor attractions or other places that charge for entry

ON OR IN WATER
- The access rights apply to non-motorised crafts only, and open water swimming
- Respect anglers and their desire for peace
- Take care when entering or exiting water so as not to damage the environment
- Avoid areas of commercial fishing unless you have spoken to the landowner
- Access rights extend to swimming (subject to any local bylaws)

IN WOODLAND
- Never light fires during dry periods in woodlands or on peaty ground
- Never cut down or damage trees
- Pay attention to signs, and follow any advice from the forester or land manager

ON FARMS
- Access rights do not usually apply to farmyards. However, if a right of way or core path goes through a farmyard, you can follow this at any time
- Use a gate or stile where one has been provided. Do not climb over walls or hedges unless there is no alternative
- Leave gates as you find them, even if they are open
- Keep away from fields of farm animals or growing crops
- Do not take your dog into fields containing growing crops, calves, lambs, or other young animals

HILLS AND MOUNTAINS
- Avoid areas where red stag stalking is taking place. This is usually between July and October. and notices will give full details of restricted areas
- The same applies to grouse shooting
- Do not let your dog roam near ground-nesting birds, or worry sheep or cattle
- Take responsible care when walking in hills and mountains so as not to damage the environment or disturb wildlife

WILD CAMPING
Scotland's generous outdoor access rights extend to wild camping, except where there are seasonal camping restrictions such as on the shores of the east side of Loch Lomond
- Wild camping should be lightweight, done in small numbers, and only for two or three nights in any one place

Wonderful walks from dog-friendly campsites

- Always responsibly consider where you are camping, and try to avoid causing problems for local people and land managers by not camping in enclosed fields of crops, or near farm animals
- Take extra care to avoid disturbing deer stalking or grouse shooting. If you wish to camp close to a house or building, seek the owner's permission

LEAVE NO TRACE
- Take away all your litter
- Remove all evidence of your tent pitch, and of any open fire
- Not cause pollution

Country Code
www.gov.uk/government/publications/the-countryside-code/the-countryside-code

RESPECT OTHER PEOPLE
Please respect the local community and other people using the outdoors. Remember your actions can affect both lives and livelihoods.

CONSIDER THE LOCAL COMMUNITY, AND OTHERS ENJOYING THE OUTDOORS
Respect the needs of local people and visitors alike: for example, don't block gateways, driveways or other paths with your vehicle.

When riding a bike or driving a vehicle, slow down or stop for horses, walkers and farm animals, and give them plenty of room. By law, cyclists must give way to walkers and horseriders on bridleways.

Co-operate with people at work in the countryside: for example, keep out of the way when farm animals are being herded or moved, and follow directions from the farmer.

Busy traffic on small country roads can be unpleasant and dangerous to local people, visitors and wildlife: slow down and, where possible, leave your vehicle at home; consider sharing lifts and use alternatives such as public transport or cycling. For public transport information, phone Traveline on 0871 200 22 33 or visit www.traveline.info.

LEAVE GATES AND PROPERTY AS YOU FIND THEM, AND FOLLOW PATHS, UNLESS WIDER ACCESS IS AVAILABLE
A farmer will normally close gates to keep in farm animals, but may sometimes leave them open so the animals can reach food and water. Leave gates as you find them, or follow instructions on signs. When in a group, make sure the last person knows how to leave the gates.

Follow paths unless wider access is available, such as on open country or registered common land (known as 'open access land').

If you think a sign is illegal or misleading such as a 'Private – No Entry' sign on a public path, contact the local authority.

Leave machinery and farm animals alone – don't interfere with animals even if you think they're in distress. Try to alert the farmer instead.

Use gates, stiles or gaps in field boundaries if you can – climbing over walls, hedges and fences can damage them, and increase the risk of farm animals escaping.
Our heritage matters to all of us: be careful not to disturb ruins and historic sites.

PROTECT THE NATURAL ENVIRONMENT

We all have a responsibility to protect the countryside, now and for future generations, so make sure you don't harm animals, birds, plants or trees, and try to leave no trace of your visit. When out with your dog, make sure he is not a danger or nuisance to farm animals, horses, wildlife or other people.

LEAVE NO TRACE OF YOUR VISIT, AND TAKE HOME YOUR LITTER

Protecting the natural environment means taking special care not to damage, destroy or remove features such as rocks, plants and trees. These provide homes and food for wildlife, and add to everybody's enjoyment of the countryside.

Litter and leftover food doesn't just spoil the beauty of the countryside; it can be dangerous to wildlife and farm animals – so take it home with you. Dropping litter and dumping rubbish are criminal offences.

Fires can be as devastating to wildlife and habitats as they are to people and property – so be careful with naked flames and cigarettes/pipes at any time of the year. Sometimes, controlled fires are used to manage vegetation, particularly on heaths and moors between 1 October and 15 April, but if a fire appears to be unattended report it by calling 999.

KEEP DOGS UNDER EFFECTIVE CONTROL

When you take your dog into the outdoors, always ensure he does not disturb wildlife, farm animals, horses or other people by –
- keeping him on a lead, or
- keeping him in view at all times, being aware of what he's doing, and confident that he will return to you promptly on cue
- ensure he does not stray off the path or area where you have a right of access

Special dog rules may apply in particular situations, so always look out for local signs: for example –
- dogs may be banned from certain areas that people use, or there may be restrictions, bylaws or control orders limiting where they can go
- the access rights that normally apply to open country and registered common land (known as 'open access' land) require dogs to be kept on a short lead between 1 March and 31 July, to help protect ground-nesting birds, and all year round near farm animals
- at the coast, there may also be local restrictions that require dogs to be kept on a short lead during bird breeding season, and to prevent disturbance to flocks of resting and feeding birds during other times of year

It's always good practice (and a legal requirement on 'open access' land) to keep your dog on a lead around farm animals and horses, for your own safety and the welfare of the animals. A farmer may shoot a dog who is attacking or chasing farm animals without being liable to compensate the dog's owner.

However, if cattle or horses chase you and your dog, it may be safer to let your dog off the lead. Your dog will likely be much safer if you let him run away from a farm animal without impedence from you – and so will you.

Everyone knows how unpleasant dog mess is, and a health hazard to boot, so always clean up after your dog and get rid of the mess responsibly – bag it and bin it (don't leave it hanging from a branch ...) Make sure your dog is regularly wormed to protect him, other animals, and people.

ENJOY THE OUTDOORS

Even when going out locally, it's best to get the latest information about where and when you can go. For example, your rights to go onto some areas of open access land and coastal land may be restricted in particular places at particular times. Find out as much as you can about where you are going, plan ahead, and follow advice and local signs.

PLAN AHEAD AND BE PREPARED

You'll get more from your visit if you refer to up-to-date maps or guidebooks and websites before you set off. Visit Natural England on GOV.UK, or contact local information centres or libraries for a list of outdoor recreation groups offering advice on specialist activities.

You're responsible for your own safety and for others in your care – especially children – so be prepared for natural hazards, changes in weather, and other events. Wild animals, farm animals and horses can behave unpredictably if you get too close, especially if they're with their young, so give them plenty of space.

Check weather forecasts before you leave. Conditions can change rapidly, especially on mountains and along the coast, so don't be afraid to turn back if in doubt. When visiting the coast, check tide times on EasyTide: don't risk being cut off by rising tides, and take care on slippery rocks and seaweed.

Part of the appeal of the countryside is that you can get away from it all. You may not see anyone for hours, and there are many places without good mobile phone signals, so let someone know where you're going and when you expect to return.

FOLLOW ADVICE AND LOCAL SIGNS

England has about 190,000 km (118,000 miles) of public rights of way, providing many opportunities to enjoy the natural environment. Get to know the signs and symbols used in the countryside to show paths and open countryside. See the Countryside Code leaflet for some of the symbols you may come across.

KENNEL CLUB COUNTRYSIDE CODE

Wherever you go, following these steps will help keep your dog safe, protect the environment, and demonstrate that you are a responsible dog owner.
* Control your dog so that he does not scare or disturb farm animals or wildlife

- When using the new access rights over open country and common land, you must keep your dog on a short lead between 1 March and 31 July – and all year round near farm animals – and you may not be able to take your dog at all on some areas or at some times. Please follow/abide by any official signs.
- You do not have to put your dog on a lead on public paths, as long as he is under close control. As a general rule, though, keep your dog on a lead if unsure about how reliably he will do as you ask. By law, farmers are entitled to destroy a dog who injures or worries their animals.
- If cattle or horses chase you and your dog, it may be safer to let your dog off the lead. Your dog will likely be much safer if you let him run away from a farm animal without impedence from you – and so will you.
- Take particular care that your dog doesn't scare sheep and lambs, or wander where he might disturb birds nesting on the ground and other wildlife: eggs and young will soon die without protection from their parents.
- Everyone knows how unpleasant dog mess is, and a health hazard to boot, so always clean up after your dog and get rid of the mess responsibly – bag it and bin it (but don't leave it hanging from a branch ...) Make sure your dog is regularly wormed to protect him, other animals, and people.

Visit Hubble and Hattie on the web:
www.hubbleandhattie.com • www.hubbleandhattie.blogspot.co.uk • Details of all books
• Special offers • Newsletter • New book news

233

Appendix ii
Campsite details

(All details and prices correct at time of going to press)

Wales

Monmouthshire

Pyscodlyn Farm Caravan and Camping Park, Llanwenarth Citra, Abergavenny, Monmouthshire NP7 7ER
Tel: 01873 853271 • mb: 07816 447942 • email: via website
• website: www.pyscodlyncaravanpark.com
Open April to October
N: 51.835709 W: 3.070202

Directions
Using the post code, my satnav found the campsite easily. The entrance is on the left, two miles west of Abergavenny on the A40 Brecon Road. From the other direction it is four miles after Crickhowell on the right, 200 metres after a large brown sign.

Charges
Pitch+2 people – £15.00-£17.00
Electric hook-up – £3.00
Dogs – free
Additional adult – £4.00
Children – £2.00

Pembrokeshire
Lleithyr Farm Holiday Park, Lleithyr Farm, Whitesands, St Davids, Pembrokeshire SA62 6PR
Tel: 01437 720245 • email: via website • website: www.lleithyrfarm.co.uk
Open March to October
N: 51.896590 W: 5.278753

Directions
My satnav took me to the campsite entrance. Follow A487 to St Davids, then B4583 to Whitesands. At crossroads between St Davids and Whitesands is a campsite signpost.

CHARGES
Adult – £5.00-£9.00
Electric hook-up – £4.00
Dogs – free
Children – £2.50-4.00
Awning – £1.00

POWYS

Elan Oaks Camping and Caravan Site, Elan Valley, Rhayader, Powys LD6 5HN
Tel: 01597 810 326 (daytime); 01597 810 610 (evening) 0777 1524 634 (emergency)
• email: via website • website: www.elanoaks.co.uk
Open all year
N: 52.279844N W: 3.558114W

DIRECTIONS
My satnav directed me straight to Rhayader. From the Clock Tower in the centre of the town, proceed to West Street (B4518) over River Wye and follow signs to Elan Valley. Continue for just over two miles past Elan Valley Hotel. The site is on the left just before the cattle grid. If booking on the day, register first at the electric shop on North Street in Rhayader. There is a pay and display opposite but parking is tricky.

CHARGES
Pitch+electric+2 adults+awning+2 dogs – £17.00-£22.00
Additional person – £4.00
(Charges vary according to different sections of the site)

North East
YORKSHIRE (EAST)

Wold Farm Campsite, Bempton Lane, Flamborough, Bridlington, East Yorkshire YO15 1AT
Tel: 01262 850 536 • mb: 07429 604 782 • email: woldfarmcamping@live.com
• website: www.woldfarmcampsite.com
Open March to November
N: 54.131757 W: 0.138186

DIRECTIONS
Do NOT rely on a satnav! At Bempton take the B1229 Flamborough Road signposted Flamborough. In two miles turn left at a sharp right bend. There are some signs at the junction (none for the farm). At the top of a very bumpy track, 0.8ml (1.29km), is Wold Farm.

CHARGES
Pitch+2 people – £14.00-£16.00

Electric hook-up – £4.00
Dogs – free
Single occupancy – £2.00
Bank Holidays – +£5.00

YORKSHIRE (NORTH)

Thirsk Racecourse Caravan and Motorhome Club Site, Station Rd, Thirsk, North Yorkshire YO7 1QL
Tel: 01342 327490 • email: via website • website: www.caravanclub.co.uk
Open March to November
N: 54.231311 W: 1.350573

DIRECTIONS
Caravans are prohibited on A170 at Sutton Bank. Take A61 to Thirsk. Campsite entrance is next to Lidl.

CHARGES
Pitch+electric hook-up – £5.20-£5.80
Adult – £4.40-4.80
Dogs – free

NORTHUMBERLAND

Herding Hill Farm, Shield Hill, Haltwhistle, Northumberland NE49 9NW
Tel: 01434 320175 • email: bookings@herdinghill.co.uk • website: www.herdinghill.co.uk
Open all year
N: 54.977917 W: 2.450338

DIRECTIONS
DO NOT follow satnav, especially if towing a caravan.
A69 East – Take A68 north and then B6318 towards Chollerford.
A69 West – Take Greenhead turn off to B6318 (before Haltwhistle). Follow brown tourist signs at Milecastle Pub.

CHARGES
Pitch+2 adults+electric hook-up – £24.00-£34.50
Dogs – free
Additional adult – £4.40
Child – £2.20
Awning – £3.00

North West
CHESHIRE
Delamere Forest Camping and Caravanning, Club Site, Station Road, Delamere,

Northwich, Cheshire CW8 2HZ
Tel: 01606 889231 • email: via website
• website: www.campingandcaravanningclub.co.uk
Open all year
N: 53.2288 W: 2.6681

DIRECTIONS
My satnav took me straight to the campsite. From M6 take A556 west to B5152 towards Delamere Railway Station. The campsite is adjacent.

CHARGES
Pitch+1 adult+electric hook-up – £12.60-£25.00
Dogs – free

CUMBRIA
Castlerigg Hall Caravan and Camping Park, Keswick, Cumbria CA12 4TE
Tel: 01768 774499 • email: info@castlerigg.co.uk • website: www.castlerigg.co.uk
Open March to November
N: 54.592521 W: 3.11149

DIRECTIONS
Using the post code, the satnav found the campsite easily. From M6 exit junction 40 Penrith; follow A66 to Keswick. Take A591 signposted Windermere. After one mile (1.6km), take minor road on right signposted to campsite.

CHARGES
Pitch+2 adults+electric hook-up – £21.65-£37.10
Dogs – £1.70-£2.50 (each)
Additional person – £3.35-£4.45
Children (4yrs and under) – free

Castlerigg Farm Camping and Caravan Site, Keswick, Cumbria. CA12 4TE
Tel: 01768 772479 • email: info@castleriggfarm.com
• website: www.castleriggfarm.com
Open March to November
N: 54.592521 W: 3.111491

DIRECTIONS
Using the post code the satnav found the campsite easily. From M6 exit junction 40 Penrith; follow A66 to Keswick. Take A591 signposted Windermere. After one mile (1.6km), take minor road on right signposted to campsite.

Wonderful walks from dog-friendly campsites

CHARGES
Pitch+2 adults – £18.00-£22.00
Electric hook-up – £2.00-£2.50
Dogs – free
Additional persons – £3.50-£4.00

LANCASHIRE
Lower Greenhill Caravan Park, Kelbrook Road, Salterforth, Lancashire BB18 5TG
Tel: 01282 813067 • email: lowergreenhill@btconnect.com
• website: www.lowergreenhillcaravanpark.com
Open all year
N: 53.902580 W: 2.165173

DIRECTIONS
My satnav had no problems finding site. From Burnley take the A56 north to Kelbrook.
At roundabout take first exit (B6383 signposted Barnsoldwick). Campsite is half-a-mile
(0.8km) on the left.

CHARGES
Pitch+adult+electric hook-up – £17.00
Dogs - Free

Central England
CAMBRIDGESHIRE
Waterclose Meadows National Trust campsite, Houghton Mill, Near Huntingdon,
Cambridgeshire
Tel: 01480 466716 • email: houghtonmillcampsite@nationaltrust.org.uk
• website: www.nationaltrust.org.uk/houghton-mill
Open March to November
N: 52.330915N W: 0120617W

DIRECTIONS
My satnav directed me straight to Houghton village. From the A123, turn along road
signposted Houghton/Houghton Mill. Drive into the village, and continue straight ahead
through the square into Mill Street (signposted Houghton Mill). Pass church on the right.
Campsite entrance is on the left, immediately before the last house. (Entrance to the site
involves a tight turn for long outfits.)

CHARGES
Pitch+electric hook-up – £8.00-£9.00
Adult (16+) – £8.00-£9.00

Dogs – free
Child (6yrs+) – £2.00

DERBYSHIRE

Rivendale Holiday Park, Buxton Rd, Alsop-en-le-Dale, Ashbourne, Derbyshire DE6 1QU
Tel: 01335 310311/310441 • email: enquiries@rivendalecaravanpark.co.uk
• website: www.rivendalecaravanpark.co.uk
Open February to January
N: 53.106198 W: 1.760040

DIRECTIONS

My satnav took me to Buxton Road without problem. The campsite entrance is on the main A515, so do not turn off into the village of Alsop-en-le Dale. Travelling south, leave the M1 at junction 28; travelling north, leave M1 at junction 25. Take the A52 towards Derby, then Ashbourne. Take A515 to Buxton and campsite entrance.

CHARGES

Pitch+2 adults+electric hook-up – £21.00-£35.70
Dogs – £2.00 (each)
Additional adult – £2.50
Child – £2.00
Awning/pup tent – £2.00

SHROPSHIRE

Easthope Caravan and Camping, Easthope, Much Wenlock, Shropshire TF13 6DN
Tel: 01746 785434 • mb: 0797 1085 762 • email: info@easthopecaravanandcamping.
co.uk • website: www.easthopecaravanandcamping.co.uk
Open March to October
N: 52.553356 W: 2.642366

DIRECTIONS

Units, especially caravans, should enter the campsite coming down the hill from the B4371. From Much Wenlock take the A458 towards Shrewsbury; then the B4371 signposted Church Stretton. In approximately 4 miles (6.4km) turn left at crossroads opposite signpost for Easthope Woods. From Church Stretton take B3471 signposted Much Wenlock. In approximately 8 miles (12.9km) turn right at Easthope Wood junction. Campsite is accessed via a gate on the left a few hundred yards down the hill. Caution: proceed slowly as road is narrow.

CHARGES

Pitch+electric hook-up – from £12.00
Dogs – free

Wonderful walks from dog-friendly campsites

STAFFORDSHIRE
Willow Brook Farm Certificated Site, A38 Southbound, Alrewas, Burton-On-Trent, Staffordshire DE13 7BA
Tel: 01283 790217
Open March to October
N: 52.73819 W: 1.72988

DIRECTIONS
Entrance only from the south side of the A38 dual carriageway that runs from Burton-On-Trent to Lichfield. Just after a bridge over a river is a very small brown campsite sign on a lampost: a few yards further on is the entrance.

CHARGES
Unit+2 adults – £9.00-£10.00
Electric hook-up – £3.00
Dogs – free

BUCKINGHAMSHIRE
Town Farm Camping & Caravanning, Ivinghoe, Leighton Buzzard, Buckinghamshire LU7 9EL
No telephone number as all bookings have to be made online (difficult to extend stay).
Email: via website • website: www.townfarmcamping.co.uk
Open March to October
N: 51.838631 W: 0621777

DIRECTIONS
As long as postcode LU7 9EL is used, the satnav will take you to the correct Town Farm on the outskirts of Ivinghoe. From the B488 through Ivinghoe, take the B489 signposted Dunstable and Ashridge. Campsite is on left, signposted. Go up driveway to top by grain silos and wait by blue check-in sign.

CHARGES
Pitch+2 adults+electric hook-up – £22.50 for one night; £20.00 for two+ nights
Dogs – £2.00
Additional adults – £10.00 (each)
Children – £5.00
Awnings – £5.00

ESSEX
Fen Farm Caravan Site, Fen Farm, Moore Lane, East Mersea, Colchester, Essex CO5 8FE
Tel: 01206 383275 • email: havefun@fenfarm.co.uk • website: www.fenfarm.co.uk

Open March to October
N: 51.790012 W: 0.984560

DIRECTIONS
Follow the B1025 over bridge called 'The Strood' onto Mersea Island. Take left fork signposted East Mersea. Continue along East Mersea Road and two miles (3.2km) along cul-de-sac to Dog & Pheasant Pub. Take first turning on the right to Fen Farm.

CHARGES
Pitch+up to 5 people+electric hook-up – £19.00-30.00
Dogs – free
(Prior booking essential as same-day bookings not accepted)

WEST SUSSEX
Graffham Camping and Caravanning Club Site, Great Bury, Graffham, Petworth, West Sussex GU28 0QF
Tel: 01798 867476 • email: via website
• website: www.campingandcaravanningclub.co.uk
Open April to November
N: 50.956807 W: 0.671034

DIRECTIONS
My satnav took me straight to the campsite. Be aware that some roads are unsuitable – use Chichester to Petworth A285. Turn off along minor road signposted Selham, Graffham. Turn left signposted Graffham, and with a small brown campsite sign. Turn left onto campsite driveway by a very small club signpost.

CHARGES
Unit+1 adult+electric hook-up – £12.00-£30.50
Dogs – free

South West
CORNWALL
Pentire Haven Holiday Park, Stibb Road, Bude Cornwall EX23 9QY
Tel: 01288 321 601 • email: holidays@pentirehaven.co.uk
• website: www.pentirehaven.co.uk
Open all year
N: 50.872888 W: 4.493385

DIRECTIONS
My satnav did not recognize the postcode. Drive through Kilkhampton on A39 towards Bude. Road to the campsite, on the right, is well signposted just outside the village.

Wonderful walks from dog-friendly campsites

CHARGES
Pitch+2 adults+electric hook-up – £18.00-£37.00
Dogs – £2.00-3.00
Additional adults – £4.00-£7.00 (each)
Child – £4.00-£6.00
Awning – £1.00-£2.00
(An expensive site for a solo traveller, but, because it is open all year, it is possible to take advantage of the much cheaper off-peak prices)

SOMERSET
Exe Valley Caravan Site, Mill House, Bridgetown, Exmoor, Dulverton, Somerset. TA22 9JN
Tel: 01643 851432 ● email: info@exevalleycamping.co.uk
● website: www.exevalleycamping.co.uk
Open March to October
N: 51.087365N W: 3.540042W

DIRECTIONS
My satnav directed me to straight to Bridgetown: some of the roads, being minor ones, are rather narrow. Exit M5 at junction 27. Take A361 to Tiverton, then A396 signposted Bampton. Stay on the A396 as it twists and turns beside the river Exe to Bridgetown. Turn left immediately past the Badgers Holt Inn. The site entrance is on the right, and this involves a tight turn. It is not recommended for outfits in excess of 32 feet (9.75m).

CHARGES
Pitch+2 adults – £14.50-£21.50
Electric hook-up & TV – £3.50
Dogs – £1.00
Additional adults – £5.00 (each)
Awning – £1.00
(An adults-only site)

Burrowhayes Farm Caravan and Camping Site and Riding Stables, West Luccombe, Porlock, Minehead Somerset TA24 8HT
Tel: 01643 862463 ● email: info@burrowhayes.co.uk ● website: www.burrowhayes.co.uk
Open March to October
N: 51.204241 W: 3.578021

DIRECTIONS
Five miles (8km) west of Minehead on the A39, turn left at Allerford signposted Horner and West Luccombe. Campsite is ¼ mile (0.4km) on the right just before the humpback bridge.

CHARGES
Pitch+2 adults+electric hook-up – £20.00-£25.00

Dogs – free
Additional adults – £7.00 (each)
Children – £3.00
Awnings – £1.50

WILTSHIRE
Summerlands Caravan Park, College Farm, Rockbourne Road, Coombe Bissett,
Salisbury, Wiltshire SP5 4LP
Tel: 01722 718259 • email: enquiries@summerlandscaravanpark.co.uk
• website: www.summerlandscaravanpark.co.uk
Open April to October
N: 51.012203 W: 1.854168

DIRECTIONS
Using the post code the satnav found the campsite easily (do not confuse it with the one
at Salisbury racecourse). Take the A354 south through Coombe Bissett. At a right-hand
bend take a minor road to the left (drive slowly as the road very soon becomes a bumpy,
stony track). Pass riding school on the right, then turn left. Campsite is on the left.

CHARGES
Pitch+2 adults – £14.85-£16.50
Electric hook-up – £2.70-£3.00
Dogs – free
Additional adults, children and awnings – £2.25-£2.50

Scotland
BORDERS
Melrose Gibson Park Caravan and Motorhome Club Site, High St, Melrose, Scottish
Borders TD6 9RY
Tel: 01896 822969 • email: via website • website: www.caravanclub.co.uk
Open all year
N: 55.598894 W: 2.725262

DIRECTIONS
The satnav takes you directly to the campsite. Proceed with caution through the town as it
is easy to miss the entrance, which is down a cul-de-sac opposite the Rugby Club.

CHARGES
Pitch+electric hook-up – £6.80-£11.20
Adults – £6.10-£8.70 (each)
Dogs – free
Children – £1.00-£3.10

Wonderful walks from dog-friendly campsites

HIGHLANDS

Glen Nevis Caravan and Camping Park, Fort William, Highlands. PH33 6SX
Tel: 01397 702191 • email: holidays@glen-nevis.co.uk
• website: www.glen-nevis.co.uk/caravans
Open March to September
N: 56.804474 W: 5.073954

DIRECTIONS

Using the postcode the satnav found the campsite easily. From the A82 north of
Fort William, at a mini roundabout exit junction signposted Glen Nevis. Campsite is
approximately two miles (3.2km) along the road on the right.

CHARGES
Pitch+electric hook-up – £19,00-£20.00
Adults – £3.50 (each)
Dogs – free
Children – £2.50

MORAY

Burghead Beach Holiday Park, Station Road, Burghead, Moray IV30 5RP
Tel: 01343 830084 • email: ritchie.helen@yahoo.co.uk
• website: lossiemouthcaravans.co.uk/burghead.asp (not very informative)
Open May to October
N: 57.697727 W: 3.488023

DIRECTIONS

My satnav located this campsite. From Elgin take the A96 to Forres. Turn right along the
B9013 signposted Burghead, and follow road into the town. Turn left along Bridge Street
signposted Beach, Car Park. Campsite entrance is on left past houses.

CHARGES
Pitch+adult+electric hook-up – £16.00-£25.00
Dogs – free

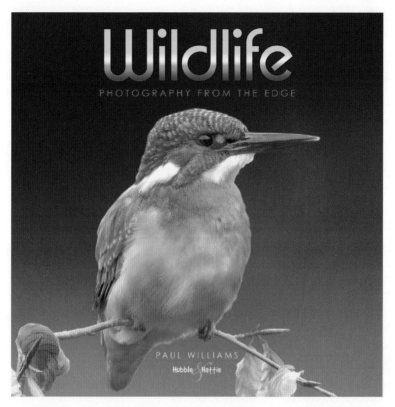

Index